The Children's Table

E S T. 75 1938
YEARS
THE UNIVERSITY OF GEORGIA PRESS 2013

The Children's Table

Childhood Studies and the Humanities

EDITED BY ANNA MAE DUANE

The University of Georgia Press   Athens and London

© 2013 the University of Georgia Press

Athens, Georgia 30602

www.ugapress.org

Set in Adobe Caslon Pro and Minion Pro by Graphic Composition, Inc.

Manufactured by Sheridan Books

The paper in this book meets the guidelines for
permanence and durability of the Committee on
Production Guidelines for Book Longevity of the
Council on Library Resources.

Most University of Georgia Press titles are
available from popular e-book vendors.

Printed in the United States of America

18 17 16 15 14 P 6 5 4 3 2

Library of Congress Cataloging-in-Publication Data
The children's table : childhood studies and the humanities /
edited by Anna Mae Duane.

viii, 265 p. : ill. ; 23 cm.

Includes bibliographical references and index.

ISBN 978-0-8203-4521-5 (hardcover) — ISBN 0-8203-4521-0 (hardcover) —
ISBN 978-0-8203-4522-2 (paperback) —
ISBN 0-8203-4522-9 (paperback)

1. Children—Research. 2. Children—Study and teaching.
I. Duane, Anna Mae, 1968–

HQ767.85.C488 2013

305.23072—dc23   2012047747

British Library Cataloging-in-Publication Data available

Contents

Acknowledgments

At times, editing this book did indeed feel like sitting at the children's table—a bit chaotic perhaps, but a lot of fun, nonetheless. My goal was to create a collection that readers would experience as a lively conversation, and I was very fortunate to have such smart and dedicated interlocutors along the journey. It has been an enormous pleasure collaborating with such a talented group of scholars, and I'm enormously grateful to every one of them for their part in this project. I'm particularly indebted to Lucia Hodgson, without whom this volume would have never gotten off the ground; to James Marten, a remarkable editor himself, who provided such helpful advice, and to Sarah Chinn and Sophie Bell, whose canny comments on an early version of the introduction improved it greatly. Karen Sánchez-Eppler inspired this volume through her own pioneering scholarship, and it was her willingness to contribute to the book that was the impetus for me to take the leap and begin the project in earnest.

In addition to benefiting from fruitful collaborations with the writers within this volume, I profited from the remarkable generosity of many writers and editors outside of it. Witnessing Lenny Cassuto's remarkable skill at editing *The Cambridge History of the American Novel* was as instructional as it was inspirational. At the University of Connecticut, Kate Capshaw Smith provided very useful feedback on several aspects of this project. I'm also grateful to colleagues Alexis Boylan, Martha Cutter, Nina Dayton, Wayne Franklin, Liz Hart, Sherry Harris, Kathy Knapp, Cathy Schlund-Vials, and

Chris Vials, whose collegiality and intelligence are always a spur to new and better thinking. Interns Laura Blackburn and Amanda Norelli were both paragons of organization and efficiency. I'm grateful for nourishing conversations with scholars and friends, including Rachel Adams, Robin Bernstein, Mary Burke, Christina Carlson, Brigitte Fielder, Bill Gerke, Jennifer Gilchrist, Ken Monteith, Leah Richards, Marion Rust, Jonathan Senchyne, and Joanne Van Der Woude about a host of subjects, childhood among them. At the University of Georgia Press, I'm grateful to Erika Stevens for first believing in this project, and to Nancy Grayson and Beth Snead for helping me to improve it so greatly. John Joerschke did a wonderful job stewarding the manuscript through production. M. J. Devaney's keen eye was essential to the copyediting process. I owe many thanks to the anonymous readers of the manuscript for their careful and insightful readings.

As always, my greatest debt is to my family. My sisters Susie and Helen were the ones who first taught me how to really whoop it up at the children's table in the first place. I'm grateful to my parents for teaching us how to treasure lively, challenging conversations. And most of all, I am continually delighted by my great good fortune at getting to sit down at my own table each night with my partner Matthew and my son Connor.

The Children's Table

The Children's Table

Childhood Studies and the Humanities

As anyone who has attended a Thanksgiving dinner can attest, the children's table is not usually an A-list destination. Denied the good china, seated at a wobbly folding table, placed out of earshot of the juicy adult gossip, the guests at the children's table know that they occupy a marginal space. In many ways, the children's table is an apt metaphor for the role childhood studies has played in the humanities and, more discomfortingly perhaps, for the role the humanities sometimes seem to play within the academy. Yet, as in many marginalized spaces, there can be an intense sense of freedom and creativity precisely because one's voice is out of earshot. This book provides an overview of the innovative work being done in childhood studies—a transcript, if you will, of what they've been saying at the children's table. But this volume is also an argument for rethinking the seating arrangement itself. The study of children, often seen as peripheral to the important work of understanding social, political, national, and ethnic structures, allows us to rethink the very foundations underlying these structures. The chapters in *The Children's Table* share a unifying premise: to include the child in any field of study is to realign the very structure of that field, changing the terms of inquiry and forcing a different set of questions.[1] Because defining childhood is a means of defining and distributing power and obligation, studying childhood requires a radically altered approach to the questions of what constitutes knowledge and what animates the work of power and resistance.

In short, we argue that engaging children as individuals worthy of study inevitably complicates how we process knowledge about the human subject.

For at least a generation, the humanities have been in a state of continual self-evaluation (some might say self-recrimination) about how to define the field and the value of what lies within those parameters. Charles Frankel, the first director of the National Humanities Center, characterizes the humanities as "that form of knowledge in which the knower is revealed." For Frankel, all "knowledge becomes humanistic when we are asked to contemplate not only a proposition but the proposer, when we hear the human voice behind what is being said."[2] Geoffrey Harpham takes another tack, focusing on methodology and motivation. "The humanities," he argues, take "'the text' as their object, humanity as their subject, and self-understanding as their goal."[3] Perhaps the most pervasive—if largely unarticulated—definition stipulates that the humanities are what the sciences are not. In her article "Defining the Humanities" Anna Wierbicka writes that whereas the focus of science is things, the "subject-matter of 'the humanities' is 'people,' and people studied not in the way in which 'things' can be studied."[4] In sum, science purports to focus on objects, and thus to be objective, while the humanities are a messier enterprise. Echoing Frankel's assertion, this argument suggests that the voice of the knower, replete with that knower's political and aesthetic beliefs, can be heard in the humanities but is largely undetectable in scientific inquiry.

Within a model that defines the humanities and the sciences as antithetical, childhood studies can function as an important corrective. Willem Koops, a developmental psychologist, contends that children pose questions that science cannot answer. For Koops, the empirical approach favored by science cannot, by itself, provide the capacious approach necessary for fully understanding the experience of children. Further, empirical knowledge does not attempt to trace how the experiences of children shape our larger culture. "Normative issues," writes Koops, "cannot be solved empirically."[5] *The Children's Table* goes still further, arguing that ideas of normativity themselves often get in the way of accurate knowledge.[6] The pull of the normative still needs to be questioned, and humanists are well positioned to do the asking.

A brief history of the evolution of childhood studies reveals that the field does not just function as a corrective to scientific essentialism but that it also reveals how profoundly interdependent scientific and humanistic knowledge are in the first place. As an endeavor that focuses on children with the intent of locating and studying their agency, childhood studies defies the easy divisions of biology and culture, body and book. More precisely, childhood studies demonstrates how the science we apply to children and, by extension, to human development has been shaped by cultural narratives about independence and autonomy—stories that were forged in opposition to an imagined child.

Although we can trace interest in childhood back to any number of historical moments, many practitioners locate the origins of contemporary childhood studies in the Enlightenment, as part of that era's interest in human nature. Within Enlightenment thought, the child was deployed to represent everything from the state of nature to the power of the environment to the benefit of perpetual progress. John Locke and Jean-Jacques Rousseau, philosophers whose work roamed freely between "scientific" pronouncements on diet and exercise, social scientific speculations about human psychology, and political meditations on parental obligations, took the child both as an object and as a metaphor for their ideas of governance. The romanticized notion of the child—perhaps best exemplified by Wordsworth's odes to childhood innocence—took hold in the early nineteenth century and would manifest itself in Victorian culture's fathomless fascination with the sentimental child whose beauty and fragility wrung hearts and evoked tears. In turn, this beautiful, if perpetually endangered, child of sentimental literature occupied the very heart of the social scientific child-saving movements of the late nineteenth and early twentieth centuries. As these medical and scientific movements developed, they evolved in cultural conversation with contemporary cultural and literary narratives that rendered childhood a battleground for racial supremacy.[7] For instance, G. Stanley Hall argued that one could look to the growth of children to trace the development of racial types from the supposedly primitive races to the supposed pinnacle of evolution—the white race.[8] We need look no further than the American "Better Baby" contests of the early twentieth century for evidence of how the biases manifested in literary and popular culture shaped the early days of genetic/hereditary science that focused so intensely on producing (racially and ethnically) "strong" children.[9]

Sigmund Freud brought another level of attention to the child. The founder of psychology—a field that currently encompasses a blend of social and hard sciences such as neuroscience and psychotherapy—drew much of his theoretical inspiration from classical art, literature, and folklore. "Not only did the serious study of children's literature start with Freud," Kenneth Kidd has argued, but "we may also say that psychoanalysis developed in part through its engagement with children's literature."[10] Anthropology— a field that likewise spans the traditional humanities, social sciences, and the natural sciences—has been one of the leading fields in furthering our understanding of the child as a position contingent on history, culture, and other environmental factors. Human rights advocates are among the many who have realized we must embrace a model that realizes the reciprocal relationship between what we have traditionally called the humanities and what we have traditionally called science. UN documents such as the 1989 Convention on the Rights of the Child express a carefully crafted vision that address children's biological and cultural needs, drawing from medical, anthropological, and political perspectives.

To reiterate, the history of childhood studies demonstrates how cultural narratives about what children *should* be shape what experts—in both the humanities and the sciences—have found to be "true" about childhood. As cognitive scientists, forensic psychologists, and others continue to open up new ways of understanding children's bodies and minds, this new knowledge will be disseminated through narratives that will, in turn, shape the directions that research takes in the larger culture. "The humanistic turn of mind," Cathy Davidson has argued, "provides the historical perspective, interpretive skill, critical analysis, and narrative form required to articulate the significance of the scientific discoveries of an era" and "show how they change our sense of what it means to be human."[11] In short, because the child has always been a deeply narrativized subject, any useful study of childhood and children must be willing to draw on the "humanistic turn of mind" and its ability to illuminate, critique, and ultimately transform the narratives that both influence and occlude the lives of actual young people.

Over the past twenty years, scholars have done much to reveal how these narratives have shaped our constructions of childhood and to trace how those constructions have affected our concepts of humanity.[12] A particularly rich vein of inquiry asks how ideas about childhood have influenced larger cultural attitudes toward dependence and has explored the political implications of those attitudes in illuminative studies about children's roles in political, cultural and even military life.[13] The political, sexual, and cultural work of children's literature has become a major field within literary studies.[14] It is precisely because of the recent publication of these powerful and well-received texts that we must now rigorously consider the child's wide-ranging impact beyond discrete studies of particular subjects. In short, childhood studies, a vibrant but largely self-contained niche within humanities scholarship, is ready to assume its place as an epistemological game changer.

The Children's Table takes on the ambitious task of charting how childhood studies transforms how we ask a number of questions about the relationship between science and story, biology and culture, data and narrative. The work of childhood studies, this volume argues, is not to simply correct the essentialist pull that undergirds scientific notions of the child. Rather we must rigorously engage science's biological parameters in relation to, rather than treat them as the ontological opponent of, other forms of knowledge. As the authors in this collection move back and forth between, in Frankel's words, the "knowledge and the knower," they offer a different perspective on this relationship between representations of childhood and young people's experiences as they live within those formulations.

For if scientific inquiry is shaped by embedded narratives about the child, rethinking childhood as a critical category within the humanities also promises to overturn some of the foundational structures of thought within the humanities itself. The figure we now recognize as a child was created in tandem with forms of modernity that the Enlightenment generated and that the humanities are working to collectively rethink. As I've been arguing, the child has long served as the model for progress—from savagery to civilization, from murky past to fully realized present—that provides a cornerstone of contemporary work within the humanities. John Locke's child figure, the irrational subject incapable of giving full consent, still looms large over the scholarship that seeks to recover the voices and experiences of those who have been infantilized. Passive, victimized, silent, and sheltered, the child is the placeholder for what full citizen-subjects need to define themselves against. Consider, for example, James Beattie's 1770 deployment of the wellworn analogy between children and savages in his argument that "one may as well say of an infant, that he can never become a man, as of a nation now barbarous, that it can never be civilized."[15] On both sides of the comparison, the state of childhood is antithetical to full humanity—the child, like the barbarous nation, may have the potential for future rational autonomy, but both must undergo rigorous training to overcome their current state of incompleteness. Thomas Jefferson follows a similar line of argument when he laments that freeing slaves would be analogous to "abandoning a child."[16] His argument is based on the unquestioned premise that a child is inherently dependent on others and therefore must forgo his or her rights in order to gain the supposedly benevolent protection of "adults."

Much of the most exciting work in the humanities today seeks to recover the voices of those who, like Jefferson's rhetorical slave, have been infantilized because of their gender, ethnicity, or sexual orientation. This work often makes the case for removing the excluded group from the childish realm to which it had been consigned and for including it within the parameters of our imagined ideal citizen—an autonomous private agent. Yet this expansion of the class of the citizen-subject often stops short of engaging the child figure against which the citizen-subject continues to be measured. To take one example, feminist scholars have made us realize that strategies of derogatory feminization only work if there is an implicit understanding that to be female is to be inherently weak, emotional, and insufficient.[17] We know that a feminizing comparison is not simply unjust to the subject being feminized; it also functions through an inherently oppressive—and illusory—conception of the feminine itself. When it comes to infantilizing images, however, many scholars have focused only one part of the equation: they decry the unjust analogy without engaging the very figure on which metaphors of infantilization rely.[18] African American studies, queer studies, and disability studies have all argued persuasively that infantilizing metaphors are unjust and disempowering when deployed against members of their community. Yet, childhood studies insists, without rethinking the structures of thought that render childhood an implicitly shameful position in the first place, we are at an intellectual impasse. If scholars are to do the work of engaging people whose experiences necessitate allowing for authentic interdependence, rather than an illusory independence, whose literature speaks with mediated voices rather than through romanticized authorship, we can no longer stand on the crumbling theoretical ground that assigns partial, dependent, mediated subjectivity *only* to childhood, that defines childhood as a state that needs to be outgrown.

As Annette Appell, John Wall, Sarah Chinn, and other contributors argue persuasively, the work of gender and queer studies have done much to problematize the naturalized biological differences between bodies that have been used to justify discrimination and coercion. Foucault's now-classic assertion that subjects are created through power acting on and through them and Judith Butler's argument that identity—particularly gendered identity—is created through performance are just two of the revolutions in thought that reveal the extent to which we are all humans-in-the-making, perpetually in flux, continually responding to authoritative forces beyond our own minds and bodies.[19] There's arguably no better way to understand this form of subjectivity than through the child, a term often used uncritically as a placeholder for the dependence and malleability we still seek to partition off from adult autonomy. Rather than denying the child's fragility, we insist that bringing a critical eye to childhood will teach us to better conceive of a realistic human subject.

Joan W. Scott has argued that an "interest in class, race, and gender signal[s] first, a scholar's commitment to a history that included stories of the oppressed and an analysis of the meaning and nature of their oppression, and second, scholarly understanding that inequalities of power are organized along at least three axes."[20] *The Children's Table* not only makes the case that age needs to be added to the categories of race, gender, and class but also that adding conceptions of childhood to this critical trinity requires rethinking what qualifies as oppression and identity in the first place. Childhood, after all, both cuts across and encompasses all three categories in this analytic triptych. Disqualifying those on the "wrong" side of race, gender, and class is often accomplished by comparing them to children. Yet actual children occupy positions on both the privileged and disadvantaged sides of these three coins. Rather than arguing for moving children over to the empowered side of the equation, this collection contends that childhood studies offers new ways of engaging interdependence as a social reality and offers new frameworks for thinking about how to negotiate the obligations incurred across the very real gaps of power that do, and will, exist. Very young children are not autonomous, nor should they be. For scholars dedicated to charting and celebrating resistance to authority, childhood studies pushes us to reconsider when, if at all, it is just for the dominant to impose their will on the less powerful. In short, actual children raise uncomfortable questions that complicate the stance that authority is inherently oppressive and that subversion and resistance are unqualified positives. It is precisely because childhood skews this critical equation that it is essential that we engage with it, along with our own possible discomfort with the implications that follow. By engaging the liminality of childhood, we are pushed to a more nuanced understanding of and engagement with dependence and the way such dependence can generate unequal distributions of power.[21]

If, as I have been arguing, certain stylized and largely unquestioned assumptions about childhood undergird many pursuits in the humanities, then when we allow the insights of childhood studies to work through the theory and practice of particular disciplines, many possibilities emerge. The chapters in this volume explore some of those possibilities. Individually, these chapters exist as discrete instruments in a theoretical toolbox: by applying the insights of childhood studies to their particular field of study (such as queer theory, historical inquiry, or philosophical ethics) the authors provide new ways of thinking about both fields. Taken as a whole, the chapters collected here emerge as a cumulative thesis, arguing that, at this key moment in the state of the humanities, rethinking the child is both necessary and revolutionary.

Rather than providing a broad overview of all the work being done in this capacious and growing field, this volume has carefully chosen case studies from across disciplines to provide a sense of the questions childhood studies asks of scholars working in the humanities. To begin, although childhood studies is undoubtedly an international field, this volume has chosen to focus largely on the United States in order to provide a carefully contextualized account of how the insights of this field can function in response to the particular pressures wrought on the humanities in light of U.S. political culture's increasingly tight grip on the fantasy of independence and its rejection of communal forms of obligation.[22] Thus this book orbits around key foci of current humanities thought and scholarship as they emerge in imagined subject positions of particular, though certainly not exclusive, weight in the United States: the autonomous agent-actor, the object of the disciplinary gaze, the subject of moral and sexual panic, the negotiating (and negotiated) member of the community. As the chapters constellate around these centers of epistemological gravity, they necessarily cross back and forth over contradictory representations of childhood—over questions of dependence and independence, of agency and submission, of citizenship and disenfranchisement. Because we've envisioned this collection as a series of conversations revolving around a different but interrelated set of questions in the humanities, each section is headed by a brief introduction that situates the arguments of the individual chapters in relation to one another. This general introduction thus sketches the organizational schema in broad strokes; the section headings provide more detailed analysis.

Our first group of chapters takes on the sine qua non of modern liberal thought—the independent, consenting subject. When John Locke wrote that children are "not born in [a] full state of equality, though they are born to it," he simultaneously changed the terms of government and created a means of excluding some from it.[23] As Holly Brewer has argued, Locke's emphasis on consent rendered children—and, I would add, those who could be likened to children—incapable of participating in the contractual obligations that would come to occupy center stage in liberal democratic thought.[24] The social contract effectively excludes those who do not come to it as fully consenting, independent subjects.[25] These chapters bring the perspective of childhood studies to the Enlightenment triad of reason, consent, and autonomy to make the case that none of these terms are as stable as their place in legal, social, and scholarly discourses would imply. As Annette Appell asks in her contribution, what does consent mean for an eight-year-old in a court system designed to give everyone an adult set of rights? Lucia Hodgson takes on another set of Enlightenment presumptions as they emerge in problematic analyses about how race and childhood intersect in moral development. Her argument, like Appell's, reveals the deep injustice done to actual children when we impose fictional frameworks on their experiences and then punish them for not conforming to those fictions. James Marten examines another venue, that of war, in which the Lockean model of the fully consenting rational subject does a disservice to our understanding of the effects of conflict on both adults and children. In the final piece in this section, John Wall suggests that we need to engage in a "childist" ethics, one that avoids the neat binaries of adult and child, of the reasoning and unreasoning subject. Childist ethics rejects the idea of a straight line leading from child to adult (or put another way, from them to us) and instead decenters the Lockean subject and replaces it with an elliptical perspective. In this ethics neither observer nor observed holds a place of privilege; rather each learns from orbiting the other, always rethinking their own assumptions. As these authors indicate, when we put a realistic approach to childhood at the center of these inquiries, we are led into new territory in the analysis of both citizenship and subjectivity.

While the first group of chapters revolves around the antipode of the child-figure—the independent, consenting liberal subject, the second and third sections analyze the disciplined subject—a character often aligned with childhood—and the problems the child figure raises for identity studies. The child, after all, is the quintessential subject of discipline, the site where even the most conservative commentator celebrates the powerful work of social construction. These chapters build on the rich cadre of theories by Michel Foucault, Judith Butler, Kathryn Bond Stockton, and others to demonstrate how childhood studies can add to our understanding of how social forces shape individual interiors. As a whole, the chapters argue that we cannot fully understand how communal pressures construct identity without examining the structures explicitly designed to discipline emerging personalities—the very institutions designed to accommodate childhood.

More specifically, section 2 illuminates the work of the schoolroom to illustrate how social discipline pivots on an imagined child who lives on two temporal planes simultaneously. The schoolchild is the student of the present moment, who needs particular materials, such as the pedagogical tracts Lesley Ginsberg discusses and the physical schoolrooms Roy Kozlovsky analyzes. This child is also at the same time the future citizen, whose role as a state subject is created and projected in the lessons he or she learns, lessons that adhere to certain beliefs about race, gender, and class. As Ginsberg and Sophie Bell illustrate, educational practice was always in productive tension with the legal and cultural structures that insisted some children (such as girls and African Americans) would never be able to move through the lessons of the schoolroom to the contracts of adulthood. Kozlovsky focuses on physical structures designed for eduction in order to trace how the horrors of World War II helped to create new means of imagining and educating children through architectural practices.

The third section continues its exploration of the disciplined subject by exploring how affect can be enhanced and repressed through social, familial, and educational structures. Both Sarah Chinn's and Susan Honeyman's contributions think through what happens when childhood studies and queer/gender theory are put in conversation. Chinn suggests that the work of childhood studies would benefit from the theoretical daring of queer theory's speculations about love, sex, and reproduction—all topics essential to how we formulate childhood but often subjects that are overlooked in historical attention to children's agency. Susan Honeyman makes the case that an emphasis on children's reading practices can open up new possibilities in gender theory. She explores how the transgendering apparent in much of children's literature and the transreading enjoyed by many children offers a fertile place to theorize gender without reifying the stubborn binaries of male and female. Carol Singley's chapter welds adoption studies, childhood studies, and literary analysis together to suggest new ways of thinking through how Americans position childhood subjects within affective kinship relations.

Moving from theory to the archives to the classroom, the final triad of chapters demonstrates how changing ideas about childhood can fundamentally alter how we think, work, and teach in the humanities. In particular, this section cumulatively argues that rethinking childhood involves rethinking our relationship to the past, especially the individual, historical, and institutional memories of disciplinary divides and specialties. Karen Sánchez-Eppler traces how our scholarly attraction to both the archive and the child intersect and argues that our desire for origins, hidden secrets, and unclaimed treasures drives much of our attention to both subjects. Robin Bernstein draws from performance theory to provide an answer to a question that animates much debate within the field of childhood studies: How do we attend to both the physical and imaginary child? Lynne Vallone, a professor and administrator in a PhD-granting program in childhood studies, explores the concrete challenges of taking childhood studies into the next generation. In the process, these scholars work creatively to construct a child-centered vision of humanities scholarship that can move ably between theory and practice, the past and the future.

Yet like the child who is the subject of this volume, the chapters themselves resist easy classification. Rather, they enact the vibrancy of sitting at the children's table, in which conversations occur between two adjacent diners but also break out enthusiastically across the table and around the corner, as themes are picked up, realigned, and debated among an energetic group. Some of these exchanges could just as easily create their own conversational cluster. For instance, James Marten, Karen Sánchez-Eppler, and Roy Kozlovsky, placed in separate sections in this particular line-up, all speak eloquently about the work of interpreting material remnants of childhood—both what we create to accommodate real and imagined children (as with the schools and playgrounds in Kozlovsky's chapter) and what children themselves create as they find their own way in their community and culture (as with the handmade nineteenth-century card featured in Sánchez-Eppler's piece). Another equally compelling conversation occurs between Lucia Hodgson, Annette Appell, Lesley Ginsberg, and John Wall as their chapters collectively explore how legal structures organize children's realities and how those structures might be reformed to better accommodate children's particular needs. Still another exchange taking place across the classificatory boundaries of this volume emerges between Robin Bernstein, Sarah Chinn,

Susan Honeyman, and Sophia Bell, whose chapters work through—in divergent but often complementary ways—how children might navigate performative and literary expectations to first forge and then reimagine their own identities. We invite readers to move within and beyond the categories we've provided as they find their own niche in this conversation.

The object of this volume is to not simply to make the argument that invoking the child requires different questions, different methodologies, and different ways of thinking but to provide concrete examples of how those questions, methodologies, and ways of thinking function across a range of fields. In the process, these chapters reveal how we must critically assess our own scholarly and intellectual attachments to the privileges allotted to adulthood, a position propped up by the preservation of an imagined child who is "naturally" unable to access the realms of consent, resistance, and agency. Our purpose is not to replace this imagined child with a more suitable figure but to insist on the ways in which both childhood and adulthood are continually reconstructed in a host of contexts—academic, political, economic—and, in the process, to shift our scholarly analysis in ways that radically rethink these social and intellectual relationships as they affect adults, children, and all of us who occupy the spaces in between.

Notes

1. I am particularly indebted to Lucia Hodgson for providing the title of this volume and for being a part of much of the early thinking and planning that moved this book toward publication.

2. Commission on the Humanities in American Life, *The Humanities in American Life* (Berkeley: University of California Press, 1980), 2.

3. Geoffrey Galt Harpham, *The Humanities and the Dream of America* (Chicago: University of Chicago Press, 2011), 6.

4. Anna Wierbicka, "Defining the Humanities," *Culture and Psychology* 17.1 (2011): 34.

5. Willem Koops, "Imaging Childhood," in *Beyond the Century of the Child: Developmental Psychology and Cultural History*, ed. Michael Zuckerman and Willem Koops (Philadelphia: University of Pennsylvania Press, 2003), 1.

6. My thinking on this issue has been greatly influenced by the persuasive arguments put forth in disability studies, particularly by Rosemarie Garland Thomson in *Extraordinary Bodies: Disability in American Literature and Culture* (New York: Columbia University Press, 1997) and by Lennard Davis in *Enforcing Normalcy: Disability, Deafness, and the Body* (London: Verso, 1995).

7. For an insightful analysis of how childhood became a repository for a nostalgic

racism, see Robin Bernstein, *Racial Innocence: Performing American Childhood from Slavery to Civil Rights* (New York: New York University Press, 2011). For a useful analysis of the work of G. Stanley Hall, see Sarah Chinn, *Inventing Modern Adolescence: The Children of Immigrants in Turn-of-the-Century America* (New Brunswick, NJ: Rutgers University Press, 2008). For an analysis of the reciprocal relationship between childhood suffering and racial distinction, see Anna Mae Duane, *Suffering Childhood in Early America: Violence, Race, and the Making of the Child Victim* (Athens: University of Georgia Press, 2010).

8. G. Stanley Hall, *Adolescence: Its Psychology and Its Relations to Physiology, Anthropology, Sociology, Sex, Crime, Religion, and Education*, 2 vols. (New York: Appleton, 1904).

9. Steven Selden, "Transforming Better Babies into Fitter Families: Archival Resources and the History of the American Eugenics Movement, 1908–1930," *Proceedings of the American Philosophical Society* 149.2 (2005): 199–225.

10. Kenneth Kidd, *Freud in Oz: The Intersections of Psychoanalysis* (Minneapolis: University of Minnesota Press, 2011), viii.

11. Cathy Davidson, "Humanities 2.0: Promise, Perils, Predictions," *PMLA* 123.3 (2008): 707.

12. The list of venues dedicated to childhood studies continues to grow. The journal *Childhood: A Journal of Global Child Research* has been in place since 1993. In 2007, the online journal *Childhoods Today* was launched by the Centre for the Study of Childhood and Youth and the University of Sheffield. In 2008, Johns Hopkins launched the *Journal of the History of Childhood and Youth*. New York University Press and Rutgers University Press have series dedicated to childhood studies. *PMLA* has recently showcased a forum on the theories and methodologies of children's literature and childhood studies. Groundbreaking work about children's literature, itself a vibrant and growing field, continues to be produced in mainstream venues and in journals including the *Children's Literature Association Quarterly*, *The Lion and the Unicorn*, and many others.

13. Karen Sánchez-Eppler, *Dependent States: The Child's Part in Nineteenth-Century American Culture* (Chicago: University of Chicago Press, 2005); Patricia Crain, *The Story of A: The Alphabetization of America from "The New England Primer" to "The Scarlet Letter"* (Stanford, CA: Stanford University Press, 2005); Gillian Brown, *The Consent of the Governed: The Lockean Legacy in Early American Culture* (Cambridge: Cambridge University Press, 2001); David Rosen, *Armies of the Young: Child Soldiers in War and Terrorism* (New Brunswick, NJ: Rutgers University Press, 2005); Margaret Higonnet, "War Toys: Breaking and Remaking in Great War Narratives," *The Lion and the Unicorn* 31.2 (2007): 116–31; James Marten, *The Children's Civil War* (Chapel Hill: University of North Carolina Press, 1998).

14. Julia Mickenberg, *Learning from the Left: Children's Literature, the Cold War, and Radical Politics in the United States* (New York: Oxford University Press, 2006); Katherine Capshaw Smith, *Children's Literature of the Harlem Renaissance* (Bloomington: Indiana University Press, 2006); Kenneth Kidd *Making American*

Boys: Boyology and the Feral Tale (Minneapolis: University of Minnesota Press, 2005).

15. James Beattie, *An Essay on Truth on the Nature and Immutability of Truth, in Opposition to Sophistry and Skepticism*, 6th ed. (London: Edward and Charles Dilly, 1778), 508. I am indebted to Lucia Hodgson for directing me to this quote.

16. *The Writings of Thomas Jefferson*, 20 vols., ed. Andrew A. Lipscomb and Albert Ellery Bergh (Washington, DC: Thomas Jefferson Memorial Association, 1903–4), 19:41.

17. Many thanks to Sarah Chinn for helping me to clarify this point.

18. Courtney Wiekle-Mills makes a strong case for early American scholarship's reliance on an infantilizing structure to articulate arguments about private and public citizenship ("'Learn to Love Your Book': The Child Reader and Affectionate Citizenship," *Early American Literature* 43.1 [2008]: 35–61).

19. Two of the foundational works in this vein are Judith Butler, *Gender Trouble: Feminism and the Subversion of Identity* (1990) and Michel Foucault, *Discipline and Punish: The Birth of the Prison* (1975). For an analysis bringing together queer studies, performance studies, and race theory, see José Muñoz, *Disidentifications: Queers of Color and the Performance of Politics* (Minneapolis: University of Minnesota Press, 1999).

20. Joan W. Scott, "Gender: A Useful Category of Analysis," *American Historical Review* 91.5 (1996): 1054.

21. For a wonderfully nuanced exploration of how childhood articulates dependence in American culture, see Sánchez-Eppler, *Dependent States*. For an analysis of how we might rethink the demands of dependence, see Martha Fineman, "The Vulnerable Subject and the Responsive State," *Emory Law Journal* 60.2 (2010): 130.

22. As American studies scholars are well aware, any study of the United States needs to acknowledge the multiple ways that influence crosses national borders. For instance, in his chapter in this volume, Roy Kozlovsky reaches across the Atlantic in his consideration of postwar British architecture, which, he points out, influenced American ideals about the structures children needed to play and learn.

23. John Locke, *Second Treatise of Civil Government*, ed. Peter Laslett (Cambridge: Cambridge University Press, 1960), 322.

24. Holly Brewer, *By Birth or By Consent: Children, Law and the Anglo-American Revolution in Authority* (Chapel Hill: published for the Omohundro Institute of Early American History and Culture by the University of North Carolina Press, 2007).

25. For two different perspectives on how to realign our vision of rights and the social contract they are implicitly based on see Martha Nussbaum, *Frontiers of Justice: Disability, Nationality, Species Membership* (Cambridge: Harvard University Press, 2006), and Martha Fineman, "The Vulnerable Subject: Anchoring Equality in the Human Condition," *Yale Journal of Law and Feminism* 20.1 (2008–9): 1–23.

PART ONE

Questioning the Autonomous Subject and Individual Rights

Childhood studies, a field designed to dismantle inaccurate and often destructive definitions of childhood, has yet to come up with a consensus on what we mean when we say "child" in the first place. If the child is socially constructed, as Philippe Ariès has argued, and as many of our contributors take as a given, how can we possibly hope to work through those constructions to extract an authentic person? As the conversation moves between the humanities and the social sciences, between archivists and activists, childhood studies struggles with the question of how to bridge the relationship between the rhetorical child (the cultural construct of "childhood") and the historical child (actual young people making their way in the world). In many ways, the tension within this increasingly multidisciplinary field echoes the larger tension between the humanities, the social sciences, and the hard sciences, a tension too often reduced to the divide between imagination and reality, theory and practice. The autonomous subject, itself a creation of Enlightenment theory, often renders both humanist and scientific analyses of children as teleological narratives that root for the incomplete subject to evolve and grow into a self-reliant citizen. As the chapters by Annette Ruth Appell, Lucia Hodgson, James Marten, and John Wall illustrate, the fantasy of a fully autonomous person prevents us from a realistic analysis of children as individual and social subjects.

Within childhood studies, as well as in the academy as a whole, different types of work can be assigned different ethical and scholarly value. Jacqueline Rose has famously argued for the "impossibility" of children's literature, because of the partial status of the child who is the ostensible audience for those books.[1] Similarly, one might suggest, our knowledge of "real children" will always be largely speculative and deeply flawed. Perhaps, this argument runs, the most rigorous and authentic mode of scholarship is one that admits our own epistemological limitations. We can never truly move past our own constructions of children, but we can critique the damage such constructions can do and work to revise them in ways designed to promote human rights for all children. The counterargument suggests that spending scholarly resources on the rhetorical child neglects the more pressing and immediate needs of children living in dire circumstances in the developing world. In the last section of this volume, Lynne Vallone muses on this division and on the implicit assertion that "research that concentrates on children's rights in the neediest parts of the world somehow 'trump[s]' the work of those who are concerned, for example, with the social and political constructions of childhood" (243). Yet this scholarly hierarchy falsely suggests that we can indeed separate actual subjects from our literary, cultural, and political notions about them—notions deeply shaped by an investment in autonomy that renders the child's dependence and vulnerability a block to full engagement and full humanity.

The chapters in this section offer innovative and convincing responses to this perceived moral and practical imbalance between theory and practice, between "book children" and "real children," by moving with grace and rigor between theories of subjectivity and individual young people whose difficult lives are shaped by those theories. In particular, each chapter offers new ways of challenging the seductive fallacy that supposes any of us can inhabit a position of unmediated independence. Drawing from legal, ethical, and philosophical theories of personhood, each chapter demonstrates how humanist inquiry and critique of the liberal subject is vital to moving both the study and the advocacy of children forward.

Appell's contribution, the first in this section, draws from ideas cultivated in feminist thought to critique current practices of law that pose allegedly natural, objective definitions of both adulthood and childhood that are, in practice, inaccurate and damaging. She takes particular issue with the idea of the child as a primarily private subject. "With childhood safely ensconced in the family and without a voice outside of the home," Appell contends, "the polity can avoid universal questions and answers about what children, as persons, need and want, what goods children, as a class, should have, and what material conditions, opportunities, and influences are optimal for all children." She offers a new model for thinking about children as legal subjects and as citizens. Such a "jurisprudence of childhood" would give up the fantasy of a uniform childhood in favor of a contextual critical approach that acknowledges that children's agency and their needs are distributed widely across the racial, socioeconomic, and political placements of their families.

Hodgson's work on William Bennett's racially biased social "science" traces a chronology stretching back to seventeenth- and eighteenth-century theories of human development. As a literature specialist trained to understand the power of stories, Hodgson ably demonstrates the necessity of a humanist perspective that can unravel the historically racist narratives of human development that cast black children as forever stunted, unable to grow into the autonomous individual that both science and law suggests is the end result of a successful childhood. Hodgson's work demonstrates the damage these concepts wreak by tracing their influence to decisions made by those with power over the lives of African American youth caught in the twenty-first century prison system.

Marten moves skillfully between the allegedly abstract and relatively privileged realm of historical Western children and the dangerous lives of children in the developing world today as he charts the study of children in wartime. While Marten is careful to acknowledge the difficulty of finding the voices of children in the past, he argues that to the extent that doing so is possible, it revises our understanding of children's capabilities and liabilities, providing a portrait of childhood that runs counter to adult desires for it to be a realm of vulnerability and innocence. As Marten discusses the rich body of work on children in conflict, he provides evidence that children "understand war and are less shocked by it than adults might think" (57). Recalibrating our thinking about children in conflict does not simply realign adult ideas; it also demands a new way of thinking about how to advocate for young combatants.

Wall explicitly engages the larger question each chapter in this section is implicitly asking—once we become aware of how adult investments in various stories about children affect the lives of young people, what do we do? If our thinking about children has proven harmful to them, what new framework should we implement? Wall responds that we need nothing less than a "childist" ethics; "children," he argues, "will take a central place in humanities scholarship only if there is a revolution on a similar scale" to those for other "minorities." Of course, the effects of minority scholarship have exceeded the boundaries of the humanities to shape discourse in the social and hard sciences. Wall calls for a similar revolution that would permit us to engage the child as a full subject, as do the other contributors in this section and in the volume as a whole. As each chapter in this section illustrates, without a fundamental shift in how we think, even well-meaning advocates can wind up replicating the very oppressive structures they seek to undermine.

Notes

1. Jacqueline Rose, *The Case of Peter Pan; or, The Impossibility of Children's Fiction* (Philadelphia: University of Pennsylvania Press, 1992). For a persuasive response to Rose, see Perry Nodelman, "The Case of Children's Fiction; or, The Impossibility of Jacqueline Rose," *Children's Literature Association Quarterly* 10.3 (1985): 98–100.

The Prepolitical Child of Child-Centered Jurisprudence

Annette Ruth Appell

Childhood studies scholarship has revealed that childhood, the category that holds, defines, and governs children, is to be a social construct contingent on time and place.[1] While young children are, generally speaking, vulnerable and dependent, the length, contours, and extent of that dependency, as well as the assignment of children to dependency, vary greatly across time, nation, geography, and race.[2] This central insight, that childhood is not natural, has yet to gain currency in legal studies. Although legal scholars have developed critical jurisprudence regarding race and gender, illustrating how these seemingly natural categories are socio-legal constructions that create and maintain power and privilege, jurisprudential studies have not interrogated childhood or explored the work that childhood performs in law and society.

The legal construction of children in the United States as dependent—and of dependency as private, familial, and developmental—obscures both the contingency of childhood and the law's role in creating and maintaining childhood. By defining children as vulnerable and situating them in the private realm, the law defines and regulates childhood as if it were natural and universal rather than political and diverse. This construction submerges questions about how children differ as individuals and by virtue of their membership in racial, ethnic, national, age, gender, and economic groups. This construction also limits interrogation of what the public might owe these dependent persons and what public roles children play. With childhood safely ensconced in the family and without a voice outside the family, the polity can avoid universal questions and answers about what children, as persons, need and want, what goods children, as a class, should have, and what material conditions, opportunities, and influences are optimal for all children. Instead, we ask what our own children should have and what they need for success.

Childhood is a transformative site within the context of a larger system that treats dependency as both autonomy promoting, as a relational and generational matter, and autonomy limiting, as a functional matter. In other words, the privatized dependency of childhood promotes the autonomy of adults, leaving them free to employ their values through child rearing and in training their own children to become morally autonomous democratic citizens upon adulthood; this privatized dependency also limits the autonomy of the child and the caregiver—the former lacking legal or political authority by virtue of being a child and the latter rendered dependent through the provision of private, unpaid care for dependent children. Moreover, childhood is a socially constructed category deeply connected to race, gender, class, and citizenship, in which children's vulnerability and dependency perform differently along racial, class, and gender lines, factors that affect not only children themselves but also the adults on whom they depend.[3] Unlike other subordinated groups, children will outgrow their subordination as children, but whether they will be subordinated as adults depends very much on their childhood, that is, their race, class, and gender, or perhaps more accurately the race, class, and gender of their parents.

Legal theory has not systematically explored from the child's perspective the political aspects of locating this developing child in the family and then privatizing most aspects of the child's dependency. Following the lead of feminist jurisprudence, a jurisprudence of childhood might ask the same sorts of questions about how the law constructs childhood. Whom does this construction serve? Who benefits from it and who suffers? How does the relegation of our future citizens to incapacity and need serve children and adults? Who thrives under these conditions and who does not? How much of children's legal coverture is necessary and helpful? Why do children not have the right to vote? Why do children not hold political office?

Both feminist and child-centered jurisprudence share concerns about dependency and agency, but they each have different subjects (women and children, respectively) and categories of analysis (gender and youth, respectively). Feminist jurisprudence has delegitimized the legal incompetence and dependency of the female subject. By examining how law constructs gender, feminist jurisprudence has, at least in theory, denaturalized gender, taking women out of the private realm of family and situating them in the market and the polity, has shown that families are not prepolitical; removed women from dependency on fathers and husbands, and has freed them from the dependency that arises out of caregiving. In short, feminist jurisprudence treats women as moral agents and political and economic actors. Despite the significance of childhood dependency and vulnerability in feminist jurisprudence, feminist legal studies has not interrogated the structure of childhood the way it has gender. Even more surprising, child-centered jurisprudence, which addresses children's rights and representation and sometimes age, has not questioned systematically, fundamentally, or critically the dependency and vulnerability that law and society assign to children. Instead, it assumes this dependency, vulnerability, and privacy, rarely with any reference to the central insight of childhood studies—that childhood is not natural.

In interrogating the legal category of woman (and man) and, relatedly, gender relations, feminist jurisprudence has shown them to be powerful and often confining political and social constructs. A major contribution of feminism and feminist jurisprudence has been the revelation that the liberal subject—the citizen—is autonomous, free, independent, and unattached. That is, the liberal subject is not a child, not a parent, most likely not a woman, and not poor. In short, the liberal subject is a white, middle-class man.[4]

This project has proliferated and has included the disaggregation of women from motherhood and motherhood from women, the destruction of coverture, the recognition of women and increased opportunities for them in the labor market, politics, and at home, and broad recognition of women's agency inside and outside of the home and family. In a world constructed around gender roles and differences that privilege persons without dependents (we'll call them "men"), singles them out for public life and economic rewards while depending on and yet largely ignoring those who care for dependents (we'll call them "women"), dependency is problematic for women. Martha Fineman has famously and persuasively illustrated how the privatization of dependency relies on women as caregivers for dependents and, in turn, makes women dependent themselves.[5] Many others have also taken issue with the deeply embedded and all but mandatory equation of woman and caretaker and with the resulting disadvantages women face.[6]

Feminist jurisprudents have proffered a variety of resolutions for the problematic aspects of this equation. These solutions are adult centered and primarily concerned with sex or gender equality, particularly regarding the responsibility for care. For example, Fineman has proposed public support for dependent care. Maxine Eichner accepts this theory but broadens and deepens it, suggesting that employment, family, and other social systems must be reformed to reflect multiple levels of dependency, including dual parental responsibility for children, the conceptual disaggregation of women from caregiving, and dismantlement of the single breadwinner model.[7]

Critical race feminists in law and other disciplines have delved more deeply and broadly into the problematic aspects of privatized dependency, illustrating how race, gender, class, and age intersect in the privatization of dependency. These feminists examine how wealth is structurally located in and transmitted through families in a manner that maintains economic stratification and racial identification and barriers. They illustrate how this transmission is related not to family functioning but instead to the conditions of the communities in which families live. For example, the relocation of production to the suburbs, the demise of public transportation, the stratification of housing along racial lines, and the localized funding of schools all serve to create and maintain cleavages of opportunity that diminish the prospects for children in families without economic capital and connections while reinforcing the prospects for children in families with such capital. This analysis challenges the myth of the autonomous liberal subject by illustrating how much of adulthood is predicted by the location of childhood rather than by personal choice and motivation.[8] This is true for both the child and caregiver, because the parents, whether biological or social, transfer their social capital, race, and class to the child, while the caregiving constrains the parent's options and resources.[9]

Nevertheless, feminists note that despite these dynamics, legal regulation rewards and blames mothers for the status of their children, putting "bad" mothers at risk of losing their children.[10] Thus, these structural conditions that serve to all but monopolize wealth and poverty challenge feminists to view children not as a burden but as a privilege that has been and continues to be hard won for poor women and women of color. African American women in particular have fought for generations to rear their children free from state or state-sanctioned interference and to prevent their children from being removed. In contrast to those feminists who view the domestication and privacy of child rearing as isolating and burdensome, critical race feminists value the opportunity to care for their children in the home and want better present lives and futures for their children.[11]

Feminism's illumination of both the oppressiveness of the mandatory association of women with child care and the power and privilege of motherhood renders feminist jurisprudence's relationship with children complicated. The vulnerability of children creates dependency, which can be a burden for the caregiver, who in turn becomes dependent because of the caregiving. The "natural" connection between women and children, through the operation of motherhood, causes other problems for women because it conflates womanhood and motherhood, binds women to constricting social scripts that relate to ideal images of mothering, and effectively undermines women's "full and equal political and economic participation."[12] Feminists have also exposed the interrelated patriarchal, male-centered structures of the home and market, structures that are built on, and sustained by, the assignment of domestic labor to women.

Despite their disagreements regarding children, race, and class, feminists have made progress in disaggregating women from compulsory motherhood, dismantling many aspects of patriarchy within this system, and achieving political power and authority. These achievements have no doubt changed women's lives, even if feminism has not been successful in dislodging men (noncaregivers) from the center of social organization. These successes can be attributed to many things, not the least of which is women's leadership in the intellectual, legal, and political movements that have led to these reforms.

Feminist jurisprudence also may have helped children by helping caregivers, but feminists have not systematically applied feminist methodologies to children.[13] On the contrary, as Leena Alanen has observed, feminists have largely failed to critically examine childhood, and this failure has limited both the advancement of children and of feminism.[14] To the extent that feminism seeks to politicize children, it is as dependents, not agents. In regarding children as dependents, feminist jurisprudence has, somewhat ironically, assumed childhood to be primarily a privatized space. It is not surprising then that feminists have continued to struggle with liberatory and inhibitory aspects of dependency and the woman-child relationship.

While feminist legal theorists have recognized that motherhood—the privilege of rearing children—is an important aspect of autonomy and constitutes political action, they continue to struggle with the burdens of dependency because feminist jurisprudence does not confront childhood. Childhood studies exposes the artifice of childhood itself and asks why children do not have moral or political claims or authority. It also asks what it might mean for women if children did have these claims. If feminist jurisprudence viewed childhood as political, and not natural, private, or dependent, it might gain insights into why children's care is privatized and why this care requires so many trade-offs for caregivers, what children gain and lose from this seclusion, and who else gains and loses under this regime. Once the child is at the center, the political subject or citizen does not have to be understood as the unattached liberal subject but can become something or someone else—a dependent being, a caregiver, or a developing child. Feminist jurisprudence might also imagine what care and caregiving would be if needing or receiving care was privileged.

Child-centered jurisprudence has also failed to apply lessons from childhood studies to children and, like feminist jurisprudence, has embraced the psychological model of childhood as a private place of need, vulnerability, and development. While feminist jurisprudence's fundamental method of denaturalizing women is to distinguish sex and gender, child-centered jurisprudence has not sought to distinguish age and childhood. Instead, it has assumed children's dependency and privacy. In contrast to feminist jurisprudence, which asks political questions regarding the law's construction of women as private and dependent (and also at the same time as care giving), child-centered jurisprudence is generally concerned with narrow legal questions of children's rights and children's representation; that is, it addresses what rights children have or should have vis-à-vis the state or their caregivers and what duties their legal representatives owe them. This inevitably (i.e., naturally) private, vulnerable, and dependent child is reminiscent of the naturally private, vulnerable woman of the prefeminist past.

There is no self-conscious, named, or well-developed school or methodology regarding childhood jurisprudence. This is not to say there are no legal writings or critiques regarding children and the law; however, unlike feminist jurisprudence, which has deconstructed woman, existing child-centered jurisprudence has not deconstructed the child, childhood, or dependency. Instead, child-centered jurisprudence has focused primarily on children's dependency and vulnerability in the context of their relationships with parents, the state, and educational systems. As a result, child-centered jurisprudence is largely unconcerned with the political nature and purpose of childhood and assumes dependency and privacy as givens. Unlike the woman at the center of feminist jurisprudence who is complex, multifaceted, and autonomous, the child at the center of child-centered jurisprudence is a developing being in need of protection and education during a legally and perhaps cognitively defined period of childhood. Moreover, it is not uncommon for child-centered jurisprudence to construct the family as the problem. Owing to the feminization of family, the problem in some strands of child-centered jurisprudence may be the mother, because these strands reflexively accept the privacy of childhood and uncritically place both responsibility and blame on the caregiver.

Child-centered jurisprudence thus misses opportunities to empower children and their caregivers. It does not question why children have so little authority outside the family, why caregivers are often disadvantaged through the caregiving, and why children are not more central in the law. Instead, child-centered jurisprudence extends to two primary inquiries: children's rights and children's legal representation. Children's rights jurisprudence generally consists of and comments on two types of rights: quasi civil rights and dependency rights. Both categories construct children as dependents and measure their freedom and rights accordingly. Quasi civil rights are like adult civil rights but may be cabined by children's youth. These rights include the right to be free from coercive state intervention and to receive equal treatment among dependents, to receive procedural due process protection, and to be granted modified versions of several of the constitutionally guaranteed substantive freedoms adults enjoy. Dependency rights center on children's vulnerability and dependency and sometimes overlap with quasi civil rights, particularly in the context of educational rights or in the case of those who advocate that children have a right to be free "from the shackles of their parents' authority."[15]

Quasi–civil rights jurisprudence seeks to preserve and protect the child's voice and conscience, as in freedom of choice and speech cases or in freedom from coercive intervention cases.[16] Children's dependency and vulnerability, however, often circumscribe the full extent of constitutional freedom. For example, girls do not receive women's right to (relatively) autonomous decisions regarding termination of pregnancy; instead, girls have a right to bypass their parents and convince a judge that they are mature enough to decide for themselves whether or not to terminate a pregnancy.[17] At the same time, this perceived decision-making vulnerability afforded greater freedom to children in *Roper v. Simmons*, in which the Supreme Court ruled that because of children's youth (i.e., their underdeveloped brains), it is unconstitutionally cruel and unusual to subject them to the death penalty or mandatory life without parole.[18] Children's quasi civil rights also extend to children's rights to attend schools that are not de jure racially segregated, to attend school regardless of their immigration status, and to be treated as legally legitimate regardless of their parents' marital status.[19] These rights represent attempts to liberate children from the oppressive or discriminatory arm of the state.

Dependency rights are also centered on the child, but they are concerned with the protection and socialization of children. These rights apply to what the parents and the state owe children as dependents who must be cared for and reared to adulthood. They govern adult responsibilities to children regarding education, basic sustenance, and physical and medical care. Although dependency rights promote children's long-term freedom and interests as adults, they are not aimed at emancipating children as children. Moreover, in the context of many dependency rights, it is adults who define the terms of these rights and the occasions on which they are invoked. For example, it is adults who choose whether they want a legal relationship with children, what choices children can make regarding custody, which school children attend and what they will study, and to what care they are entitled. Here, although child-centered jurisprudence might call for children's voices to dictate, or at least bear on, these outcomes and choices, these rights are concerned wholly with children's care and custody as children. This jurisprudence does not take issue with the category of childhood itself but instead assumes the attributes of childhood—vulnerability, dependency, and immaturity—and then operates in accordance with them.

More critical jurisprudential approaches to children's rights acknowledge the limitations of children's rights as well as the adult purposes they serve and the dissembling they perform.[20] This jurisprudence recognizes that children's rights, like rights more generally, tend to be "individualistic, individualizing, legalistic, and to reinforce existing power structures and socio-economic inequities."[21] This critical wing has also studied the content, purposes, and work of children's rights—approaches that have laid bare the very adult and even political work that lawyers and policy makers perform on the backs of children. For example, adults politicize teen pregnancy, school choice, adoption, and custody as part of larger societal fissures around birth control, race, gender, and wealth. Self-identified children's rights advocates rarely address structural changes to remedy sources of childhood risks, such as racism, poverty, poor schools, lack of economic opportunity, and lack of access to health care. These rights-based approaches tend to be confined by inherently conservative law and legal systems and so do not typically draw on critical or social justice approaches that might challenge the very structural conditions that the law both creates and naturalizes.

Children's rights advocates have tried to denaturalize and delegitimize parental control over children, but they have not, for the most part, interrogated the naturalness of children's dependency or childhood's private locale. In fact, child-centered jurisprudence has assumed a natural childhood even as it has called for the law to apply specifically, contextually, and with nuance to children. This jurisprudence has not engaged in a sustained examination of how legal and social norms regarding children shape society and conceptions of justice for children and adults. Instead, it is simply taken as a given that the child at the center of this jurisprudence is a developmental being in need of protection and education during a legally defined period of childhood. Yet the regulation of children—what and who a child is, what a child can and cannot do, to whom children belong, and who is responsible for children—has deep and broad implications for children themselves, the adults to whom they relate, and the adults they will become.

Child-centered jurisprudence also examines how children are represented before the law, raising questions in particular about who represents children and what role children play in this representation. This work is both academic and political; it is undertaken in the academy for theoretical and normative purposes as well as in policy-making fora.[22] Here, the primary debates are over whether children can determine the objectives of the representation or whether these objectives are guided by children's best interests. These debates also center on children's vulnerability and dependence.

Research and advocacy in this area invoke metrics of child development, capabilities, and capacities and the safety of the child. This work is also concerned with the disparities between lawyers and their child clients.

The legal literature regarding children's representation is deeply concerned with the balance between children's voices and their vulnerability. The law routinely, although not always, assigns legal representatives for children who will represent and advocate for their best interests and not necessarily what the children want. Even attorneys appointed to serve in the traditional lawyer role may not represent their child clients' wishes.[23] Attorneys, academics, policy makers, and judges continue to debate the proper role of children's attorneys, and they struggle with the contradictions in representing clients who may not have authority to dictate the objectives or scope of the representation or to pursue substantive rights.[24]

This wing of child-centered jurisprudence includes a significant call for children's agency in the representation. This call, represented in standards and theory regarding the legal representation of children and youth, recommends that attorneys allow the child to direct the objectives and means of the representation. The child representation wing also advocates that children have a direct voice in legal matters relating to them or their interests, even if the child's wishes will not be determinative. This wing has developed methodologies for representing a child who cannot direct all or portions of the representation or who simply may be unable to control his or her lawyer because he or she is too young, he or she is unable to hire or fire the lawyer, or the lawyer is appointed to represent an abstraction—the best interests of the child—rather than the child's own wishes.[25] Some child-centered jurisprudents have suggested how law and legal representation might embrace, or at least reflect, what children need and want, advocating respect for and engagement with the child as a moral being whose perspective is both valid and helpful to the decision makers. This perspective is worthy of expression because of the child's personhood, even if the child's competence to make decisions is not settled. These approaches have seriously and vigorously interrogated presumptions that children lack agency and voice in the law and legal proceedings and have articulated schemata to empower children and bring their wishes to bear on matters affecting them even as they acknowledge children's dependency and vulnerability.[26]

It would be difficult to identify a common methodology or shared objectives among these schools of thought regarding children and the law. Most of this very important and foundational child-centered jurisprudential work acknowledges and responds to children's development, dependency, agency, and vulnerability, but it has not taken on, in a systematic way, the questions childhood studies would raise: structural questions about what purposes the designation of childhood serves, how the law constructs it, and why children are domesticated. Instead, child-centered jurisprudence, as vital and important as it is, confines itself primarily to legalistic or individualizing approaches to rights, agency, and representation, never reaching an analysis of what political and cultural work the legal category and regulation of childhood performs.

Even as children's rights "move children into the public realm," child-centered jurisprudence is only occasionally engaged with substantive questions surrounding the privacy and dependency of childhood outside of legal representation, education, and custodial matters.[27] Although child-centered jurisprudence is concerned with children's participation in their own legal representation and sometimes their direct voice in court, it is not yet heavily engaged with other questions that childhood studies asks. These questions would bear on children's role in forming or informing public policy, children's voices when they are the subjects of study, and children's right to vote. These questions engage childhood scholars in other parts of the world and in other disciplines in this country, but not, for the most part, the U.S. legal academy.[28]

Moreover, child-centered jurisprudence equates progress with the transition of children from property to persons, but, unlike childhood studies, sheds little light on what personhood means for children outside of their dependent status. In other words, the personhood of the child of child-centered jurisprudence exists only within the boundaries of dependency, vis-à-vis parent, state, and school. Under this approach, the question of what this cabined personhood means for children in material, social, and economic terms is folded into their dependency, which is in turn privatized and assigned to parents or guardians and to various public entities designed to address children's vulnerability. In this way, child-centered jurisprudence internalizes the privacy and dependency of children and contemplates children within the bounds of childhood—the structural site that defines and regulates children—rather than interrogating this site itself in order to explore the role of childhood in distributing power, agency, and opportunity.

When child-centered jurisprudence critiques the private family, it does so without accounting for either the social inequalities or the value pluralism that undergirds liberal theory. That is, in a liberal democracy, rearing children in private families that propagate and preserve value pluralism while fostering private allegiances will, in theory, produce critically thinking citizens with the requisite distance from the state to govern. This private aspect of the political child has great utility, particularly for protecting the moral autonomy of marginalized women and children. At the same time, however, the material aspects of privatized dependency serve to reify and naturalize multiple inequalities, limiting the political and economic roles and options of certain children and families. This is an insight that has been largely absent from child-centered jurisprudence.

In these ways, child-centered jurisprudence, while extraordinarily important, tends to be confined by the contours of dependency, which prevents it from systematically interrogating the beneficial and harmful conditions of this construction. For the most part, child-centered jurisprudence does not challenge the structure of dependency or the relegation of that dependency to the private realm. For example, child-centered jurisprudence rarely challenges the legal norm that children are raised in families or the fact that public investment in children is primarily centered on children's caregivers. Child-centered jurisprudence does not ask whom and what purposes privatized dependency serves.

The childhood studies field has illuminated childhood as partly, if not entirely, an artificial social category, framed and reinforced by the law to create, define, and maintain power. Childhood studies has further illustrated that the elasticity and contingency of childhood and its norms respond to changing material and ideological conditions over time and place. This artificial construction of childhood formulates the child as raceless (i.e., white) and middle class. As such, the child is very much like the raceless (i.e., white) middle-class male liberal subject that feminist and critical theorists have exposed and contested.[29] No matter who this child is or whence she or he comes, she or he is expected to become the white, male, middle-class, adult liberal subject upon reaching adulthood. The three pillars of the legal definition of the child as developing, dependent, and private mask the differences among children while reinforcing the normative middle-class child as the measure of childhood; moreover, these characteristics further obfuscate the inequalities among the adult liberal subjects children are expected to become. This standardization effectively serves to reproduce poverty, race, and wealth because the privacy and dependency of childhood ensures that children will step into the adult shoes their childhoods provide. A jurisprudence of childhood might begin with a critique of these three pillars.

Despite the extensive political work that childhood performs, childhood is not viewed as a powerful or agential site but instead as a private and developmental state of nature. This equation is central to the American understanding of a liberal, republican democracy in which government is created by (reasoned) consent and remains in the hands of enlightened republican citizens who can exercise their consent in the name of the public good. In this equation, children are the opposite of this citizen, but are also capable of becoming this citizen through the process of maturation and education. The liberal child is, strangely, both the precursor to and the opposite of the liberal subject (adult).[30]

Constructed primarily as developing beings, children are understood as having needs that are immediate and time limited. The developmental child needs basic care and education—nutrition, school, and protection from their physical, emotional, and cognitive vulnerabilities—in order to reach adulthood. Homing in on this narrow, scientific version of development, the law both universalizes childhood through developmental standards and individualizes childhood by regulating only for physical, moral, and cognitive development. This scientific approach carries the appearance of objectivity, truth, and universality. Possessing only individual and personal needs, children inhabit a childhood that relies on professionals to identify, measure, and assess what developmental milestones they must achieve to become liberal citizens. This developmental view of childhood, in turn, permits a suspension of questions regarding other conditions that affect children's lives and chances, such as the quality and safety of their housing, neighborhoods, and schools, how many hours their parents have to work to support them, and to what cultural cornerstones they are exposed.

This legally codified scientific approach is culturally bound and tied to middle-class norms, even as the experience, terms, and objectives of child development vary according to class.[31] Tethered to the middle-class child, assessments of what children need and what constitutes development contemplate only one type of child, one who has middle-class resources and that are available at home or in the community to satisfy needs that are individual and personal. Yet mental health professionals establish measures and interventions for all children without regard for other conditions that affect children's lives and chances and without regard for how developmental trajectories and needs might differ according to socioeconomic status and geographic location.

Childhood's dependency effectively subsumes children's identities. A variety of adults have authority over children. These adults range from their parents to teachers, health care providers, and, for some children, lawyers. These adults, with varying levels of knowledge of and authority over the specific child, have great power in a child's life but little accountability to the child because of the child's lack of authority. In addition, this absence of legitimated authority inhibits direct public accountability to children both because of children's lack of authority and because this scheme expects the child's adult agents to promote children's interests. These agents, however, are not equally situated (in the case of parents) when it comes to knowing what children need or equally inclined (in the case of professionals) to advocate for them.

This equation of childhood and dependency disaggregates childhood from adulthood even though childhood evokes, and terminates in, adulthood. Adulthood and childhood remain in a binary, or at most tangential, relationship because of the centrality of child development in defining and regulating childhood. In other words, despite the deep, pronounced connections between childhood and adulthood and the fact that the transformation from child to adult is gradual, the legal transition is abrupt. Once children become adults, they are the liberal citizen: autonomous, independent, unattached, and self-sufficient. They are no longer entitled to care and support but are responsible for their own lot, their own achievements, and their own resources. This is true even though children experience their dependency in widely disparate conditions.

The construction of childhood as natural and dependent has left all children without a direct political voice and relegated them to the privacy of the family and, therefore, they are able to make few affirmative claims against the state. At the same time, this privatized childhood promotes important liberal goals: it provides a private site of value creation and promulgation that supports pluralism, strengthens democracy, and preserves the liberty of adults. Privacy also provides protection for the most vulnerable and marginalized parents and children who might be at greater risk of family dissolution and loss of identity if child rearing were more public.

On the other hand, the privatization of childhood and its assignment to families serve to individualize social and economic needs and goods and to mask the political nature of resource distribution. As Caroline Levander explains, in addition to forming the basis of the distinction between the self (the individual) and the state, "the child also works to facilitate a shift of social responsibility from the state onto the self."[32] The legal construction of childhood as private and personal rather than structural has still larger repercussions. It has contributed to the impoverishment of women who are caregivers and to the personalization and individualization of wealth and poverty. Moreover, this privacy both accounts for and masks the distributive functions of childhood by naturalizing and individuating childhood.

Thus, children's needs are private, both because their needs are not publically accounted for and because what children "need" is very much tied to their families. As Patricia Hill Collins has observed, "Despite ideas that social mobility is widespread, U.S. children routinely enjoy or suffer the economic status of their parents. Families constitute important sites for inheritance, not solely of cultural values, but of property."[33] Because children's dependency resides in families who live in a country with great variations in wealth, some children will have tremendous economic resources and want for nothing, while other children will need more. What social goods children have and need depends very much on their families, which dictate to a large degree what they have, what they can and should achieve, and what their social capital will purchase. This privatized childhood does not place children on a level playing field and thus produces (and reproduces) inequality among adults that derives from their privatized upbringing but for which they are accountable as political citizens.

A jurisprudence of childhood might approach the regulation of childhood contextually and critically, taking into account the benefits and deficits of the political, ideological, and distributive placement of children in families. Analyzing the foundational, liberatory, and repressive aspects of the legally private, vulnerable, and dependent child and the relationships between childhood and adulthood might propel the legal study of childhood to imagine what justice for children would mean during their childhood and what children will need as children to have substantive equality as adults.

Such a set of inquiries regarding children might lead to a childhood jurisprudence that breaks out of a narrow focus on dependency and vulnerability while appreciating and bolstering the public role of childhood and its deep connections to adulthood—both to the adults who support children and through the adults the children will become. In addition, this intergenerational and politicized jurisprudence would likely benefit women, who continue, despite many advances, to be intimately and deeply connected to and bound by dependency. Toward that end, existing child-centered jurisprudence might be pushed to view children's moral and political claims, rights, welfare, and identity as standing outside of but also as being part of families.[34]

Notes

This chapter is an edited excerpt of "The Pre-political Child of Child-Centered Jurisprudence," *Houston Law Review* 46.3 (2009): 703–57.

1. Chris Jenks, *Childhood* (London: Routledge, 1996); Holly Brewer, *By Birth or Consent: Children, Law, and the Anglo-American Revolution in Authority* (Chapel Hill: published for the Omohundro Institute of Early American History and Culture by the University of North Carolina Press, 2005); Paula S. Fass and Mary Ann Mason, eds., *Childhood in America* (New York: New York University Press, 2000); Linda Gordon, *The Great Arizona Orphan Abduction* (Cambridge, MA: Harvard University Press, 1999); Joseph M. Hawes, *The Children's Rights Movement* (Boston: Twayne, 1991); Caroline F. Levander, *Cradle of Liberty: Race, the Child, and National Belonging from Thomas Jefferson to W. E. B. Du Bois* (Durham, NC: Duke University Press, 2006); Mary Ann Mason, *From Father's Property to Children's Rights* (New York: Columbia University Press, 1994); Karen Sánchez-Eppler, *Dependent States: The Child's Part in Nineteenth-Century American Culture* (Chicago: University of Chicago Press, 2005); Steven Mintz, *Huck's Raft: A History of American Childhood* (Cambridge, MA: Harvard University Press, 2004). See also Anna Mae Duane's introduction to this volume as well as Robin Bernstein's, Lucia Hodgson's, and Carol J. Singley's chapters.

2. David Archard, *Children: Rights and Childhood*, 2nd ed. (London: Routledge, 2004), 25–27; Allison James, Chris Jenks, and Alan Prout, *Theorizing Childhood* (Cambridge, UK: Polity, 1998), 124–31. See also Lucia Hodgson's and Carol Singley's chapters in this volume.

3. Berry Mayall, *Towards a Sociology for Childhood* (Buckingham, UK: Open University Press, 2002), 122.

4. Monique Lanoix, "The Citizen in Question," *Hypatia* 22.4 (2007): 113, 114–15; Susan Moller Okin, "'Forty Acres and a Mule' for Women: Rawls and Feminism," *Politics, Philosophy and Economics* 4.2 (2005): 233.

5. Martha Fineman, *The Autonomy Myth* (New York: New Press, 2004), 169.

6. See, for example, Zillah R. Eisenstein, *The Female Body and the Law* (Berkeley: University of California Press, 1988), 130, Susan Moller Okin, *Justice, Gender, and the Family* (New York: Basic Books, 1989), 139, Catharine A. MacKinnon, "Reflections on Sex Equality Under Law," *Yale Law Journal* 100.5 (1991): 1281, Robin West, "Jurisprudence and Gender," *University of Chicago Law Review* 55.1 (1988): 1, 47, and Dorothy E. Roberts, "The Unrealized Power of Mother," *Columbia Journal of Gender and Law* 5.1 (1995): 141, 143.

7. Maxine Eichner, "Dependency and the Liberal Polity: On Martha Fineman's *The Autonomy Myth*," *California Law Review* 93.4 (2005): 1285, 1294; Martha Fineman, "The Vulnerable Subject: Anchoring Equality in the Human Condition," *Yale Journal of Law and Feminism* 20.1 (2008): 1, 8–10.

8. See Patricia Hill Collins, "African-American Women and Economic Justice: A Preliminary Analysis of Wealth, Family, and African-American Social Class," *University of Cincinnati Law Review* 65.3 (1997): 825, Patricia Hill Collins, "It's All in the Family: Intersections of Gender, Race, and Nation," *Hypatia* 13.3 (1998): 62, 64–65, Maxine Baca Zinn, "Feminism and Family Studies for a New Century," *Annals of the American Academy of Political and Social Science* 571 (September 2000): 42, Maxine Baca Zinn, "Family, Race, and Poverty in the Eighties," *Signs* 14.4 (1989): 856, Angela Harris, Margaretta Lin, and Jeff Selbin, "From 'The Art of War' to 'Being Peace': Mindfulness and Community Lawyering in the Neoliberal Age," *California Law Review* 95.5 (2007): 2073, and Val Gillies, "Perspectives on Parenting Responsibility: Contextualizing Values and Practices," *Journal of Law and Society* 35.1 (2008): 95, 100.

9. Even in the context of transracial families, a child's race may be contingent on his or her location. For example, African Americans may perceive a phenotypically black child raised by white parents to be white, while that same child might be constructed as black when with white peers. See Annette Ruth Appell, "Controlling for Kin: Ghosts in the Postmodern Family," *Wisconsin Journal of Law, Gender and Society* 25.1 (2010): 102–6, and Sandra Patton-Imani, *Birth Marks: Transracial Adoption in Contemporary America* (New York: New York University Press, 2000), 173.

10. Peggy Cooper Davis, "The Good Mother: A New Look at Psychological Parent Theory," *New York University Review of Law and Social Change* 22.2 (1996): 346, 356, 365; Annette Ruth Appell, "Disposable Mothers, Deployable Children," *Michigan Journal of Race and Law* 9.1 (2004): 421, 442–44.

11. Dorothy E. Roberts, "Racism and Patriarchy in the Meaning of Motherhood," *American University Journal of Gender Social Policy and Law* 1.1 (1993): 1, 13–15.

12. Susan Moller Okin, *Justice, Gender, and the Family* (New York: Basic Books, 1989), 56; Susan Moller Okin, "Humanist Liberalism," in *Liberalism and the Moral Life*, ed. Nancy L. Rosenblum (Cambridge, MA: Harvard University Press, 1989), 39, 52.

13. Among the exceptions are Martha Minow, "Rights for the Next Generation: A Feminist Approach to Children's Rights," *Harvard Women's Law Journal* 9 (1986): 1,

and Barrie Thorne "Re-Visioning Women and Social Change: Where Are the Children?" *Gender and Society* 1.1 (1987): 85.

14. Leena Alanen, "Gender and Generation: Feminism and the 'Child Question,'" in *Childhood Matters*, ed. Jens Qvortrup (Aldershot, UK: Ashgate, 1994), 34.

15. Martin Guggenheim, *What's Wrong with Children's Rights?* (Cambridge, MA: Harvard University Press, 2005), 220.

16. For example, *Carey v. Population Services International* 431 U.S. 678 (1977), *Goss v. Lopez*, 419 U.S. 565, 584 (1975), *Tinker v. Des Moines Independent Community School District*, 393 U.S. 503 (1969), and In re Gault, 387 U.S. 1, 33–34, 41, 55, 57 (1967).

17. *Hodgson v. Minnesota*, 497 U.S. 417 (1990).

18. *Roper v. Simmons*, 543 U.S. 551, 568–70 (2005); see also, *Miller v. Alabama*, 560 U.S. ___ (2012) (8th Amendment's prohibition on cruel and unusual punishment precludes mandatory life without parole for juveniles) and *Graham v. Florida*, 130 S. Ct. 2011 (2010) (8th Amendment prohibits sentencing children to life sentences without parole for noncapital crimes because minors do not have sufficient culpability).

19. *Plyler v. Doe*, 457 U.S. 202, 230 (1982); *Levy v. Louisiana*, 391 U.S. 68, 70–72 (1968); *Brown v. Board of Education*, 347 U.S. 483, 495 (1954).

20. See Guggenheim, *What's Wrong with Children's Rights*, 243–44, Robert H. Mnookin, *In the Interest of Children: Advocacy, Law Reform, and Public Policy* (Cambridge, MA: PON Books, 1996): 152–54, 244, Jane M. Spinak, "When Did Lawyers for Children Stop Reading Goldstein, Freud and Solnit? Lessons from the Twentieth Century on Best Interests and the Role of the Child Advocate," *Family Law Quarterly* 41.2 (2007): 393, 401, Kim Taylor-Thompson, "Girl Talk—Examining Racial and Gender Lines in Juvenile Justice," *Nevada Law Journal* 6.3 (2006): 1137, 1140–42, and Barbara Bennett Woodhouse, "'Who Owns the Child?' Meyer and Pierce and the Child as Property," *William and Mary Law Review* 33.4 (1992): 995, 1051–52, 1056–59.

21. Annette Ruth Appell, "Children's Voice and Justice: Lawyering for Children in the Twenty-First Century," *Nevada Law Journal* 6.3 (2006): 692, 701.

22. Bruce A. Green and Annette Ruth Appell, "Representing Children in Families—Foreword," *Nevada Law Journal* 6.3 (2006): 571; Bruce A. Green and Bernardine Dohrn, "Foreword: Children and the Ethical Practice of Law," *Fordham Law Review* 64.4 (1996): 1281.

23. Child Abuse Prevention and Treatment Act of 1974, 42 USC 5106a(b) (2006); Kristin Henning, "Loyalty, Paternalism, and Rights: Client Counseling Theory and the Role of Child's Counsel in Delinquency Cases," *Notre Dame Law Review* 81.1 (2005): 245, 246–48.

24. Jane M. Spinak, "Simon Says Take Three Steps Backwards: The National Conference of Commissioners on Uniform State Laws Recommendations on Child Representation," *Nevada Law Journal* 6.3 (2006): 1385, 1386–88.

25. "Recommendations of the Conference on Ethical Issues in the Legal Representation of Children," *Fordham Law Review* 64.4 (1996): 1301–11; "Recommendations

of the UNLV Conference on Representing Children in Families: Child Advocacy and Justice Ten Years after Fordham," *Nevada Law Journal* 6.3 (2006): 592, 593–97.

26. See, for example, Jean Koh Peters, *Children in Child Protective Proceedings*, 3rd ed. (Albany, NY: Matthew Bender 2007), 385–87, Barbara Atwood, "The Voice of the Indian Child: Strengthening the Indian Child Welfare Act through Children's Participation," *Arizona Law Review* 50.1 (2008): 127, 135–38, Linda D. Elrod, "Client-Directed Lawyers for Children: It Is the 'Right' Thing to Do," *Pace Law Review* 27.4 (2007): 869, 889–94, Elizabeth S. Scott and Thomas Grisso, "Developmental Incompetence, Due Process, and Juvenile Justice Policy," *North Carolina Law Review* 83.4 (2005): 793, 831–32; David B. Thronson, "Kids Will Be Kids? Reconsidering Conceptions of Children's Rights Underlying Immigration Law," *Ohio State Law Journal* 63.3 (2002): 979, and Franklin E. Zimring, "The Common Thread: Diversion in Juvenile Justice," *California Law Review* 88.6 (2000): 2477, 2481–83.

27. Samantha Brennan and Robert Noggle, "The Moral Status of Children: Children's Rights, Parents' Rights, and Family Justice," *Social Theory and Practice* 23.1 (1997): 1, 15.

28. See Francis Schrag, "Children and Democracy: Theory and Policy," *Politics, Philosophy and Economics* 3.3 (2004): 365, 370–76 (analyzing the effect of children's disenfranchisement), and "Theorising Children's Participation: International and Interdisciplinary Perspectives," special issue, *International Journal of Children's Rights* 16.3 (2008): 281.

29. Okin, "'Forty Acres and a Mule' for Women," 233, 236–39.

30. Brewer, *By Birth or Consent.*

31. Annette Lareau, *Unequal Childhoods* (Berkeley: University of California Press, 2003), 13; Gillies, "Perspectives on Parenting Responsibility," 95, 102.

32. Levander, *Cradle of Liberty*, 15.

33. Collins, "It's All in the Family," 62, 73.

34. See Guggenheim, *What's Wrong with Children's Rights*, 243–44, Mnookin, *In the Interest of Children*, 152–54, 244, Spinak, "When Did Lawyers for Children Stop Reading Goldstein, Freud and Solnit?," 393, 401; Thompson, "Girl Talk," 1137, 1140–42, and Woodhouse, "'Who Owns the Child?,'" 995, 1051–52, 1056–59.

Childhood of the Race

A Critical Race Theory Intervention into Childhood Studies

Lucia Hodgson

The popular defense of processing children under eighteen in the adult criminal justice system instead of the juvenile justice system turns on the nature of the offense: children who commit adult crimes should do adult time. This position highlights the ways in which American cultural constructions of the child are not exclusively child based. That is to say, adult constructions of the child often do not correspond to what children themselves say and do. Paradoxically, children can lose their child status when they do not act *like children*. The definitions of the child that inform academic inquiry and social policy are not simply objective: a child is what a child does. They function more like standards to which actual children must conform than the empirically based descriptions they purport to be.

If childhood studies hopes to be what John Wall (in this volume) aptly describes as a "child-inclusive humanistic methodology," then it must interrogate the politics of adult constructions of childhood, especially when these constructions overtly conflict with the words and behaviors of individuals under eighteen (68). Here I examine the rhetoric surrounding the growing trend in the criminal justice system of trying children as adults in order to make the point that critical race theory is an essential component of a viable childhood studies methodology. Annette Ruth Appell argues in this volume that a true jurisprudence of childhood must include "an analysis of what political and cultural work the legal category and regulation of childhood performs" and that, ideally, it will "approach the regulation of childhood contextually and critically" (29, 33). As I attempt to show, critical race theory can provide many of the critical tools needed to achieve such a child-centered jurisprudence.

According to the advocacy group Campaign for Youth Justice, "An estimated 250,000 youth are tried, sentenced or incarcerated as adults every year across the United States."[1] Processing children in the adult system instead of the existing juvenile justice system is counterintuitive. American law does not treat minors as adults; minors are denied most civil rights on the grounds that they lack the intellectual, psychological, and physical capacity to function in society as adults. In addition, juveniles tried as adults do not simultaneously accrue other adult civil rights, such as the right to vote or to consent to medical treatment. In addition, trying children as adults isolates their legal offenses from their social circumstances in a system that usually considers circumstances to be crucial to the nature of a criminal offense. For example, the legal system construes the taking of human life in a variety of ways depending on whose life is taken by whom under what circumstances and classifies that act along a spectrum ranging from murder in the first degree to manslaughter to self-defense to state-administered execution. Being under eighteen years old in a society in which minors have much less power than legal adults over their own living conditions is necessarily a significant circumstance. For example, many minors are incarcerated with adults simply for having been present at the scene of a crime committed by someone else, even though children as a group have much less control than adults over where they are and with whom they spend their days.

Existing child-centered critiques of processing juveniles in the adult criminal justice system have not been particularly effective in stemming the proliferation of state laws that facilitate the practice. Conventional critiques rely on social science research that emphasizes the differences between children and adults: they draw on neurological research on adolescent brain development to argue that children lack the impulse control and foresight of adults. They point to higher rates of suicide among and rape and physical assault of juveniles in adult jails and prisons to argue that children are too vulnerable to be fairly treated in adult confinement settings. And they document incarceration with adults as a factor in the corruption of youth and higher recidivism rates.[2] These approaches can (and should) garner sympathy and even exoneration for particular children. However, they cannot explain why our legal system engages in a practice that is not only clearly harmful to children but also, as child advocates point out, inherently contradictory in the sense that it violates its own determination that (in legal terms) the child is not the same as the adult.

Through critical race theory (CRT), childhood studies can focus on the racial disparities in sentencing children as adults to elucidate how the practice draws on racist theories of child development that ultimately rationalize and implement legal maneuvers that impact all children. CRT can identify and contextualize the fundamental premise of processing minors as adults: that certain children, mainly children of color, are innately prone to criminal behavior and cannot be rehabilitated. The dramatic overrepresentation of African Americans in the population of juveniles processed in the adult criminal justice system points to the deployment of racist myths, particularly the belief that the development of black youth stagnates in early adolescence. This myth fueled the regressive laws that now sweep up children of all colors, shapes, and sizes into the adult prison industrial complex. CRT can explain how racism has undermined the effectiveness of social science evidence. As Appell argues, juridical discourse "formulates the child as raceless (i.e., white) and middle class" (30), and child development discourse does the same.[3] Yet trying juveniles as adults has historically been framed as a practice designed to protect society from African American youth, rendering seemingly irrelevant those critiques based on white child development and welfare.

Critical race theory is a body of scholarship that seeks to understand and combat the impact of American racism on individual members of society and on the social fabric as a whole. It emerged as a discipline in the mid-1970s in response to the sense that the gains of the 1960s civil rights movement were being lost. Many legal theorists believed that "new approaches were needed to understand and come to grips with the more subtle, but just as deeply entrenched, varieties of racism that characterize our times." CRT argues that racism is a constitutive feature of American culture, that American laws construct a society that benefits whites at the expense of blacks and other people of color, and that "white elites will tolerate or encourage racial advances for blacks only when such advances also promote white self-interest."[4] CRT has not systematically investigated children's issues in the same concerted way it has theorized women's and GLBT studies, but children's representations and experiences abound in CRT scholarship. The centrality of configurations of the child and childhood to CRT discourse is apparent in the contents of the leading anthologies such as *Critical Race*

Theory: The Key Writings That Formed the Movement and *Critical Race Theory: The Cutting Edge*.[5] The words "child" and "childhood" rarely appear in the indices, but many of the anthologized articles call attention to the legal injustices experienced by children of color, particularly African American children.

The criminalization of black children is a major component of their social oppression, and it is one logical point of entry into an attempt to connect critical race theory to childhood studies. According to Donna M. Bishop, professor of criminal justice at Northeastern University, racial disparities in the juvenile justice system are well documented:

> Nationally, youths of color—especially African Americans and Hispanics—are arrested in numbers greatly disproportionate to their representation in the general population. They are overrepresented among young people held in secure detention, petitioned to juvenile court, and adjudicated delinquent. . . . And . . . prosecutors and judges are more apt to relinquish jurisdiction over them, transferring them to criminal court for prosecution and punishment as adults.[6]

The American Civil Liberty Union's (ACLU) Racial Justice Program has identified a "school-to-prison pipeline," which the civil rights organization defines as "a disturbing national trend wherein children are funneled out of public schools and into the juvenile and criminal justice systems."[7] This criminalization of children's behavior in educational institutions affects African American children disproportionately. According to the ACLU, "African-American students are far more likely than their white peers to be suspended, expelled, or arrested for the same kind of conduct at school."[8] According to Henry A. Giroux, professor of English and cultural studies, youth is ever more criminalized because "the racial disparities in school suspensions, expulsions, and arrests feed and mirror similar disparities in the juvenile and criminal justice systems."[9] Economic, social, and legal injustice work together to mark African American children as disposable; their collective "deprivation" is recoded as individual "depravity."[10]

The overrepresentation of African American youth in the criminalization of juveniles helps to explain the widespread public support for trying, sentencing, and incarcerating children as adults; it illuminates the role of anti-black racism in implementing policies hostile to children in general. In the mid-1990s, William Bennett, former secretary of education under Ronald

Reagan and author of *The Children's Book of Virtues*, was instrumental in promoting the prosecution of juveniles as adults. He was the lead author of *Body Count: Moral Poverty—and How to Win America's War against Crime and Drugs* published by Simon and Schuster in 1996.[11] This purportedly scientific study argued that "America is now home to thickening ranks of juvenile 'superpredators'—radically impulsive, brutally remorseless youngsters, including ever more preteenage boys, who murder, assault, rape, rob, burglarize, deal deadly drugs, join gun-toting gangs and create serious communal disorders."[12] Bennett and his coauthors argued that "superpredators" were overwhelmingly African American. According to the study, the disproportionate number of African Americans in the justice system confirmed their racialized superpredator hypothesis.

The theory presented by *Body Count* that this new "breed" of "superpredators" would lead to a spike in juvenile crime by the end of the century has been discredited, but it nonetheless led to a spike in juvenile and adult incarceration facilities and juveniles to fill them. "The Rest of Their Lives," a 1996 Human Rights Watch study that documents the plight of children sentenced to life without parole, reported that "the specter of 'super predators' created much of the national furor over youth violence." This furor led to more stringent juvenile justice policies and a corresponding decrease in support for preventive programs.[13] *Body Count* capitalized on the momentum generated by the case of the Central Park jogger in which four African American and one Latino youth, ages fourteen to sixteen, were accused of rape and given seven- to eleven-year sentences. The five youths spent a combined total of forty years in prison. They were exonerated in 2002 when DNA testing proved that a previously convicted adult serial rapist and murderer was guilty of the crime. According to the Campaign for Youth Justice (CFYJ), the Central Park jogger case triggered new laws in almost every state and on the federal level to facilitate the process of trying juveniles in the adult criminal justice system.[14]

As the Central Park jogger case and the *Body Count* study suggest, the trend of processing juveniles as adults relies heavily on the myth that African American youth are more like predatory animals prone to violence than adolescent humans capable of reform. In 2005, Bennett told a caller to his nationally syndicated morning radio show that aborting African American babies would lower the national crime rate. He called the strategy "morally reprehensible" but he repeated his claim that the "crime rate would go down."[15] William Bennett's comments about terminating black fetuses traffics in the racist discourses that both generate and are generated by the criminalization of black youth. They emphasize the connection between African Americans and immorality, eliding systemic environmental factors including white supremacism and economic injustice. According to *Body Count*, the explanation for juvenile criminality is "not institutionalized racism, and . . . not material want."[16] The polemical study acknowledges "racial disproportionalities in the system" but does not address the racism that produces the "real differences in crime rates" it refers to.[17] *Body Count*'s claims perpetuate a common American discourse that, on the one hand, denies racist social policies and practices and, on the other, propagates fallacious theories of essentialist race-based explanations for criminal behavior.

Any explanation for racial disparity in the justice system that denies systemic explanations is necessarily racist in that it must locate the origins of the disparity in theories of innate racial difference. *Body Count* purports to be both prochild and antiracist. It claims that the "true culprit" of juvenile criminality is "moral poverty" — "the poverty of growing up severely abused and neglected at the hands of deviant, delinquent, or criminal adults," and it avers that if we "give black children, on average, the level of positive adult social support enjoyed by white children, the rates [of criminal offense] would reverse themselves."[18] This "moral poverty" explanation claims to link juvenile behavior to social circumstances, not racial identity, but it relies on the myth that the African American adults who raise African American children are less capable of prosocial child rearing than their white counterparts and that African American children acquire immorality as they would a virus or genetic disorder. The study makes the unsupported claim that "on average, black children are more likely than white children to grow up without two parents or other adults who supervise, nurture, and provide for them."[19] One of the book's solutions to juvenile crime is to repeal adoption laws that have restricted "whites seeking to adopt nonwhite babies."[20] According to Bennett and his coauthors, the proposed origin of racial disparity in juvenile crime rates is actually racial disparity in adult morality that is passed on to children through child rearing, almost as if inherited.

Critical race theory encourages scholars to recognize racial disparity rather than genetics as the legacy of United States history. CRT provides an intellectual framework for analyzing current racialized inequities in education, employment, and incarceration, among other areas, in terms of the racist ideologies and practices of American slavery. Critical race theorists seek "to understand how society goes about constructing and inventing racial differences."[21] The theories of racial difference that rationalized the slave system into the nineteenth century currently rationalize endemic and persistent racial inequalities in American social institutions. CRT scholars trace the continuities between ideologies of racial difference evident in debates about the legitimacy of slavery with strikingly similar ideologies evident in debates about, for example, the legitimacy of racialized disparities in secondary school funding, in employment income, and in legal sentencing.

An explicit focus on the child presents a potentially effective way to raise critical awareness about systemic racism and its consequences. We can ask, for example, why researchers, lawmakers, judges, and the public are so tolerant of racialized disparities in juvenile arrests, charges, sentencing, and conditions of incarceration given how closely these disparities mirror socioeconomic disparities. The superpredator theory suggests that we criminalize individual children in order to obscure and naturalize systemic inequality. Like the law, social science purports to be universal and nondiscriminatory. But like the law, the social science of childhood in the United States has roots in a past that entrenched racist theories of human difference, and like the law, it contains vestiges of that past. As William S. Bush, author of *Who Gets a Childhood? Race and Juvenile Justice in Twentieth-Century Texas*, argues, "Highly charged words such as 'super-predator' do not appear in a cultural and historical vacuum. They resonate with the public for reasons involving collective historical memory, real and imagined."[22] It is because of these cultural and historical memories that social scientific explanations of child behavior must also be subjected to the scrutiny of critical race theory.

A child-centered analysis that draws on critical race theory and critical developmental psychology can identify some of the ways that the superpredator theory echoes past myths about racial difference. Critical developmental psychology, a field that dates from the mid-1980s, offers a framework for historicizing and deconstructing narratives of child development. In "Beyond Developmentalism?," Valerie Walkerdine argues for locating child development narratives "in historically and geographically specific practices" rather than assuming that they simply reflect the truth about children.[23] The superpredator thesis that underwrites adult processing of juveniles resonates as well as it does with the American public in part because it rehearses the theory popular at turn of the twentieth century that African-descended children could not transcend the "savage" traits that all people displayed in early childhood.[24] Late nineteenth-century child development experts argued that the development of African American children stagnated in early adolescence. According to the 1884 edition of the *Encyclopaedia Britannica*, "Nearly all observers admit that the Negro child is on the whole quite as intelligent as those of other human varieties, but that on arriving at puberty all further progress seems to be arrested."[25] This myth supports the conclusion that there is paradoxically no point in processing African American juveniles as juveniles because they cannot be rehabilitated.

A childhood studies methodology informed by critical race theory can position contemporary myths about African American youth in an illuminating historical context. In many ways, the racist ideologies that supported the institution of slavery worked on and through the bodies of children. In "The Genetic Tie," Dorothy E. Roberts considers "the historical interplay between concepts of race, social status, and genetic connection."[26] According to Roberts, current belief in a "genetic tie" of race that determines treatment by the legal system stems from two related legal practices of American slavery: the enforcement of "racial purity" laws (such as antimiscegenation laws) and the inheritability of slave status. By the 1680s, all British colonies subscribed to the policy of *partus sequitur ventrem*, which mandated that children born to enslaved women were born slaves whether or not the biological father was white—a pronounced break from traditional British legal ideology, specifically "the long-standing patriarchal tenet that the social status of the child followed the male line."[27] Any postulated African ancestry nullified white genetic ties and resulted in the denial of full legal personhood. The law associated African ancestry with "pollution, taint, blemish, corruption, and contamination."[28] *Body Count*'s racialized theory of "moral poverty" emanates from the myth enshrined in the law that "the genetic tie to a black parent automatically passed down a whole set of inferior traits."[29] In early American legal discourse, black skin "was irretrievably associated with loss of control over the baser passions, with weakening of traditional family ties, and with breakdown of proper social ordering."[30] Despite the formal illegality of slavery and racist discrimination, contemporary laws continue to figure African American youth as the inheritors and carriers of antisocial immorality.

Myths about inherited immorality embodied in African American youth displace the realities of inherited socioeconomic inequality. According to a recent report by the Insight Center for Community Economic Development, "children of color are four times more likely than white children to be born into the most economically fragile households."[31] African American youth, on average, are statistically much more likely than white children to have poor parents and to live in socioeconomically impoverished environments.[32] Poverty does not signal or cause immorality, but it does contribute significantly to involvement with the criminal justice system. The exclusion of African American families from the wealth generated by their historical enslavement puts today's African American youth at much greater risk for incarceration. The myth of equal opportunity in America conflicts with entrenched racialized socioeconomic inequality that is causally related to the criminalization and incarceration of African American children.

Critical race realism, a branch of CRT, argues that what is constituted as a crime and who is constituted as a criminal are directly related to lack of socioeconomic privilege.[33] Critical race realism, "a synthesis of critical race theory, empirical social science, and public policy," makes the point that the field of psychological criminology neglects environmental factors."[34] In response to Bennett's implication that black children are prone to criminal behavior (which rationalizes his genocidal "solution" to crime), critical race realism argues that the disproportionate representation of African American youth in the juvenile justice system signals racialized socioeconomic disparity much more so than "individual-level features (e.g., genes)."[35] In "Towards a Radical Psychology: Psychology, Race, Environment, and Crime," Shayne Jones and Michael J. Lynch critique psychological criminology's emphasis on the role of genetics in the etiology of criminal behavior over the role of the environment (defined broadly to include cultural discourses and material circumstances). The central premise of the "radical criminology" theorized by Jones and Lynch is that "the root causes of crime are to be found in the social structure."[36] Social factors rather than innate individual traits determine what is constituted as criminal behavior and under what circumstances and also dictate who is punished for criminal infractions.

Critical race realism can highlight the role of white-collar crime in rising incarceration rates of African American youth. For example, exposure to lead in childhood can cause "psychological states criminologists have correlated with crime, including attention-deficit/hyperactivity disorders, conduct disorder, neuropsychological deficits, impulsivity, disruption of the central nervous system, and various cognitive and learning disorders."[37]

However, the corporations that knowingly allow dangerous levels of lead to be present in structures where there are young children (such as public housing, schools, and detention centers) do not routinely face criminal charges. Corporations that endanger children are sanctioned, if at all, by administrative and regulatory agencies. Thus, we end up with two separate systems, "the criminal justice system," which focuses primarily on the crimes of poor minorities and responds with (increasingly) harsh punishments," and a system comprising "various, nonintegrated regulatory agencies," which focuses on "the crimes of the wealthy and responds with comparatively exculpatory actions."[38]

Though the human and financial costs of white-collar violations are much greater than those exacted by street crime, white-collar criminals are rarely incarcerated or made to pay punitive damages. In addition, both the criminal justice and regulatory systems are shaped by racial disparities. Individuals affected by lead poisoning and prosecuted in the criminal justice system are disproportionately African American. Those white-collar "criminals" regulated by agencies are mainly white elites who break the law in the course of doing their jobs. In some corporate environments, groups make harmful and sometimes deadly decisions, and individuals often evade accountability. "Deindividuation" loosens ethical restraints and allows situational forces, such as the drive for profit, to dominate decision making.[39] In other words, the criminal justice system essentially punishes African American youth for being the victims of corporate greed.

Another major factor in the economics of the racialized juvenile justice system has been the increasing privatization of incarceration facilities over the past three decades. Companies like Corrections Corporation of America profit from building and operating facilities including prisons, jails, and detention centers.[40] In 2009, the egregious case of judges Mark A. Ciavarella Jr. and Michael T. Conahan provoked widespread outrage, but the principle of the privatization of juvenile justice has not received similar condemnation. The two judges pleaded "guilty to wire fraud and income tax fraud for taking more than $2.6 million in kickbacks to send teenagers to two privately run youth detention centers."[41] The news coverage of the case underscores the way in which injustice is most visible to the public when it affects white people. Although the majority of youth affected by detention privatization are black and male, the *New York Times* story leads with a picture and anecdote of a white teenage girl sentenced to three months detention for a spoof of her assistant principal posted on a social networking site. She is quoted as saying: "I felt like I had been thrown into some surreal sort of nightmare. . . . All I wanted to know was how this could be fair and why the judge would do such a thing."[42] This remark encapsulates the myth that the criminal justice system is inherently just and that injustice is exceptional; this myth is more true for white Americans than for African Americans.

Those elites who benefit financially from the criminalization of youth support the critical racial realist's claim that "the purpose of law, at least as it is practiced, is to maintain the status quo of controlling the behaviors of the poor and promoting the interests of the powerful."[43] Proponents of for-profit facilities, jails, and prisons are like the "white-collar" criminals whose actions perpetuate policies that disadvantage minorities. Jones and Lynch conclude that "the crimes of the powerful are themselves linked to the crimes of the poor."[44] A critical race theory reading of the Ciavarella and Conahan case suggests that the public is more tolerant of legal injustice toward children of color than toward white children. This reaction can be explained in part by what Joyce E. King calls "dysconcious racism," the resistance of her white students to a critical examination of "culturally sanctioned assumptions, myths, and beliefs that justify the social and economic advantages white people have as a result of subordinating others."[45] In other words, white Americans resist the argument that racial disparity in juvenile sentencing is partially motivated by economic incentives. Punitive policies and practices that disproportionately affect youth of color are less likely to be questioned, challenged, or resisted.

Racial disparities in processing children and adults expose the way our society holds individual children accountable for social circumstances and forces that are far beyond their control. Processing teenagers as adults forecloses on the question of child agency in two important and contradictory ways. On the one hand, the practice assumes that children have the same amount of self-determination as adults and that they must take full responsibility for participating in the activities prevalent in their community, such as the illicit drug trade. On the other, the practice implies that the self-determination of certain adolescents, particularly African American adolescents, is fundamentally undermined by innate dispositions. Neither model of agency allows for recognition of systemic socioeconomic deprivation, and neither acknowledges the political valences of children's behavior and the theories we invent to explain it. Racial disparities in the treatment of children are signposts that identify contradictions in the logic of the social sciences and in the practices of our social institutions. These contradictions in turn can help to make visible the politics embedded in social constructions of children of all colors. Critical race theory is a crucial tool for accomplishing this visibility.

Notes

1. "Facts and Research," *Campaign for Youth Justice*, www.campaignforyouthjustice .org/facts-a-research.html.

2. See, for example, *Juvies*, directed by Leslie Neal (Santa Monica, CA: Chance Films, 2004), DVD.

3. Valerie Walkerdine, "Beyond Developmentalism?," *Theory and Psychology* 3.4 (1993): 455, 459.

4. Richard Delgado and Jean Stefancic, eds., introduction to *Critical Race Theory: The Cutting Edge*, 2nd ed. (Philadelphia: Temple University Press, 2000), xvi–xvii.

5. Kimberlé Crenshaw, Neil Gotanda, Gary Peller, and Kendall Thomas, eds., *Critical Race Theory: The Key Writings That Formed the Movement* (New York: New Press, 2010); Delgado and Stefancic, introduction.

6. Donna M. Bishop, "The Role of Race and Ethnicity in Juvenile Justice Processing," in *Our Children, Their Children: Confronting Racial and Ethnic Differences in American Juvenile Justice*, ed. Darnell R. Hawkins and Kimberly Kempf-Leonard (Chicago: University of Chicago Press, 2005), 23.

7. "School-to-Prison Pipeline," American Civil Liberties Union, www.aclu.org/ racial-justice/school-prison-pipeline.

8. "School-to-Prison Pipeline: Talking Points," American Civil Liberties Union, www.aclu.org/racial-justice/school-prison-pipeline-talking-points.

9. Henry A. Giroux, "Locked Up: The Youth Crime Complex and Education in America," *Journal in Advanced Composition* 30.1–2 (2010): 35.

10. Giroux, "Locked Up," 19.

11. William J. Bennett, John J. Dilulio Jr., and John P. Walters, *Body Count: Moral Poverty—and How to Win America's War Against Crime and Drugs* (New York: Simon and Schuster, 1996).

12. Bennett, Dilulio, and Walters, *Body Count*, 17.

13. Alison Parker, *The Rest of Their Lives: Life without Parole for Child Offenders in the United States* (New York: Human Rights Watch/Amnesty International, 2005), www.hrw.org/reports/2005/10/11/rest-their-lives. For an analysis of the role of the corporate media in promoting the super-predator myth, see Lucia Hodgson, *Raised in Captivity: Why Does America Fail Its Children?* (St. Paul, MN: Graywolf Press, 1997), 141–50.

14. Liz Ryan and Jason Ziedenberg, introduction to *The Consequences Aren't Minor: The Impact of Trying Youth as Adults and Strategies for Reform*, Campaign for Youth Justice Report (Washington, DC: Campaign for Youth Justice, 2007), 3.

15. "MediaMatters Exposes Bennett," MediaMatters for America, http://mediamatters.org/mmtv/200509280006.

16. Bennett, Dilulio, and Walters, *Body Count*, 56.

17. Bennett, Dilulio, and Walters, *Body Count*, 45.

18. Bennett, Dilulio, and Walters, *Body Count*, 56, 22–23.

19. Bennett, Dilulio, and Walters, *Body Count*, 22.

20. Bennett, Dilulio, and Walters, *Body Count*, 203.

21. Richard Delgado, foreword to Gregory S. Parks, Shayne Jones, and W. Jonathan Cardi, eds., *Critical Race Realism: Intersections of Psychology, Race, and Law* (New York: New Press, 2008), xi–xii.

22. William S. Bush, *Who Gets a Childhood? Race and Juvenile Justice in Twentieth-Century Texas* (Athens: University of Georgia Press, 2010), 3.

23. Walkerdine, "Beyond Developmentalism?," 451.

24. Diana Selig, "Hall, Granville Stanley (1844–1924)," in *Encyclopedia of Children and Childhood: In History and Society*, vol. 2, ed. Paula S. Fass (New York: Macmillan Reference USA, 2004), 413.

25. H. M. Bracken, "Essence, Accident and Race," *Hermathena: A Dublin University Review* 116.1 (1973): 89.

26. Dorothy E. Roberts, "The Genetic Tie," *University of Chicago Law Review*, 62.1 (1995): 223.

27. Roberts, "Genetic Tie," 226.

28. Roberts, "Genetic Tie," 226.

29. Roberts, "Genetic Tie," 230.

30. Roberts, "Genetic Tie," 230.

31. Trina Shanks, *Diverging Pathways: How Wealth Shapes Opportunity for Children* (Oakland, CA: Insight Center for Community Economic Development, 2011), 2.

32. Shanks, *Diverging Pathways*, 3–4.

33. Parks, Jones, and Cardi, introduction to *Critical Race Realism*.

34. Shayne Jones and Michael J. Lynch, "Towards a Radical Psychology: Psychology, Race, Environment, and Crime," in *Critical Race Realism*, 234.

35. Jones and Lynch, "Towards a Radical Psychology," 225.

36. Jones and Lynch, "Towards a Radical Psychology," 225.

37. Jones and Lynch, "Towards a Radical Psychology," 227.

38. Jones and Lynch, "Towards a Radical Psychology," 233.

39. Jones and Lynch, "Towards a Radical Psychology," 231–32.

40. Randall G. Shelden, *Controlling the Dangerous Classes: A Critical Introduction to the History of Criminal Justice* (Boston: Allyn and Bacon, 2001), 275–80.

41. Ian Urbina and Sean D. Hamill, "Judges Plead Guilty in Scheme to Jail Youths for Profit," *New York Times*, February 13, 2009.

42. Urbina and Hamill, "Judges Plead Guilty in Scheme to Jail Youths for Profit."

43. Jones and Lynch, "Towards a Radical Psychology," 225.

44. Jones and Lynch, "Towards a Radical Psychology," 233–34.

45. Joyce E. King, "Dysconscious Racism: Ideology, Identity and Miseducation," *Journal of Negro Education* 60.2 (1991): 135.

Childhood Studies and History

Catching a Culture in High Relief

James Marten

"Childhood," writes Joseph M. Hawes, "is where you catch a culture in high relief."[1] This deceptively simple statement reveals the possibilities created by the merger of childhood studies and history. Although children and youth do not make laws, declare wars, manage corporations, or write books and plays—although they do not feature in traditional measures of progress—they are at the center of many kinds of cultural markers, including support for education, respect for the family, and provision for adequate health care, all of which not only measure the status of children and youth but also reveal the ways in which a society sets its priorities. That insight has led scholars to exploit the opportunities offered by the intersection of childhood studies and history. The first section of this chapter samples a few areas in American history that reflect this combination of fields. The second explores the special value of combining childhood studies and history in the study of war. Finally, the third section highlights selected primary sources to show how my own work on Civil War–era children can provide more nuanced approaches to that much-studied period.

Two distinct approaches to the history of children and youth developed as the field grew and prospered: many historians, mainly because of the nature of the source material, had to be satisfied with talking *about* children. Children may be among the least articulate of all members of society. By the time they are fully literate and aware of the possibilities and challenges posed by their surroundings, they are hardly children at all. And they are, it goes without saying, literally without political power. As a result, it is very difficult to get at their points of view, and most treatments examine institutions, ideas, or policies that shape the lives of children and youth rather than flesh-and-blood youngsters. On the other hand, a few historians, taking advantage of unusual sources, casting fresh eyes on traditional sources, or simply exerting more imagination than most scholars, provide at least glimpses of the points of view of the children they study.

When they are done well, these histories help us better understand both the lives of children and youth and the times in which they lived. Rooted in the early Republic, Jacqueline S. Reinier's research shows how the junction of history and childhood studies can tell us something new about each. The founders and their successors, Reinier writes, developed "the staggering notion that one could mold the human personality in a desired direction."[2] This, in turn, "generated optimism that a truly new affectionate and voluntary society could emerge."[3] Few human institutions were untouched by this confidence. "In a general revolt against tyranny and patriarchy, philosophers, physicians, journalists, and printers championed and publicized the affectionate nuclear family," which stressed "voluntary ties" and functioned, in their view, as "a kind of school for citizenship."[4] In addition, Enlightenment notions of the "malleable child" led to the belief that youngsters could be "shaped by affectionate parents and educators" into "material for the virtuous, autonomous adult."[5] All would help create and sustain the republican experiment. Moreover, because the "republican virtue" that inspired both revolution and nation building depended on a disinterested, engaged, and incorruptible citizenry, Americans consciously built institutions and developed child-rearing strategies to inculcate those virtues in their offspring.[6] Reinier argues that a number of institutions and ideas aimed to instill the values of hard work, modesty, independence, and other distinctive traits that formed the American "character." They included Protestant theology and the creation of Sunday schools, the development of public schools as laboratories for republican behavior, and the integration of children into the free market workplace.[7] Not all historians can make such direct links between traditional topics in American history and the history of children and youth, but Reinier nevertheless provides a model for the value of child studies.

Two of the "founding documents" in the modern historiography of children and youth came out of the wave of New England town studies and the rise of family history. In his famous 1970 book on Plymouth Colony, John Demos foreshadowed his later interest in children by making them central to the work of creating family structures that would sustain the "little commonwealth" developed by the earliest settlers of New England. A few years later Philip Greven showed how we can come to a better understanding of the religious, class, and cultural dynamics of the developing nation by articulating the patterns of child rearing in the first century and a half or so of European settlement.[8] Even after the explosion of books published in the last few decades of the twentieth century that explored the complexities of American slavery, two historians found new ways of viewing the peculiar institution through the eyes of children. Wilma King's *Stolen Childhood* and Marie Jenkins Schwartz's *Born in Bondage*—the titles say it all, of course—complicate our view of an institution we thought we understood. Slave children did have a childhood, it turns out, however abbreviated and unstable, and their lives were both less awful and even worse than we imagined. For instance, despite the general fragmentation of slave families, most children did spend much of their young lives with at least one parent and other family members. By the same token, over and above the horrific living conditions that led to an infant mortality rate of as much as 30 percent, the split loyalties forced on slave children—between their families and their owners—created unimaginable psychological burdens on young slaves.[9]

Although they address very different expressions of culture, both Anne Scott MacLeod's *American Childhood* and Karin Calvert's *Children in the House* show the ways in which parents, educators, and writers sought to limit and shape children's freedom, whether through exposing them to didactic short stories and descriptions of youngsters' death-bed scenes or by putting them in restrictive clothing or furniture. Texts for children and the household items used by children and their parents have always been, of course, literally under the noses of historians. Taking a fresh look at these rather mundane materials opens whole new vistas into the interior and exterior lives of children and the adults responsible for them.[10]

David Wallace Adams, Devon A. Mihesuah, and Brenda Child get below the well-known surface of broken treaties and open warfare to show how "assimilation" policies were supposed to work by examining the experiences of Native Americans at the boarding schools established for them in the late nineteenth century. Less obviously brutal than winter campaigns and trails of tears, they were nevertheless important parts of the policy aimed at crushing the native cultures of North America. Although these accounts use to great effect the reminiscences and oral histories of former students to show the heartbreak of the cultural imperialism imposed by boarding schools, they also provide examples of resilience and agency, large and small, as the students—as Native Americans and as teenagers—resisted their teachers and the expectations of the culture to which they were supposedly being assimilated.[11]

A quartet of books deserve closer attention—not because they are necessarily more important than those already mentioned but because they are representative of those works that realize the potential of children and youth studies to expand our knowledge of history. All four deal with American children since the end of the Civil War, and all four are models of how historians of children and youth can find novel things to say about seemingly well-understood themes and issues. Elliott West's *Growing Up with the Country* and David Nasaw's *Children of the City* are among the best examples of books that capture the points of view of children. Through memoirs and the oral histories gathered by state historical societies, West explores the lives of children who, with their parents, settled the far West in the late nineteenth century. With the help of scores of autobiographies and the testimony of children and youth interviewed by Progressive-era "child-savers," Nasaw examines the largely immigrant children who populated eastern and a few midwestern cities between the 1880s and the 1910s. Both historians emphasize the tension in these children's lives between school and work, but they also describe family dynamics and the relationship between children and their environment.

The children and youth who appear in Nasaw's and West's wonderfully written books could not seem less alike. Western children roamed for hours without seeing another human being, fought prairie fires and rattlesnakes, traveled miles to attend school or to receive medical treatment, and slept under a big sky carpeted with stars or filled with towering thunderstorms or blizzards. Nasaw's children roamed streets filled with other people as well as streetcars and dray horses, brawled with boys from other ethnic groups or neighborhoods, and crowded into hard-pressed urban classrooms. But despite their vast differences, their similarities are more important for historians of children: they were the first generations to grow up in their respective milieu. West argues that the parents of pioneer children were simply easterners transplanted to places in which the elder emigrants rarely grew comfortable; Nasaw suggests that the mothers and fathers of his city children, themselves the products of the Russian steppes or southern Italy or other parts of southern and eastern Europe, never adjusted to life in American cities. Both sets of children and youth paved the way for entirely new kinds of Americans. They embraced their environments, took them at face value, and exerted agency in the most powerful ways imaginable.[12]

Jennifer Ritterhouse's *Growing Up Jim Crow* offers an alternative approach to a well-worn issue: race relations in the American South. By stepping away from the adult worlds of violence and courtrooms and into the child-sized universe in which racial interactions were less dangerous but no less fraught with meaning, Ritterhouse shows how black and white children between the Gilded Age and the 1950s "learned race." Although youngsters were clearly schooled by their parents and other elders to subscribe to traditional assumptions and strictures, she shows that children had minds of their own. White children, she argues, actually expanded segregation when they became adults, creating new boundaries and separations. Black children, on the other hand, frequently used the relative safety of youthful interactions with whites to stand up for themselves, foreshadowing later generations' civil rights activism.[13]

Finally, Paula Fass, whose earlier books explore the complexities of Americans' attitudes about youth, casts a wider net in a collection of essays published as *Children of a New World: Society, Culture, and Globalization.* Although the word "globalization" is, indeed, nearly ubiquitous in discussions of economic, immigration, or political issues, Fass gets beneath the surface of these typical applications of the term to argue that childhood provides a perfect lens for understanding the connections between cultures and populations around the world. That lens leads her to define globalization as a growing awareness of other cultures and as an acceptance of the fact that similar issues challenge and define peoples regardless of borders and ethnicities. Despite its subtitle, *Children of a New World* is really about American children, who, Fass argues, were among the first nations of youngsters to experience the sometimes jarring, sometimes liberating processes of migration, ethnic accommodation and assimilation and to live through the development of new technologies, evolving and competing child-rearing strategies, and changing attitudes and assumptions about the nature of childhood.[14]

Unfortunately, war is one of the global experiences of children, and nothing puts more pressure on a society and its children than war—wartime truly is, to paraphrase Joe Hawes's words once again, a time when many facets of a society can be seen in "high relief." A number of books published in recent years have explored the many ways in which armed conflict affects youngsters. Most of these books, even when they do not cite them directly, implicitly accept the work of Anna Freud and Dorothy Burlingame, who, in their pathbreaking study of children's reactions to the German bombing campaign against Britain during the Second World War, suggested that, far from being frightened by the destruction of war, children were engaged by "primitive excitement," joyfully playing amid wreckage and debris and actually becoming rather heedlessly destructive themselves. Perhaps because their own lives are seemingly always characterized by small conflicts—disciplinary restrictions, arguments with siblings, the tension caused by the imposition of moral codes that run up against more primitive desires—they instinctively understand war and are less shocked by it than adults might think. Put simply, the responses of children to war are far more complicated than we had imagined, which makes it a likely topic for productive study by scholars of childhood. Accordingly, many historians have come to see children as more than simply victims of war. They do not simply remain bystanders; nature, desperation, familial and even national loyalty push them to insist on becoming actors in wars large and small. They absorb the politics that lead to war, they exploit the sometimes jarring freedoms offered by wartime, and, as in so many other facets of life, they make the experience their own.[15]

Not surprisingly, a number of books have focused on the Second World War. Perhaps the most stunning victimization of children in any war of the twentieth century was the murder of one and a half million Jewish youngsters in Nazi concentration camps. Drawing on diaries, drawings, and oral histories, Deborah Dwork's *Children with a Star* demonstrates how Jewish children fought to retain some sense of their humanity amid a catalogue of abuses and humiliations. Similarly, *Children and Play in the Holocaust* by George Eisen shows that even in these worst of conditions children were still children, going so far as to invent games that revolved around the harsh conditions in concentration camps.[16] There were also less obvious forms of victimization. Although the evacuation of children from London and other British cities during the Second World War has become a part of the legend of English wartime pluck and determination, historians approaching the subject from the viewpoint of the evacuees themselves and with modern sensibilities about child welfare and abuse have criticized the policy. Among them are Martin Parsons and Penny Starns, who have suggested that political considerations weighed heavier than humanitarian concerns and, through interviews with survivors, chronicle the danger, hardships, and potential abuse to which the children were exposed.[17]

Far from the fighting and physical suffering but not immune from shortages, uncertainty, and demands on their labor and patriotism, American children experienced the war very differently than many children in Europe or Asia did. William M. Tuttle Jr. offers a fresh approach to the children of the greatest generation in *Daddy's Gone to War: The Second World War in the Lives of America's Children.* Tuttle makes mention of all of the activities one expects to be covered in a book on the World War II home front — scrap drives, comic books, movies, war toys — but also sensitively explores how the war affected family dynamics and the ways that children and youth of different ages reacted to war. Utilizing insights gleaned from developmental psychology and over a thousand autobiographical letters sent to him by adults who had been children during the war, Tuttle provides a nuanced analysis of the varied ways that children responded to the war. The most moving aspect of his study, and perhaps the most useful, is his examination of how children were affected by the absence of fathers and how they reacted to their reappearance after the war.[18]

Other historians have investigated the effects of wars and their aftermaths on fairly typical childhood concerns from education and relationships to government and child welfare institutions, child rearing, health, and popular culture. These scholars have shown that wars sometimes inspire nations to question basic assumptions and values; in other cases, the expansion of government power that inevitably accompanies mobilization for war can lead to the formation of institutions and government agencies that provide the impetus for "reforming" the lives of children. For instance, Susan Pedersen, in *Family, Dependence, and the Origins of the Welfare State*, places the two world wars in the contexts of feminism, trade unions, and economic development to explain the creation of government social welfare programs, especially those aimed at aiding children. Juvenile delinquency, a vital field of inquiry for historians and social scientists alike, gets a new look in a wartime context in Sarah Fishman's *The Battle for Children: World War II, Youth Crime, and Juvenile Justice in Twentieth-Century France*, which argues that wartime conditions led officials in the Vichy criminal justice system to see juvenile delinquents as victims rather than criminals, inspiring the change from a punitive to a therapeutic model of disciplining youngsters.[19] Still other writers peer into the effects of wars and of warlike militarism on education, for example, the effects of Victorian Britain's attempt to inculcate military values into working-class schools, the Soviet Union's early efforts to make communists out of Russian children, and the ways in which East and West German educators and policy makers during the Cold War tried to politicize children in ways supportive of their respective regimes.[20]

Although many of the children described in these books exert agency in any number of ways, most remain, at least ostensibly, "behind the lines"— however meaningless that term has become in modern warfare. At the very least they are officially noncombatants. Fewer studies of children and youth who go to war are available.[21] Perhaps the most useful account of child soldiers in the twentieth century is David M. Rosen's *Armies of the Young: Child Soldiers in War and Terrorism*, which is, in many respects, a model of the intellectual alchemy that can be performed when one mixes childhood studies with history. Rosen integrates youth into the larger cultural, political, and economic contexts that shape their lives, recognizing them as actors rather than simply victims.

In three case studies—1940s Poland, 1990s Sierra Leone, and contemporary Palestine—Rosen focuses less on the atrocities endured or committed by youthful soldiers than on the ways in which their participation was, in some ways, inevitable, given the dynamics of the times and places in which they lived. Many Jewish resistance fighters in Poland came out of the radical Zionist youth organizations of the 1920s and 1930s. Refusing to succumb to Nazi persecution without a fight, they carried out brutal ambushes and assassinations. In Sierra Leone, the desperate economic situation of the 1990s, combined with the region's longtime economic exploitation of children and youth, the glorification among young men of violent gangs, and the political manipulation of youth organizations, created a perfect storm of terror that devastated the country and made thousands of young men and a few women into brutal killers or their victims. The participation of Arab children in the ethnic violence and warfare that has plagued Palestine since the 1920s likewise came out of the politicization of youth movements, which, in this case, was encouraged by the rise of an apocalyptic religious movement unwilling to share Palestine with the Jews.

Rosen seeks to understand the forces that have pulled youth into the conflict. At the center of *Armies of the Young* is a chilling account of the agency of youth—that quality that historians eagerly seek when studying the past lives of the youngest members of our societies. In the case of young Polish Jews, for instance, even as their doomed lives narrowed, they "struggled to control their own identity and destiny. . . . If they were almost certain to die, they wanted to die under circumstances of their own choosing. They wanted to die in a way that would give meaning to their lives. As soldiers, children and youth fighters made it clear that they would be killed with dignity."[22]

Wars create conditions that help historians access the lives of children and parents in ways that peacetime rarely offers. My own research on Civil War children would not have been possible without the outpouring of documents produced because Civil War–era men, women, and children, separated from loved ones for extended periods of time, and conscious of the fact that they were living through unprecedented times, chose to keep diaries or save letters or write memoirs. In short, the virtually universal literacy of white Americans during the Civil War era ensured that the stories of parents and children would be preserved, providing windows into the ways that this war, the bloodiest in American history, affected children. Although social historians long ago rejected the "drums and bugles" version of Civil War history that still remains popular, it is somewhat surprising that historians of children and youth did not "discover" the Civil War until a decade ago.[23]

The unprecedented opportunity—and personal instinct—to record not only major events but also the mundane details of everyday life has provided historians with the resources to address many common assumptions both about the war and about gender roles, regionalism, and children's agency. For instance, the letters of an Indiana soldier to his three sons—letters that would never have been written if the war had not intervened—challenge common assumptions about domesticity and child rearing. The diaries of a boy and a girl articulate in homely and eloquent ways the vast differences between the experiences of northerners and southerners during the conflict. And memoirs of a feminist who during the war grew from a teen to a young woman on the Michigan frontier undermines the celebratory version of the war and offers a fresh take on what "freedom" meant outside of emancipation.

We do not know much about James Goodnow. He was an officer in an

Indiana regiment who served in the Union army for about two years before returning home. Like most men who went away to fight, this was his first extended period away from his family, which by this time consisted of three sons ranging in age from about fifteen to three or four and a daughter who may have been just a baby when he left. Goodnow's wartime missives challenge the rather outdated but still powerful belief that mid-nineteenth-century, middle-class men and women separated into public and domestic "spheres," revealing that he had been a constant presence in his children's lives, not only as a disciplinarian but as a source of comfort and even entertainment. Goodnow was committed to continuing his role as guide and confidant to his boys, to whom he wrote separate letters as often as he could. "I want that you and I should be regular correspondents during my absence," he wrote Sam, in his first letter home. He urged him to "tell your mind freely," in weekly letters, to "tell me all about what you are doing—and all about your cares and troubles—and you may be Sure I will always feel an interest in whatever interests or affects you." He felt the same way about his younger sons.[24]

Goodnow's letters to his boys tended toward straightforward bits of advice and manly affection, but they were never generic or clichéd; he shaped his letters around the interests and needs of each. As the oldest, Sam received most of the general news about Goodnow's unit, including information about their travels in Tennessee and Alabama, speculations about military strategy, and a detailed description of the only battle in which Goodnow fought. More important, however, were the pieces of fatherly advice and hints of affection that Goodnow freely distributed. His letters to Sam frequently, if gently, nudged him toward adulthood. He naturally urged him to work hard at school, for it "will not be long before you will have to go out in the world to make your own way, and you will then be too busy to study." At one point Sam apparently complained about a simmering conflict with his teacher; James sympathized and assured Sam that he was clearly in the right but also urged him to take the high road and apologize. It was a step toward manhood, and would be a good lesson as he went forward in the world.[25]

The two younger sons received messages tailored to their ages. Goodnow's first letter to "Master Daniel Goodnow," who must have been about nine or ten, began with small talk about Christmas, but quickly moved to what Dan was no doubt pining to hear about: the war. "You ought to be out here and See our big armies," James wrote at the start of a passage that must have made the war like the grand adventure that young Dan imagined it to be. He described his army on the march out of Memphis and in camp. "If you would have been there you would have thought there was going to be a battle there was So much noise. The men Cheered and yelled and the mules brayed loud enough to make you jump out of your boots." Yet Goodnow made sure his boys knew that the war was not simply a big adventure. Despite the excitement and drama, he was glad they were safe at home rather than with him, "for wherever the large armies go here they drive the people away from home and take all they have to eat and all their corn and then burn their houses and fields—and a great many little boys down here do not have enough to Eat and often have no home." Dan also received advice, but of a very different sort from Sam's. Whenever he felt like quarreling or crying, suggested Goodnow, "just run out into the wood Shed and Saw a few Sticks of wood and See if you don't get in a good humor before you get done." The youngest son, Johnny, whose mother had to read his letters to him, received much shorter but no less affectionate notes. "I have been wanting to See you for a long time," wrote James, "but I am too far away to go home often." Like countless fathers throughout the Union and Confederate armies, he promised that when he returned, "we will have a big talk." In the meantime, he said, "I want you to be the best little boy. . . . I don't want you to Say any bad words—or cry much—I want you to be a man." Goodnow's letters suggest a much more intimate familiarity with child rearing than scholarship on domesticity might suggest. His letters to Sam are reasonably close to form—although they seem shrewder and gentler than we might expect from a Victorian father—but the nuances and gentleness of his letters to the little boys suggest a surprising involvement with their lives.[26]

Few Civil War–era children's diaries have survived, but two extraordinary documents produced by a boy and a girl—both about seven when the war began—provide first-person accounts of the war as it happened from the unusual points of view of children. Gerald Norcross, son of a prosperous Boston merchant and Republican alderman, kept his diary throughout the war. Carrie Berry lived in Atlanta; the available portion of her diary begins during the battle for Atlanta and continues throughout the siege and evacuation and their aftermath. Gerald's and Carrie's diaries can be viewed in a number of ways, but one constructive line of analysis is material culture; contrasting the possessions and activities of these two young children as described in their own words provides two extreme examples of the ways in which the war affected children in their daily life, as they playfully or grimly adapted their lives to their circumstances.

Gerald's diary is primarily a chronicle of fun: trips and walks, books and games, toys and scrapbooks, snacks and parties, fireworks and kittens. By May 1863 he was recording the many war books he had read, which ranged from dime novels like *War Trails, Vicksburg Spy*, and *Old Hal Williams; or, The Spy of Atlanta* to better-known factual narratives such as *Life and Campaigns of Gen. McClellan, Days and Nights on the Battlefield, Following the Flag*, and trilogies about two teenaged brothers by the well-known writer of juvenile wartime adventures, Oliver Optic: *Sailor Boy, The Yankee Middy, The Brave Old Salt, Soldier Boy, The Young Lieutenant*, and *Fighting Joe*.

The war entered Gerald's world as another source of diversions and pastimes, and he incorporated it seamlessly into his normal routine, adapting previous joys and occupations to the war. For instance, in addition to attending Goodwin and Wilbur's circus, he also attended military parades, political rallies, and the National Sailors' Fair. Like many kids, he was a collector: Gerald's collection of seashells and other curiosities, which numbered well over three hundred items by the end of the war, came to include a piece of army hardtack and a tiny, pea-shooting cannon. Tucked into his reports of peaceful play were references to making army hats and playing with paper soldiers named for prominent Massachusetts officers.[27]

Carrie Berry's life could not have been more different from Gerald's. On the same night in the fall of 1864 that Gerald had to endure a disappointing simulation of the fight between the USS *Monitor* and CSS *Virginia* on Boston Common, Carrie was "fritened [*sic*] almost to death" when "some mean soldiers set several houses on fire in different parts of the town." Not surprisingly, she could not go to sleep for fear her own house would be next, and she spent the next several days watching Yankees methodically burn the city until theirs was among the handful of homes still standing. Later that fall, on the same day that Gerald spent some of his pocket change on souvenirs at the Soldiers and Sailors Fair, Carrie told her diary that "Papa and Mama say that they feel very poor." The ten-year-old had spent her days chasing the family's last hog (driven off by soldiers), "plundering about" the ruins of the city, trying to find anything that they might be able to use, and sifting through the ashes for nails. In contrast to Gerald, who refers to many possessions, including his three hundred-piece collection, Carrie mentions only a doll or two—indeed, she goes six weeks in the fall of 1864 without mentioning play at all—and celebrates her tenth birthday by ironing clothes and running for the bomb shelter. At one point, she is ecstatic when a resourceful aunt somehow obtains a bunch of grapes. The simplest things in a child's life—the toys they owned, they games they played—come to represent far deeper differences in these diverging tales of wartime childhoods.[28]

A very different kind of source—the autobiography of Anna Howard Shaw, who as an adult would become a pioneering Methodist minister, doctor, and president of the National Woman Suffrage Association—provides a reflective narrative of a northern girls' war that focuses more on the plight of the women and children left behind than on the political and military events of the period. Although Shaw's childhood was long gone by the time she wrote her memoir, her memory of the war was shaped by her sometimes bitter recollection of how it had narrowed her teenage years. As such, her memoir provides a northern, feminist counterpoint to the more typical outcomes of Civil War memory studies in recent years by historians: the Confederate "Lost Cause," sectional reconciliation, and emancipation.[29]

Anna was twelve when the Civil War began, but her family had already endured two years of hardship on the Michigan frontier. Her impractical father, who, "like most men . . . should never have married," had delivered her mother and siblings to their remote homestead and then returned east, forcing the family to confront "the relentless limitations of pioneer life . . . on every side, and at every hour of the day." He finally joined them—just in time for the beginning of the war. By mid-1862, two brothers and her father had enlisted in the army, and at the age of fifteen, Shaw became "the principal support of our family, and life[,] . . . a strenuous and tragic affair." She taught school and helped her mother sew and wash; they also took in boarders. A sister married, gave birth to a child, and died. Life "grew harder with every day." It was "an incessant struggle to keep our land, to pay our taxes, and to live." Her health began to fail, as she walked several miles to and from the country school where she taught every day.[30]

"These were years I do not like to look back upon," Shaw wrote fifty years later. They were "years in which life had degenerated into a treadmill whose monotony was broken only by the grim messages from the front." After Appomattox the men returned home and the pressure lifted. She was eighteen, and "the end of the Civil War brought freedom to me, too." She began saving some of her money for college and eventually freed herself from the responsibilities that had limited her young life. Yet one gets the feeling that Howard never forgot the scars of "her" war. Her self-conscious comparison of herself to slaves emancipated by the war and her harsh feelings about her father sparked by his irresponsibility in deciding to go off to war are just two of the insights gained from this document by a Civil War child.[31]

The preceding only hints at the richness of the literature produced by historians of American children over the last two decades. Like all well-researched and thoughtful histories, these accounts of children and youth as they participate in and are acted on by the great forces of history offer original perspectives that add the experiences of the usually inarticulate youngsters that, in the nineteenth century, made up as much as 50 percent of the population of the United States. Indeed, without the stories and points of view of children, no culture's history can truly be understood.

Notes

1. Dale Russakoff, "On Campus, It's the Children's Hour," *Washington Post*, November 13, 1998.

2. Jacqueline S. Reinier, *From Virtue to Character: American Childhood, 1775–1850* (New York: Twayne, 1996), ix.

3. Reinier, *From Virtue to Character*, ix.

4. Reinier, *From Virtue to Character*, ix.

5. Reinier, *From Virtue to Character*, ix.

6. Reinier, *From Virtue to Character*, xi.

7. Reinier, *From Virtue to Character* xii.

8. John Demos, *A Little Commonwealth: Family Life in Plymouth Colony* (New York: Oxford University Press, 1970); Philip J. Greven, *The Protestant Temperament: Patterns of Child-Rearing, Religious Experience, and the Self in Early America* (New York: Knopf, 1977). In subsequent books, Demos investigates elements of the history of children and youth; see *Past, Present, and Personal: The Family and the Life Course in American History* (New York: Oxford University Press, 1986) and *Entertaining Satan: Witchcraft and the Culture of Early New England* (New York: Oxford University Press, 1982). See also Greven's *Spare the Child: The Religious Roots of Punishment and the Psychological Impact of Physical Abuse* (New York: Knopf, 1992).

9. Wilma King, *Stolen Childhood: Slave Youth in Nineteenth-Century America* (Bloomington: Indiana University Press, 1995); Marie Jenkins Schwartz, *Born in Bondage: Growing up Enslaved in the Antebellum South* (Cambridge, MA: Harvard University Press, 2000).

10. Anne Scott MacLeod, *American Childhood: Essays on Children's Literature of the Nineteenth and Twentieth Centuries* (Athens: University of Georgia Press, 1994);

Karin Calvert, *Children in the House: The Material Culture of Early Childhood, 1600–1900* (Boston: Northeastern University Press, 1994).

11. David Wallace Adams, *Education for Extinction: American Indians and the Boarding School Experience, 1875–1928* (Lawrence: University Press of Kansas, 1995); Devon A. Mihesuah, *Cultivating the Rosebuds: The Education of Women at the Cherokee Female Seminary, 1851–1909* (Urbana: University of Illinois Press, 1993); Brenda Child, *Boarding School Seasons: American Indian Families, 1900–1940* (Lincoln: University of Nebraska Press, 1998).

12. David Nasaw, *Children of the City: At Work and At Play* (New York: Oxford University Press, 1985); Elliott West, *Growing Up with the Country: Childhood on the Far Western Frontier* (Albuquerque: University of New Mexico Press, 1989).

13. Jennifer Ritterhouse, *Growing Up Jim Crow: How Black and White Southern Children Learned Race* (Chapel Hill: University of North Carolina Press, 2006).

14. Paula Fass, *The Damned and the Beautiful: American Youth in the 1920s* (New York: Oxford University Press, 1977); Paula Fass, *Kidnapped: Child Abduction in America* (New York: Oxford University Press, 1997); Paul Fass, *Children of a New World: Society, Culture, and Globalization* (New York: New York University Press, 2007).

15. Anna Freud and Dorothy Burlingame, *War and Children* (New York: Ernst Willard, 1943), 23–24.

16. Deborah Dwork, *Children with a Star: Jewish Youth in Nazi Europe* (New Haven, CT: Yale University Press, 1991); George Eisen, *Children and Play in the Holocaust: Games among the Shadows* (Amherst: University of Massachusetts Press, 1988). See also Richard C. Lukas's look at how the German occupation affected all Polish children in *Did the Children Cry? Hitler's War against Jewish and Polish Children, 1939–1945* (New York: Hippocrene Books, 1994).

17. Martin Parsons and Penny Starns, *Evacuation: The True Story* (London: DSM, 1999).

18. William M. Tuttle Jr., *Daddy's Gone to War: The Second World War in the Lives of America's Children* (New York: Oxford University Press, 1993). For a more traditional narrative of children's experiences during the Second World War, see Jay Kirk, *Earning Their Stripes: The Mobilization of American Children in the Second World War* (New York: Peter Lang, 1994).

19. Susan Pedersen, *Family, Dependence, and the Origins of the Welfare State: Britain and France, 1914–1945* (New York: Cambridge University Press, 1993); Sarah Fishman, *The Battle for Children: World War II, Youth Crime, and Juvenile Justice in Twentieth-Century France* (Cambridge, MA: Harvard University Press, 2002).

20. Stephen Heathorn, *For Home, Country, and Race: Constructing Class, Gender and Englishness in the Elementary Classroom* (Toronto: University of Toronto Press, 2000); Lisa A. Kirschenbaum, *Small Comrades: Revolutionizing Childhood in Soviet Russia, 1917–1932* (London: Routledge Falmer, 2001); Thomas Davey, *A Generation Divided: German Children and the Berlin Wall* (Durham, NC: Duke University Press, 1987).

21. An exception is Ian Brown's Khomeini's *Forgotten Sons: The Story of Iran's Boy Soldiers* (London: Grey Seal, 1990).

22. David M. Rosen, *Armies of the Young: Child Soldiers in War and Terrorism* (New Brunswick, NJ: Rutgers University Press, 2005), 55.

23. See, for instance, James Marten, *The Children's Civil War* (Chapel Hill: University of North Carolina Press, 1998), Victoria E. Ott, *Confederate Daughters: Coming of Age During the Civil War* (Carbondale: Southern Illinois University Press, 2008), and Edmund L. Drago, *Confederate Phoenix: Rebel Children and Their Families in South Carolina* (New York: Fordham University Press, 2008).

24. James Goodnow to Sam Goodnow, November 20, 1862, and February 20, 1863, James Goodnow Papers, Library of Congress, Washington, DC.

25. Goodnow to Goodnow, November 20, 1862, James Goodnow Papers, Library of Congress, Washington, DC.

26. Goodnow to Daniel Goodnow, January 11 and February 20, 1863; Goodnow to Johnny Goodnow, February 20, 1863, James Goodnow Papers, Library of Congress, Washington, DC.

27. Gerald Norcross Diaries, American Antiquarian Society, Worcester, Massachusetts.

28. Carrie Berry Diary, entries dated November 22 and 18, 1864, Atlanta History Center, Atlanta, Georgia.

29. The most important work on Civil War memory is David Blight's *Race and Reunion: The Civil War in American Memory* (Cambridge, MA: Harvard University Press, 2002). See also Caroline Janney, *Burying the Dead but Not the Past: Ladies' Memorial Associations and the Lost Cause* (Chapel Hill: University of North Carolina Press, 2009), and William Blair, *Cities of the Dead: Contesting the Memory of the Civil War in the South, 1865–1914* (Chapel Hill: University of North Carolina Press, 2003).

30. Anna Howard Shaw, *The Story of a Pioneer* (New York: Harper and Brothers, 1915), 52–53.

31. Shaw, *The Story of a Pioneer*, 54.

Childism

The Challenge of Childhood to Ethics and the Humanities

John Wall

If the humanities focus in some way on "the human," including its mean-ings, diversities, constructions, and possibilities, then it would be curious to neglect the third of human beings who happen to be under the age of eigh-teen. This situation would appear all the more peculiar if the humanities are charged, as many argue, with challenging normative assumptions and investigating historically marginalized voices. Yet to a large extent children and youth do in fact occupy the periphery in contemporary humanities scholarship, arguably more so than any other social group. The oddness of this situation is compounded by the fact that childhood studies have be-come increasingly prominent in the social and biological sciences.

In this chapter, I take a critical look at my own field of philosophical eth-ics in order to propose a more child-inclusive humanistic methodology. I argue for what I call a new "childism" that would be somewhat analogous to recent forms of feminism, womanism, race theory, queer theory, and the like. By "childism" I mean the effort not only to pay children greater atten-tion but to respond more self-critically to children's particular experiences by transforming fundamental structures of understanding and practice for all. Children will take a central place in humanities scholarship only if there is a revolution on a similar scale to the revolutions that have occurred in connection with other "minorities." Art, literature, history, culture, philoso-phy, religion, and the like would need to be considered narrow and stunted if they did not account for age in addition to gender, sexuality, class, race, and ethnicity.

The field of philosophical ethics is a useful test case for childism because here children are rendered second-class citizens in especially profound ways. It is true that children are often considered *objects* of justice, care, and responsibility. But the field almost entirely neglects children as ethical *subjects*. The question I ask here is not how ethics can be applied to children, for ethics is adult-centered to begin with. It is rather how a fuller understanding of children's lived experiences in the world can transform basic ethical assumptions and norms, regardless of whether one is considering particular issues concerning children or not. Feminism has reconstructed ethical ideas, for both women and men, around new understandings of gender, agency, voice, power, narrative, care, and relationality. Childism should similarly rearrange the ethical landscape around experiences such as age, temporality, growth, difference, imagination, and creativity.

As long as there has been scholarship, there has been scholarship about children, from the ancient Greek academy to twentieth-century developmental psychology. What is introduced by the new field called "childhood studies" is a historically new sense of children's agency and social constructedness. What I propose to call childism grows out of recent efforts in this field, led by the social sciences, but childism also takes the field in transformative directions that the humanities are especially suited to articulate. Allow me to use the feminist metaphor of "waves" to describe how to move from childhood studies to childism.

What may be called a "first wave" of childhood studies (my own term, not one from the field) arose in the 1980s primarily among sociologists who recognized that children are actors and constructors of meaning in their own right and within diverse social and historical contexts. This idea challenged what was perceived as the dominant Western norm of childhood as a period of passive development, a presocial and premoral time of adulthood-in-the-making. As two founders of childhood studies put it, "Children must be seen as actively involved in the construction of their own social lives, the lives of those around them and of the societies in which they live."[1] Furthermore, childhoods are socially constructed, by children and adults alike, in relation to diverse and changing historical contexts.[2] Finally, as social agents, children must be seen as legitimate subjects of human rights.

A "second wave" of childhood studies can be identified with increasing efforts since the late 1990s to include children themselves as research and societal participants. The idea is that children should not just be studied and treated as objects of adult research and policy but also from the points of view of children's own concerns and agendas. Children should be empowered to help formulate research questions, contribute to academic and policy conferences, and take part in larger social and political processes. Research should take a "dialogical approach" that " engag[es] with children's own cultures of communication."[3] This new movement has given rise to a variety of innovative scholarly methodologies such as using video, narrative, drawing, and the internet. This second wave also takes up questions of social policy, investigating how children may be empowered as citizens, political participants, parliamentarians, legal self-advocates, culture makers, media users, and the like.[4]

The analogy between these first two waves of childhood studies and the first two waves of feminism is not perfect, but it does suggest a shared struggle to gain, first, social agency and then, second, social equality. My argument is that it is now time for a "third wave" in childhood studies—which I am calling "childism" proper—that is still more radical. This would be modeled in certain respects on the kind of third-wave feminism advocated by Luce Irigaray, Judith Butler, and Leslie Heywood.[5] Third-wave feminists started to argue in the 1990s that the goal of research and activism should not be limited to gaining equality to men, since equality itself is framed by a history of male power. The goal should be to restructure basic social norms and power themselves in response to excluded female experiences. Work, politics, culture, academics, family, and sexuality should be fundamentally transformed in light of the differences and diversities of gender.

Along somewhat similar lines, childism would seek not only to understand children's agency and to empower children's participation but also to ask how children's different and diverse lived experiences call for structurally transformed scholarly and social norms. This task is already under way, albeit not under the name "childism." The clearest example can be found in studies of children's citizenship, where some now argue for a "children-sized citizenship" based on the idea of broad human interdependence instead of on the idea of adult autonomy.[6] This reconstruction of historical structures does not necessarily follow the same lines for children as it has done for women and other groups, for children are not historically marginalized in exactly the same ways. But the idea is the same: that it is not enough just to include excluded groups; in addition, social spaces need to be reorganized.

I would like to distinguish this notion of childism from the only other two uses of the term that I am aware of. One is the literary theorist Peter Hunt's concept of a "childist" criticism for children's literature, in which the critic "invite[s] adults to read as children" by "taking into account personal, sub-cultural, experiential, and psychological differences between children and adults."[7] Though I am sympathetic to this idea, it remains closer to second-wave childhood studies in that it elicits children's experiences but does not go further and seek to restructure norms and practices of reading for all literature. The other is the psychoanalyst Elisabeth Young-Bruehl's use of the term on a par with negative terms such as "racism" and "sexism" as a means of identifying the ways that societies justify antichild prejudice and oppression.[8] While, again, this notion is useful, it is important to identify not only what victimizes children but also what empowers them.

A third-wave childism of the kind that I propose faces unique methodological challenges. Most obviously, children have generally had less experience than adults in standing up for themselves. One distinction of being a child is a relative inexperience in asserting one's own differences. In some areas children have more experience than adults, such as of the internal workings of educational systems or the complexities of child soldiering. But taken as a whole, the younger a human being, the less experience she is likely to bring to restructuring the social contexts in which she lives. Age actually makes a difference when it comes to the educational, economic, and political resources that are available to one for transforming socially entrenched norms. Put differently, while many groups face social marginalization, children's marginalization is compounded by having, on the whole, less experience fighting marginalization in the first place.

As a result, childism calls for a new methodological approach in the humanities and the social sciences, one that I would broadly describe as a *hermeneutical ellipse*.[9] An ellipse is a stretched out circle with two centers rather than one, like the orbit of the earth around the sun: a circle that is decentered, asymmetrical, distorted around a second focal point. This metaphor is meant to suggest an amendment to the traditional "hermeneutical circle" in which human experience is interpreted, first, in relation to its prior historical and cultural contexts and then, second, from the interpreter's own unique point of view in response to those contexts.[10] But this procedure favors the greater interpretive power of adults, of those with greater educational and social resources in the world. The notion of a hermeneutical ellipse stretches this methodological circle, in a broadly poststructuralist fashion, to make it responsive not only to social agency but also to social difference. Understanding and practice need constantly to be *decentered* around other lived experiences.[11]

The goal of scholarly and societal reflection, whether about children or not, should then involve both historical criticism and historical expansiveness. No interpreter can pretend to understand human experience without responding to the experiences of those who exercise relatively less control over the very interpretive enterprise itself. Only in this way might children be included in humanistic scholarship as not only objects but also subjects. For children participate in such a hermeneutical ellipse just as much as adults. From the moment of birth (perhaps even earlier), children begin both to absorb historically entrenched social norms *and* to respond to the differences in the experiences and understanding of others around them. Indeed, children may be faced with this methodological task even more sharply than adults, since, being newer to the world, they are called on to expand their own horizons radically. The point, however, is that social understanding depends not only on interpretive agency but also on the more complex capacity for reconstructing worlds in response to differences.

Such a hermeneutical ellipse also offers a more dynamic model for scholarly interdisciplinarity. What childism suggests is that diverse disciplines should not only work across normative boundaries but also open themselves up, in the process, to decentering and transforming their own disciplinary norms. The goal of an elliptical interdisciplinarity would be less the merging of disciplinary fields than the endless retesting of substantive and methodological disciplinary assumptions against diverse approaches to human experience.

Allow me to illustrate this childist methodology by reflecting on my own field of philosophical ethics. This field is instructive because it has in fact practiced forms of childism in its long historical past, albeit in highly limited ways. Here I would like to examine, in broad terms, how Western philosophical ethics has thereby simultaneously humanized and dehumanized children and how it may be restructured today along more radically childist lines.

The history of Western ethical reflection on children can be made visible through a three-part typology. One way childhood has been approached can be termed "bottom up." In this view, children reveal humanity's original capabilities for goodness and love, qualities that should ground all social relations and institutions. While individuals and societies tend to become corrupted over time, it remains possible to recapture humanity's original inner purity. The dominant metaphor here is of human beings as plants: we are tender shoots that need to be nurtured from the ground up if we are to have fruitful, strong, and healthy moral societies.

This narrative has informed ethical thinking throughout history; it is manifested, for example, in the very first command of the Jewish Bible to "be fruitful and multiply" (Genesis 1:28), where children are not only literal consequences but also symbolic exemplars of prefallen moral goodness. The New Testament gospels similarly describe Jesus as an infant incarnation of God and his disciples as "children of God," and Jesus himself claims that "unless you change and become like children, you will never enter the kingdom of heaven."[12] Early church theologians such as Clement of Alexandria, Origen, Cyprian, Gregory of Nyssa, and John Chrysostom consistently hold up children as images for adult imitation on account of their simplicity, freedom from desire, sexual purity, and indifference to worldly status and wealth. The seventh-century Muslim Qur'an frequently describes children as "blessings" from Allah, by which it is meant that they are models of what societies should most value. Likewise, in modernity, the romantic philosopher Jean-Jacques Rousseau pictures children as "noble savages" whose natural freedom is the true basis for just and democratic societies. And the founder of modern Protestantism, Friedrich Schleiermacher, takes children to represent "the sacred sphere of nature" and the true "image of God" in this world.

This kind of bottom-up ethics, still powerful today, has both strengths and weaknesses when it comes to responding to the experiences of children. On the one hand, it has the obvious benefit of humanizing children profoundly, since it considers children's voices and agency to be socially foundational. On the other hand, it tends, as have similar approaches in connection with groups such as women and ethnic minorities, to sentimentalize children and thereby marginalize their actual moral struggles, complexities, and diversity.

An opposed childist approach to ethics can be labeled "top down." This view understands human nature as starting out in childhood as fundamentally disordered and unruly, thus requiring an imposition from above of a rational, traditional, or divine order. Children here epitomize humanity's inborn selfishness, sin, or rebellion against moral law; because of this inborn immorality, human nature must be civilized into higher moral principles. The metaphors here are less likely to involve plants than animals: human nature needing training and discipline. The most influential ethicist here is the ancient Greek philosopher Plato, whose two great works in social theory, the *Republic* and the *Laws*, discuss childhood in depth and call for humanity's natural childish barbarism to be stamped out by a philosopher-king's imposition of rational order. Childhood is similarly understood as a model of moral disobedience in certain parts of the Bible; so we find Paul, for example, issuing an injunction to "put an end to childish ways." The early Christian theologian Augustine refers to babies' tantrums and self-centeredness as proof of humanity's "original sin." The Qur'an at times uses children as models of the need for a higher "submission" ("Islam") to spiritual discipline. The Protestant reformer Martin Luther asks: "For what purpose do we older folks exist, other than to care for, instruct, and bring up the young?"[13] And in the modern period, René Descartes describes children's irrationality as the antithesis of his "ideal of cognitive autonomy," while Immanuel Kant views moral education as the discipline of "changing [children's] animal nature into human nature."[14]

Top-down childism, also still widely influential today, has its ethical advantages and disadvantages too. The most important advantage is that it views children as engaged from birth onward in the full human moral struggle: between desire and reason, self and society, earthliness and transcendence. The disadvantage is that children are thereby dehumanized in a different way: they are seen as incapable of their own moral agency and so as in need of passive adult training.

A third childist ethics from history can be called "developmental." Here, the start of human life is viewed as neither innocent nor unruly but morally neutral or blank. What is learned from childhood is that the moral capabilities of selves and societies must develop gradually over time. Humanity's natural potential turns out well or badly depending on its progress over individual life cycles and collective history. The metaphors here tend to feature nonliving objects: blank pages, lumps of wax, uncarved statues, uncut jewels.

For example, Aristotle argues that human nature is not initially *irrational* but rather *pre*rational, containing an implicit moral potential that may become realized in stages. The twelfth-century Muslim abu Hamid al-Ghazali views children as born "soft like the soft clay in which any seed can grow" or like "a precious uncut jewel devoid of any form of carving, which will accept being cut into any shape."[15] Similarly, the Christian theologian Thomas Aquinas views ethical reasoning as developing according to "natural law" over seven-year phases of the human life cycle. The sixteenth-century humanist Desiderius Erasmus points to the ability of the child's mind to absorb both good and bad teachings over time. And, most influentially today, John Locke argues that children are not unruly animals but "blank slates" or "wax" ready to be written upon or molded in gradual phases with all the skills and discoveries of science and reason.

Ethical developmentalism is also influential today, particularly in moral psychology and the politics of "developing" nations, but it too has both its pros and its cons. A key advantage is that it refuses to either sentimentalize or demonize children but instead emphasizes their increasing moral capabilities. But its major drawback is that it views children principally through the lens of what they *are not yet*, namely fully "developed" adults. In this view, then, childhood is by definition a time of moral incompleteness or lack.

Such an analysis of history constitutes only half of our hermeneutical ellipse. It is also important, if philosophical ethics is to be transformed in light of children's experiences, to imagine new and more child-responsive understandings of ethical norms for today. Children's moral lives must not only deconstruct history but also reconstruct it more expansively. While the social sciences have much to learn from the kinds of humanistic history I have been describing, the humanities can in turn learn a great deal from social scientific descriptions of actual childhood experiences. Here I briefly sketch the outlines of a more fully childist ethics that I have formulated more extensively in my *Ethics in Light of Childhood*. I do so in response to three of the more basic ethical questions that are pursued throughout humanist history: What does childhood teach about humanity's basic moral being? What does it suggest about societies' true moral aims? And what does it require when it comes to moral obligations to one another? My answer, in a nutshell, is that being ethical means creating ever more expansive responses to one another's differences with respect to lived experience.

What can most importantly be learned about moral nature from childhood is that it is neither passively determined by social contexts nor purely free and agential but rather interdependently creative. By "interdependent creativity" I mean that, from birth to death, human beings reconstruct their already constructed moral worlds. This essentially poststructuralist view envisions human moral nature as traversing an endless moral ellipse: always already culturally constructed but always also de- and reconstructing. On this view, children are not passive recipients of top-down values, bringers of bottom-up moral agency, or blank slates developing their moral reason. Rather, they are active participants who engage in the same moral dynamics as adults by reconstructing their moral surroundings over time.

Consider the example of Ying-Ying Fry, a girl adopted from China as an infant by a family in San Francisco and author of a book titled *Kids Like Me in China*, which she wrote after revisiting her original orphanage at the age of eight.[16] Having been abandoned outside a police station when she was only a few days old, Fry is profoundly shaped by larger forces in her moral environment: the likely painful decision of her birth mother, the larger context of her biological family, Chinese cultural norms, the desires of her national government, national global economic realities, and so on, beyond any conclusive reckoning. At the same time, even as an infant, she is faced with the moral task of creating meaning for herself, which she does by reinterpreting the sights, smells, and sounds that she now encounters, forming bonds with new caregivers and other children, engaging social and cultural constructs, and in general making sense of her experiences and relationships. Likewise, when she writes her book at age eight, Fry finds herself already conditioned by all her infant experiences plus a vast range of further influences, such as U.S. cultures, the beliefs and actions of her adopting parents, their larger families, and an endless array of social, class, economic, political, and global realities. Still, her moral nature continues to consist in the ability, as her book attests, to recreate the meanings of her experiences in the context of evolving moral horizons.

Studying the experiences of children like Fry allows philosophical ethicists to arrive at more profound and complex understandings of human moral nature overall. Methodologically speaking, the ethicist's task is no different from Fry's. Both must reconstruct their own already constructed moral horizons in light of new experiences involving different others. The difference is a matter only of degree: the time an adult ethicist has had to incorporate wider reaches of life. The moral task for every human being is to create moral worlds from within a constructed, contested, and interdependent moral terrain. Or, put differently, it is to engage in moral play.[17]

If so, then childism also provides new perspectives on the age-old question of what moral life should strive to accomplish, what teleological aims or purposes it should pursue. As we have seen, various childisms of history have come to different conclusions. The moral aim can be understood variously as the achievement of higher social order, the fuller expression of inborn instincts, or the gradual progress of moral reason. My proposal is that the moral aim should be understood instead as the creation of increasingly expansive social horizons.

Let us take the example of new work in childhood studies on the diverse experiences of child soldiers.[18] Throughout history and still today, children have fought in wars, revolutions, and resistance movements and have committed acts of mass violence and terrorism. They have been both heralded as heroic and liberating agents and bemoaned as manipulated and traumatized victims. Around five hundred thousand children are soldiers today. Perhaps the most famous is Ishmael Beah, author of a memoir recounting his experiences fighting for the government army as a young teenager in the Sierra Leone civil war.[19] At age thirteen, Beah lost his entire family and village to rebel soldiers, wandered with friends for months in the countryside, was recruited to participate in countless killings, genocides, and rapes, and was eventually rescued by UNICEF and became a UN consultant.

What can be hoped for a species that, even in its earliest years, can embrace the worst kinds of violence but also achieve the heights of redemption and renewal? The answer cannot be found in collective order, individual self-expression, or developed rationality. Rather, both children and adults are called on to confront their own always-too-narrow perspectives and to struggle for more expansive relations with others around them. Like Beah, each of us is embedded in limited moral horizons that are nevertheless also capable of being broadened (or narrowed) through experience. Put differently, childhood reveals a deeper complexity to moral life's temporality. Inherited moral assumptions from the past ought to be continually decentered, over individual lifetimes and shared histories, in order, hopefully, that we might move in the direction of more fully interdependent human relations in the future.

Perhaps the most complex ethical question to consider from a childist point of view is that of obligations to each other. This question is particularly difficult today because, ever since the Enlightenment, it has primarily been answered on the basis of respect for individual autonomy. This construct tends to suggest a distinction between morally competent and independent adults and morally incompetent and dependent children. Children's supposed lack of moral autonomy has been understood in various ways: in terms of their captivity to immediate wants and desires (Kant), their weakness in the face of worldly pressures (Rousseau), and their lack of moral development (Locke). But in all cases, children become secondary players in moral relations.

Consider, however, the example of Michael, a fifteen-month-old playing with a friend, taken from Gareth Matthews's studies of children's philosophical thinking: "[Michael] was struggling with his friend, Paul, over a toy. Paul started to cry. Michael appeared concerned and let go of the toy so that Paul would have it, but Paul kept crying. Michael paused, then gave his teddy bear to Paul, but the crying continued. Michael paused again, then ran into the next room, returned with Paul's security blanket, and offered it to Paul, who then stopped crying."[20]

Michael is not acting premorally or amorally but morally. He recognizes that his friend is in distress and decides to respond. He may not respond in the same way as an older child or adult, but he recognizes at least two important things: that his own actions are causing his friend pain and that he has an obligation to come up with a creative solution that responds to his friend's particular experiences. Ethicists will miss these moral dimensions if they reduce moral obligations to mere respect for autonomy. Yes, Michael respects his friend. But, in a more complexly passive-active sense, he responds to his friend's different experience. He not only acts but also allows his friend to challenge and reshape his own thinking. His action is moral because it creates a new response to his friend's previously unseen alterity.

This more dynamic sense of moral obligation is better explained through poststructuralist ideas of responsibility to lived experiences of difference. As Emmanual Levinas puts it, "My exposure to another in my responsibility for him ... is exposure to the openness of a face."[21] I cannot enter into the details of poststructuralism here, but I would suggest that it too could use a degree of childist revision. A pure openness to otherness would still marginalize children, because, on the whole, it assumes a subject who is resistant to openness (a critique already made by feminists), and it fails to recognize that children demand not only openness to them but also agency on their behalf.[22] As the example of Michael suggests, ethical obligations are more accurately described as responsibilities. These responsibilities do not require the destruction of the self as moral center but rather the *decentering of* its existing moral horizons. This elliptical obligation is neither to find a common rationality with the other nor to allow the other to deconstruct the self altogether. It is instead to respond to one's own and others' different life experiences by creating more expansively human relations over time. In this case, like Michael, each of us is forever just starting out on a journey of moral growth.

This revisioning of ethics is of course merely an illustration of the possibility for childist scholarship. I would like now to show, very briefly, how a childist ethics might be applied to a concern that has been central in the field of childhood studies, namely, children's rights. So long as children's rights remain the province of the social sciences alone, they cannot be provided the needed fundamental critique of their historical conceptual underpinnings. More specifically, what is needed is a radical reimagining of the meaning of *human* rights. Rights language has proven vital over history to the well-being of men and women and increasingly now also children. Yet when it comes to children in particular, the very notion of rights is faced with the peculiar challenge of having historically been grounded exclusively in the experiences of adults. Such is the larger historical and ethical context of the situation described by Annette Appell in this volume. The reason children lack so many rights today is not just that rights have not sufficiently been applied to them but more fundamentally that supposedly "human" rights are in fact primarily grounded in adulthood.

Human rights were conceived of by their Enlightenment architects as demarcating an explicitly adult public realm. This argument is made in three ways that roughly parallel the three historical forms of childism I have described. Locke, the very founder of the modern concept of rights, views rights as the way governments support individuals' "self-preservation" against each other; but, owing to his developmental perspective, he argues that children must therefore be treated as the "property" of their parents until they are rational enough to hold rights to self-preservation without harming themselves or others in the process.[23] Rousseau claims, in a bottom-up way, that human rights exist to ensure that all citizens are equally included in the formation of a society's "general will," except children must be excluded because they need a prolonged seclusion in the private home in order to become strong enough to withstand being corrupted by society.[24] And Kant views rights in a top-down fashion as humanity's submitting itself to self-legislation by higher moral reason, as opposed to ruling itself by force or tradition, but, again, rights must be denied to children because children are overwhelmed by passion and desire and therefore incapable of rational autonomy.[25]

Despite this unpromising ethical groundwork, however, the lives and experiences of children have provoked child advocates, governments, and the international community to respond by increasingly applying rights language to them.[26] This is most visible in the gradual expansion of international children's rights frameworks. The very first truly global agreement in the history of humankind, in fact, is the League of Nations' 1924 Geneva Declaration of the Rights of the Child, a one-page document that calls for what have since been termed five "provision" rights for children: to receive the means for development, nutrition, health, shelter, aid relief, and education.[27] Provision rights are essentially Lockean or developmental rights to the basic social goods needed for self-preservation. On what basis are they now extended to children? The implication is that complex and globalizing societies can no longer assume that children can solely depend on families for support, which is similar to what the then growing international labor movements and antipoverty drives (both of which already included children) likewise suggested. Locke's dichotomy between independent adults and dependent children ignores the ways in which both adults and children are in fact interdependent both in families and across societies.

The next great international children's rights agreement is the United Nations' 1959 Declaration of the Rights of the Child, which calls for guaranteeing children ten rights: six "provision" rights along with four more that have been called "protection" rights.[28] These are not rights *to* something but rights *against* harm from others: including, in this case, against racial, sexual, religious, political, and other kinds of discrimination; neglect, cruelty, trafficking, and exploitation; child labor; and separation from parents. Protection rights are basically Kantian or top-down kinds of rights because they impose a larger public order upon humanity's otherwise violent tendencies. They are now, however, extended to children on the basis, it appears, not so much of children's autonomous freedom as of their passive suffering from abuse by those with greater power. The founding purpose of the United Nations, as expressed in its 1948 Universal Declaration of Human Rights (an almost entirely protection rights document), was to prevent future horrors of the kind that had been perpetrated during World War II. The mass violence and genocides of this period not only did not spare children but very often they affected children more than adults. Indeed, children may be the social group *most* in need of societies' protection rights, and so protection rights themselves must be understood less as preservers of social order than as responses to social vulnerability.

Finally, and most importantly, the United Nations' 1989 Convention on the Rights of the Child is the most widely ratified document in all of history (every country except the United States, Somalia, and South Sudan is party to it). It outlines forty children's rights and in significantly greater breadth and detail than before. Approximately eighteen are "provision" rights and approximately sixteen are extensions of "protection" rights. But it contains a third and new kind of right for children, the six so-called "participation" rights: the right to be heard, the right to freedom of expression, freedom of thought and religion, freedom of association, the right to privacy, and the right to access to media and information. Participation rights are closer to Rousseau's bottom-up model in that they seek to include in the general public will the agency, voices, and citizenship of all. The main, though not the only, reason these rights are now extended to children is because of a growing sense of children's social agency led by the then new childhood studies movement, which was instrumental in the convention's drafting.

I cannot enter here into the various explanations that have been offered for why rights should be extended to children and not just adults.[29] I would just like to observe instead these types of children's rights movements ultimately demand a fundamentally transformed understanding of human rights as such. For what is really happening, however implicitly and incompletely, is that the very notion of human rights is being expanded in response to children's previously excluded lived experiences. This shift can be described, using the ethical considerations I have outlined, as a movement toward a view of human rights as societies' creative responses to human difference. On this view, the purpose of rights is not to guarantee, encourage, or protect individual agency but to decenter collective life around humanity's widest possible experiential diversity. Existing structures of social, cultural, and power relations should constantly be deconstructed and reconstructed in order, all at once, to provide for those they exclude, protect those they do harm, and increase participation for those they silence. In short, human rights exist to help societies expand their moral imaginations and thereby grow in humanity.

I have proposed that childism offers a more transformative method for responding to children's experiences, both in scholarship and in societies. Rather than simply applying adult-constructed norms to children's lives, thinking and action should engage in a self-critical hermeneutical ellipse in which children's diverse differences are able to decenter historical assumptions and practices. What is more, childism is not just for children. It also aims to offer new methodologies for thought and action in light of considerations of age. I have shown how this method might be put to use in my own field of philosophical ethics, both as a means for gaining new perspectives on historical constructions and as a catalyst for imaginative new thinking. Ethics should move beyond its traditional adult-centered bases in autonomy, social order, and rational development to embrace more broadly humanistic bases in responsiveness to the diversity of experience. Likewise, human rights will be adequate to children's lives only if they are fundamentally reconceptualized as social responses to human difference.

Childism also has implications for larger humanistic study. The humanities, in my view, do not live up to their name if their very practices and concepts systematically marginalize a third of the planet's human beings. Given, however, that it is chiefly going to be adults who conduct humanistic scholarship, a more elliptical methodology is needed in which difference is empowered to transform historical assumptions. Childism can function similarly to feminism in many respects. But it should go beyond feminism and not finally depend on the othered group in question having to lead the scholarly and political charge. Childhood suggests that a more inclusive methodology means not only giving voice to experiences of otherness but also, in an endless cycle, expanding structures of shared understanding in response.

Finally, childism has implications for the field of childhood studies. This is an area in which the humanities can contribute to greater methodological complexity. My view is that the distinction between humanistic and scientific scholarship, while useful for establishing disciplinary boundaries, can also obscure larger scholarly goals. In the case of children, the larger goal should be not only to understand children's constructed agencies, or even to include children as research participants, but above all to respond to children's lived experiences by transforming understandings and practices. Only in this rather elliptical way, I submit, can the table be reconstructed to include children.

Notes

1. Alison James and Alan Prout, introduction to *Constructing and Reconstructing Childhood*, 2nd ed., ed. Alison James and Alan Prout (New York: Routledge Falmer, 1997), 4.

2. Philippe Ariès, *Centuries of Childhood* (New York: Vintage, 1962).

3. Pia Haudrup Christensen, "Children's Participation in Ethnographic Research: Issues of Power and Representation," *Children and Society* 18.2 (2004): 174.

4. Barry Percy-Smith and Nigel Thomas, eds., *A Handbook of Children and Young People's Participation: Perspectives from Theory and Practice* (New York: Routledge, 2010); John Wall "Can Democracy Represent Children? Toward a Politics of Difference," *Childhood* 19.1 (2012): 86–100.

5. Luce Irigaray, *An Ethics of Sexual Difference*, trans. Carolyn Burke and Gillian C. Gill (Ithaca, NY: Cornell University Press, 1993); Judith Butler, *Gender Trouble: Feminism and the Subversion of Identity* (New York: Routledge, 1990); Leslie Heywood, *Third Wave Agenda: Being Feminist, Doing Feminism* (Minneapolis: University of Minnesota Press, 1997).

6. Marc Jans, "Children as Citizens: Towards a Contemporary Notion of Child Participation," *Childhood* 11.1 (2004): 40.

7. Peter L. Hunt, *Criticism, Theory, and Children's Literature* (Cambridge, MA: Blackwell, 1991), 191, 198.

8. Elisabeth Young-Bruehl, *Childism: Confronting Prejudice against Children* (New Haven, CT: Yale University Press, 2011).

9. See John Wall, "Childhood Studies, Hermeneutics, and Theological Ethics," *Journal of Religion* 86.4 (2006): 523–48.

10. Paul Ricoeur, *Hermeneutics and the Human Sciences*, trans. John B. Thompson (New York: Cambridge University Press, 1981).

11. See my *Ethics in Light of Childhood* (Washington, DC: Georgetown University Press, 2010), 87–110 and 167–77.

12. Matthew 18:3–5; Mark 9:33–37; Luke 9:46–48.

13. Martin Luther, *To the Councilmen of All Cities in Germany That They Establish and Maintain Christian Schools*, in *Luther's Works*, vol. 45, ed. Walther I. Brandt (Philadelphia: Muhlenberg Press, 1962), 351–56.

14. Anthony Krupp, *Reason's Children: Childhood in Early Modern Philosophy* (Lewisburg, PA: Bucknell University Press, 2009), 28, 31; Immanuel Kant, *Education*, trans. Annette Churton (Ann Arbor: University of Michigan Press, 1960), 11, 6.

15. Abu Hamid Muhammad Al-Ghazali, *Revival of Religious Learnings*, trans. Fazlul Karim (Karachi, Pakistan: Darul-Ishaat, 1993), 101–2, 64.

16. Ying Ying Fry, with Amy Klatzkin, *Kids Like Me in China* (St. Paul, MI: Yeong and Yeong, 2001), 2–3.

17. See John Wall, "All the World's a Stage: Childhood and the Play of Being," in *The Philosophy of Play*, ed. Wendy Russell and Emily Ryall (New York: Routledge, forthcoming).

18. See Daniel Thomas Cook and John Wall, eds., *Children and Armed Conflict: Cross-Disciplinary Investigations* (Basingstoke, UK: Palgrave Macmillan, 2011). See also James Marten's chapter in this volume.

19. Ishmael Beah, *A Long Way Gone: Memoirs of a Boy Soldier* (New York: Farrar, Straus and Giroux, 2007).

20. Gareth Matthews, *The Philosophy of Childhood* (Cambridge, MA: Harvard University Press, 1994), 57.

21. Levinas, *Otherwise Than Being; or, Beyond Essence*, trans. Alphonso Lingis (Pittsburg, PA: Duquesne University Press, 1981), 180.

22. See my *Moral Creativity: Paul Ricoeur and the Poetics of Possibility* (New York: Oxford University Press, 2005).

23. John Locke, *Two Treatises of Government*, in *The Works of John Locke*, vol. 5 (London: Sharpe and Son, 1823), 126–33, 138, 179–80.

24. Jean-Jacques Rousseau, *The Social Contract*, trans. Charles Frankel (New York: Hafner, 1947) 4, 9.

25. Immanuel Kant, *The Philosophy of Law: An Exposition of the Fundamental Principles of Jurisprudence as the Science of Right*, trans. William Hastie (Edinburgh: Clark, 1887), 114–17.

26. I have traced this evolution in detail in "Human Rights in Light of Childhood," *International Journal of Children's Rights* 16.4 (2008): 523–43.

27. See United Nations, "Geneva Declaration of the Rights of the Child," http://www.un-documents.net/gdrc1924.htm. See also UNICEF's classification of children's rights in "Convention on the Rights of the Child," http://www.unicef.org/crc/index_30177.html.

28. See University of Minnesota Human Rights Library, "Declaration of the Rights of the Child," http://www1.umn.edu/humanrts/instree/k1drc.htm.

29. See, for example, Michael Freeman, "Why It Remains Important to Take Children's Rights Seriously," *International Journal of Children's Rights* 15.1 (2007): 5–23, and Barbara Bennett Woodhouse, *Hidden in Plain Sight: The Tragedy of Children's Rights from Ben Franklin to Lionel Tate* (Princeton, NJ: Princeton University Press, 2008).

PART TWO

Recalibrating the Work of Discipline

This section explores the structures—literary, physical, and social—that adults set up to educate children. As childhood studies argues, educational theories inevitably reflect adult desires about what children should become. Those desires in turn, exert a powerful force on the lives of children raised within these imaginative, legal, and literary configurations. The chapters here focus on the ongoing project of determining what children need from adults as they grow up. What sort of discipline and what sort of protections are necessary in order for a child to mature successfully?

In his watershed work *Discipline and Punish*—a text that influences this entire section—Michel Foucault weaves a narrative in which the classroom, the jailhouse, and the factory are given equal weight as evidence for a panoptic discipline that pins the subject fast within its gaze. In such a vision, each "individual is fixed in his place. And, if he moves, he does so at the risk of his life, contagion or punishment."[1] Since *Discipline*'s publication, a generation of scholars and even Foucault himself have interrogated this totalizing view of power. In one of his later essays, Foucault defines power as ambivalent, as a reciprocal exchange of influence, as "a mode of action which does not act directly and immediately upon others" but which instead "acts upon an action, on existing actions, or on those which may arise in the present or the future." In this definition, power "incites, it seduces, it makes easier or more difficult," but it only "constrains or forbids absolutely" in the extreme.[2]

Childhood studies scholars often vacillate between these alternating views of power as oppressive and as reciprocal. Because young children are so explicitly the objects of overt discipline, it is tempting to see them as trapped in the panopticon, pawns in a system of surveillance and correction that they cannot fully understand, resist, or escape. Other scholars, inspired by childhood studies' insistence on engaging children as social agents, have sought to locate instances in which a child resists or thwarts the disciplinary regimes imposed on him or her. Both sorts of analyses—those that chart the insidious damage wrought by adult regimes of discipline and those that celebrate children's resistance to such regimes—are essential to understanding the complex experiences of children. Yet, as the chapters by Sophie Bell, Lesley Ginsberg, and Roy Kozlovsky in this section illustrate, the study of children requires a still more nuanced engagement with discipline that moves beyond the binaries of oppression and resistance to reveal the complex interplay between adults and children that occurs during the processes we call education.[3] In all three of these chapters, the discipline aimed at children, to borrow Foucault's words once again, "makes easier" the policing and reinforcing of adult desires, and the national, racial, and class identities that emerge from them.

Bell explores how the blockbuster *Uncle Tom's Cabin* mediates between two forms of discipline—the older technique of corporal punishment and the emerging "disciplinary intimacy" so aptly described by Richard Brodhead.[4] Bell focuses on the novel's implicit arguments about education and power as manifested in the sentiment-laden disciplinary practices launched against the novel's children, particularly the children of mixed race. Stowe, she argues, "uses childhood as an experimental space in which to alternately endorse and challenge racial stereotypes, as well as to interrogate the nineteenth century's claim to have moved away from corporal punishment and toward gentle discipline" (94). Thus the naughty children of *Uncle Tom's Cabin* provide space in which adults can consider if, and how, different bodies should be corrected. Bell's explication of the racially charged disciplines undergirding Stowe's argument for love (rather than pain) as the proper way to control children allows us to bring new questions to the underlying assumptions that might populate current regimes of knowledge about which disciplinary methods are acceptable for which populations.

Ginsberg draws on changing ideas of pedagogical discipline in the nineteenth century to make the case for rethinking the workings of power in antebellum American literature and culture. Here too, the pedagogy ostensibly aimed at children emerges as a way to control adult attitudes, particularly attitudes toward women. "By understanding childhood as a way of delineating relations of power," she argues, "childhood studies allows us to rethink the ubiquitous figure of the child in the literature of antebellum America as a discursive signifier whose meanings are inherently constellated around issues of equality and mediated through pedagogy as a tool of power" (106). Ginsberg argues that foregrounding the child allows us to better understand concepts of gendered power, authorship, and personhood as they were being defined in nineteenth-century American literature.

While Bell and Ginsberg use literary representations of children to work back through the disciplinary ideals that shaped the lives of people (young and old) in the nineteenth-century United States, Kozlovsky addresses the concrete structures designed to shape children's development. His chapter triangulates children, the adults who observe and theorize about children, and the physical structures designed to both nurture and control the children those adults imagine. In a wonderfully rich example of multidisciplinarity, Kozlovsky juxtaposes Foucauldian theory with the social scientific discourses of psychology and education in order to think through the different disciplines invoked by divergent visions of the child in postwar Britain. In the process, Kozlovsky explicitly engages the issues implicitly raised by Bell and Ginsberg. If some form of discipline is necessary to help children reach their potential as both individuals and as members of a community, Kozlovsky asks, then what is the most ethical form for that discipline to take?

Notes

1. Michael Foucault, *Discipline and Punish: The Birth of the Prison* (New York: Vintage, 1979) 195.

2. Michel Foucault, "Afterword: The Subject and Power," in *Michel Foucault: Beyond Structuralism and Hermeneutics*, ed. Herbert Dreyfus and Peter Rabinow (Chicago: University of Chicago Press 1983), 220.

3. For a useful overview of the debate in childhood studies over Foucault's concept of power, see Michael Gallagher, "Foucault, Power and Participation," *International Journal of Children's Rights* 16.3 (2008): 395–406.

4. Richard H. Brodhead, "Sparing the Rod: Discipline and Fiction in Antebellum America," *Representations* 21 (Winter 1988): 67–96.

"So Wicked"

Revisiting *Uncle Tom's Cabin*'s Sentimental Racism through the Lens of the Child

Sophie Bell

After decades of critical skepticism, studies of both sentimentalism and childhood are becoming thriving areas of scholarly inquiry and analysis. In Hildegard Hoeller's recent assessment, the study of sentiment is "cooking on all burners," having overcome a century of marginality in the American literary canon to become a nimbly theorized, richly interdisciplinary body of work.[1] Her review of new scholarship finds sentimentality finally treated "as a central concept in American culture, the very vehicle through which Americans imagined themselves and defined their *identity* as a family, class, race, gender, or nation." Far from the masculine American literary canon's shrinking girl cousin, Hoeller deems sentimentalism "the necessary counterterm to individualism," a kind of dialectical interlocutor for rugged American exceptionalism.[2]

Why is sentiment powerful? In The 2007 *Keywords for American Cultural Studies*, June Howard describes sentiment as a tool "used at moments when the entanglement of the subjective and the public is implicitly or explicitly acknowledged."[3] Translating emotions into bodily sensations, sentimentality since the eighteenth century has explored how "the process of identification—how an individual puts himself or herself in someone else's place and claims knowledge of what that other person is thinking and feeling—establishes the grounds for virtuous behavior and a humane social order."[4] Howard predicts that the place of sentiment will remain central to American cultural studies, since "the sentimental is a hinge that swings between the social and the subjective—reminding us, if we are willing to listen, that they are always connected."[5] This logic, in which sentiments connect individual sensations to a larger social landscape, was most infamously articulated in the United States by Harriet Beecher Stowe, who posited that an "atmosphere of sympathetic influence encircles every human being; and the man or woman who *feels* strongly, healthily and justly, on the great interests of humanity, is a constant benefactor to the human race."[6] Stowe's injunction that each person "see to it that *they feel right*" (385) has become a catchphrase in scholarship on American sentimentalism, a touchstone for scholars debating the political efficacy of feeling.

Critical discussions of sentimentalism have traditionally deemed children corollaries to the genre's heightened pathos and emotional urgency. In fact, critics often use child figures to mark the limits of sentimentalism's political efficacy. Philip Fisher maintains that the "typical objects of sentimental compassion are the prisoner, the madman, the child, the very old, the animal, and the slave," asserting that "sentimental representation" holds a "cautious and questionable politics" in which "feeling and empathy are deepest where the capacity to act has been suspended.[7] In Fisher's formulation, children's utter dependence offers adults the means to express an overabundant empathy that is unaccompanied by a burden to act. With palpable distaste, Ann Douglas deems sentiment a "failed political consciousness" explicitly centered on the image of a child—*Uncle Tom's Cabin*'s Little Eva, who gives away locks of her hair to sobbing relatives and enslaved people on her deathbed.[8] Anna Mae Duane aptly suggests that Douglas reacts as she does to this image because she sees it as "calculated to make adults spend their time sobbing instead of thinking."[9] The child icon here, along with the sentimental logic she literally embodies—that sympathy for her spectacularly emotional death will galvanize a nation emotionally perverted by slavery—seems so dunderheaded, so simple minded, that Douglas appears offended. She allows that "sentimentalism might be defined as the political sense obfuscated or gone rancid."[10]

In the last fifteen years, however, other scholars of sentiment and childhood have found both to be increasingly complex, productive arenas for exploring social reproduction and the political power of emotion. Nancy Scheper-Hughes and Carolyn Sargent describe childhood similarly to how Howard describes sentiment. They call the child "a primary nexus of mediation between public norms and private life," central to "the transmission of genes, ideas, identities, and property."[11] Caroline Levander and Carol Singley see the child as "a compelling interpretive site precisely because it is so open and so vulnerable to competing, even opposing, claims."[12] While agreeing with Douglas about the child's centrality to nineteenth-century sentimentalism, Gillian Brown argues for a much broader range of meaning for childhood within that period, asserting that "nineteenth-century American discourse about childhood instantiates the spectrum of concerns about independence and vulnerability that children continue to epitomize in American culture."[13]

Childhood has become a productive term in feminist analyses of liberal personhood's contradictions and limitations. Karen Sánchez-Eppler asserts that childhood's "dependent state embodies a mode of identity, of relation to family, institution, or nation, that may indeed offer a more accurate and productive model for social interaction than the ideal autonomous individual of liberalism's rights discourse ever has."[14] Childish dependency also complicates and extends the place of other minoritarian identity positions, since children's very "difference" from adults is paradoxical, both uniquely temporary (children will grow up and lose this form of alterity) and universal (everyone starts out as a child), and thus works differently from other, more apparently fixed categories of social difference.[15]

Revisiting the children of *Uncle Tom's Cabin* with the sharpened tools of recent scholarship on sentiment and children allows for new insights into the puzzle it has posed for readers ever since its publication—how to reconcile the novel's abolitionist agenda and its racist epistemology. This chapter argues that the novel's contradictory modes of racial thinking collide in the behavior of naughty children. I begin by revisiting Richard Brodhead's assertion that the enslaved child Topsy is the ultimate case study in sentiment's power to discipline individuals, then take up the sentimental and antisentimental disciplinary practices launched against several mixed-race child characters, and finally return to the central scene of a child's power to wield sentiment to effect political change—Little Eva's death—to challenge existing readings of Stowe's stake on that child's sentimental power. Stowe's novel places children and emotion on the color line; revisiting this canonical text allows us to see new connections between recent trends in childhood studies and the racial politics of sentiment.

Bernard Wishy identifies children's centrality to sentiment's driving question—how communities are held together through fellow-feeling—in the pages of antebellum child nurture reform literature. Demonstrating the infusion of Enlightenment notions of rational child rearing into Calvinist approaches that emphasized "infant depravity," Wishy argues that "unruly children" became symptoms of national tensions, literally embodying "excess liberty."[16] Such a discourse foregrounded the delicacy of children's subjectivity and the importance of affection in child rearing and the need to avoid head-on conflict between parent and child. This new disciplinary paradigm in fact illuminated tensions among three historically different ideas of discipline and governance: emergent romantic ideals of childhood innocence, the dominant Lockean insistence on the child as a moral tabula rasa, and residual Calvinist assumptions of children's inherent wickedness. Such colliding views fueled parental anxieties in the pages of early nineteenth-century advice literature.

Placing sentimentalism at the center rather than the margins of American culture, Richard Brodhead grafts a Foucauldian narrative of social discipline onto this antebellum anticorporal punishment movement. He argues that the "old disciplinary mode" of corporal punishment was replaced "with new technologies—less visible but more pervasive, less 'cruel' but more deeply controlling—of modern social regulation."[17] Children were the central figures in this "purposeful sentimentalization of the disciplinary relation," this "intensification of affectional warmth" between middle-class parents or teachers and the children in their charge, scenes that Brodhead maintains antebellum Americans enacted and reenacted in order to establish sentimental cultural power.[18]

Finally, by linking more finely tuned sentimental regimens for controlling children to the antebellum abolitionist representations of the brutal physicality of slave punishment, Brodhead makes explicit a racial dimension to the outcry against children's corporal punishment in free schools and homes. Thus, his adoption of a Foucauldian-inflected "disciplinary intimacy" paved the way for studies of sentiment that foreground racial dynamics, though his own study does not. In particular, Brodhead points to Stowe's character Topsy as an example of sentiment's investment in psychological rather than physical control over children and people of color.

Topsy poses a sentimental disciplinary conundrum. Her body exposes Ophelia St. Clare's out-of-date puritanical ideas about child rearing, which hold that "children always have to be whipped" (214), especially to make them learn. Faced with a child who comically alludes to Calvinist notions of infant depravity by asserting her own "wickedness," Ophelia, a rigid abolitionist Yankee, finds that her definitive ideas about pedagogy and evangelism no longer hold up. When she sees Topsy's shocking naked body as she gives her a bath, she is deluged with conflicting sensations; the "great welts and calloused spots, ineffaceable marks of the system under which [the girl] had grown up thus far," make the woman's heart grow "pitiful within her" (209). Yet still afflicted by her disgust for the child, Ophelia exhibits an uncharacteristic ambivalence, approaching Topsy "very much as a person might be supposed to approach a black spider, supposing them to have benevolent designs toward it" (208). Topsy's body disturbs Ophelia's firm belief in puritanical child-rearing notions, which, like slavery, include whipping as a central practice.

In contrast, Topsy appears immune to the marks of bodily pain that overwhelm Ophelia even when Ophelia only imagines this pain. Topsy's alternating performances of both pain and imperviousness to pain appear to anticipate the novel's central argument for "postcorporal discipline": Uncle Tom's transcendence of pain as he is beaten to death, a transcendence that explicitly echoes the crucifixion. Yet while Topsy's increased incorrigibility in the face of whipping predicts Tom's victory over bodily discipline, unlike Tom's transcendence of the corporeal, Topsy's performances collude with a perverse disciplinary system reliant on physical pain. Initially, she demands whipping, saying, "Law, Missis, you must whip me. . . . I an't used to workin' unless I gets whipped." She then performs pain that she later denies, first "screaming, groaning and imploring," next deeming Ophelia's whippings too light to "kill a skeeter" (217). Topsy's performance of invulnerability contradicts her performance of suffering, baffling both sentimental and corporal coercion. Perhaps Stowe's use of Topsy poses a greater challenge to sentimental discipline than Brodhead suggests.

Despite the conspicuous presence of the child in the scenes of sentimental discipline Brodhead studies, I believe a more sustained focus on child figures can unmoor Brodhead's insight about "disciplinary intimacy" from several limitations, for which his work on disciplinary intimacy has come under critical fire. First, Brodhead presents children's agency as relatively simple and limited. Childhood studies urges us to focus on the child being disciplined rather than the adult inflicting discipline, and thus it disrupts Brodhead's mapping of Foucauldian disembodied surveillance onto sentimental discipline's antebellum cultural work. As Sánchez-Eppler points out, subsequent studies have suggested that "the disciplinary forces evoked by love [are] more complexly multi-directional" than Brodhead's model proposes. Indeed, she asserts, "children's imperfect or unfinished socialization" can serve as "a mark of freedom and a source of power."[19]

This duality marks Topsy's ability to pose the novel's essential discipline problem, articulated by St. Clare: "What is to be done with a human being that can be governed only by the lash,—*that* fails,—it's a very common state of things down here!" (214). The "*that* fails" appended to St. Clare's question sabotages not only his initial claim that the lash can govern but also the grammar of his sentence. Topsy causes this misstep, this exception to any disciplinary regime, gentle or cruel. Perhaps this is the syntactical equivalent the image of brutal disfigurement that Hortense Spillers uses to describe Topsy's role in Stowe's text: she is one of those "carnivalesque propositions of female character who inscribe 'growths' and 'bumps' on the surface of Stowe's fiction."[20] Topsy may inscribe bumps on the critical reception of St. Clare's assertion as well, for when Richard Brodhead calls St. Clare's query "the ultimate question of disciplinary ethics," he addresses only the intact first half of St. Clare's statement: "What is to be done with a human being that can be governed only by the lash?" (39). By removing the "bump" in St. Clare's sentence—his fragmentary self-interruption "*that* fails"—Brodhead erases the important conundrum caused by Topsy's resistance to corporal discipline. Topsy is not a "puzzler" because she is governable only by the lash; she is a puzzler because she is ungovernable by any discipline *including* the lash. This child's behavior undermines regimes of corporal *and* "postcorporal" discipline.

Foucauldian-inflected cultural analyses like Brodhead's also ought to take sentimentalism's racial logic into account.[21] As with his analysis of children, Brodhead's racial analysis remains underdeveloped. It is tempting to conclude that Stowe endorsed a bifurcated system of discipline in which white children like Eva are to be saturated with affection and black children like Topsy are to be physically abused. However, more deliberate, systematic attention is needed to discern the role of race in these portraits of sentimental solutions to social problems. I believe this kind of attention reveals Stowe using children neither to mark sentiment's disciplinary trump card nor to mark its political failure. Rather, she uses childhood as an experimental space in which to alternately endorse and challenge racial stereotypes, as well as to interrogate the nineteenth century's claim to have moved away from corporal punishment and toward gentle discipline.

Although Topsy is the most obvious symptom of racialized child discipline in the novel, she is not alone. She is joined by three other unruly children who happen to share the same name: Harry, a slave at the Shelby plantation; Cassy's son Henry, who is sold into slavery; and Henrique St. Clare, Eva's slave-beating young cousin. *Uncle Tom's Cabin* is a long novel, but the frequency with which this name appears is nevertheless remarkable. Henry, the dead son of Senator and Mrs. Byrd whose clothes are given to Harry in his northern flight, repeats the name, and even "Harris," the name given to George as the slave of Mr. Harris, echoes the name, linking this potential revolutionary to the novel's figures of childish intractability. Shirley Samuels, in "Miscegenated America: The Civil War," has commented on Stowe's "twinning" of two Georges—George Shelby and George Harris—in the novel, as well as the "twin" St. Clares, Alfred and Augustine, as part of the book's anxious exploration of miscegenation. Samuels sees twins as representing miscegenation as an act that "produces a fatal desire to pull apart one body from another, a desire that produces bodily instantiations of a house divided."[22] I want to apply Samuels's insight to my particular interest in children's centrality to Stowe's ambivalence about miscegenation, borne out by her seemingly unconscious repetition of "twinned" names for the otherwise unconnected Harry, Henry, and Henrique. There is also a very real possibility of authorial projection at work in this naming practice, since these children are, after all, acting in the name of an author called Harriet.

The whole enterprise of singular "right feeling" is made difficult by the sheer number of feelings these white-looking, racially marginal children evoke. They share several qualities that generate strong emotional responses. First, they are threatened with harm from the system of slavery. Second, they inhabit racially marginal positions, appearing, if not considered, white: Harry passes for a white girl in his northern flight, Henry believes himself to be white until he is sold to settle his white father's gambling debts; and Henrique is legally white but associated with the creole culture of Louisiana and depicted as somewhat exotic. Third, all three boys elicit a torrent of adult concern about how they should be controlled. Eliza's son Harry endangers himself by entertaining and attracting the interest of a slave trader; Cassy's son Henry endangers himself by refusing to obey the man who has purchased him; Alfred St. Clare's son Henrique endangers himself and his father's slaves by mimicking "the way papa manages" (232). The dangers facing this nominally linked, previously unremarked group of boys yoke the novel's fears about racial hybridity to an unexpected endorsement of disciplinary hybridity. Faced with these boys, the novel undermines its own condemnation of corporal punishment and endorsement of sentimental "disciplinary intimacy." Surprisingly, these boys often need *more*, not less, physical constraint. Stowe, I suggest, is working out the racial logic of her sentimental universe in the discipline of these racially marginal children.

The unrestrained mischief of a racially mixed child actually takes center stage in the novel's opening scene, after the slave trader Haley insists that Uncle Tom's sale will not cover his master Shelby's debt and suggests that Shelby choose "a boy or gal that you could throw in with Tom" (2). As if to relieve their stalemate, the "quadroon" slave boy Harry enters and solves their problem. After Shelby calls on Harry to entertain them with his "Jim Crow" dancing and mimicry of older slaves, Haley and Shelby settle their disagreement by including Harry in the sale along with Tom. Harry's amusing mischief has made up the difference between Tom's value and Shelby's debt.

I read Harry's antics as a crucial opening gesture for the novel's linked concerns about racial and disciplinary mixing. Attempting to teach readers to "feel right" toward a nearly white enslaved child, Harry's amalgamated nature elicits strong responses. The scrutiny spent on his "remarkably beautiful and engaging" (3) appearance is the first of the novel's many attempts to parse the white and black characteristics of mixed-race characters. His features are all compounded from contrasting elements: his eyes are "full of fire and softness" and he has an "air of assurance, blended with bashfulness" (3). In Harry's "Jim Crow" performances for Shelby and Haley, his elasticity and mobility become miscegenated racial characteristics, a naughty mixture that results in his sale by Shelby. Rather than tugging on sentimental heartstrings by highlighting Harry's vulnerability as an apparently white child being sold down the river, Stowe presents his race as constitutionally indeterminate and his behavior as cheeky, straight out of a minstrel hall. The fact that Stowe opens the novel with a nearly white child performing as a minstrel signals her engagement throughout the novel with racial masking. Sarah Meer argues in *Uncle Tom Mania* that Topsy derives from the minstrel show "end man," a staple character played by a white actor in blackface who engaged the interlocutor, another white actor without blackface, who was respectably attired. The energy of these exchanges derived from the end man's "mishearing and misunderstanding the interlocutor's conversational sallies" and subsequently producing "puns and surreal juxtapositions of ideas that were staples of minstrel amusement."[23] In Harry, Stowe can be seen to place the mimic-child in a kind of whiteface that both secures his freedom—he escapes dressed as a little white girl—and revises the grand tragedy of Uncle Tom's sale through minstrel mischief enacted by a "white" slave child. Harry's infinitely plastic aspect and the lowbrow ambivalence of his racial mimicry in the novel's opening scenes betray a naughty child who challenges the trumpeted sentimental narrative being deployed by Uncle Tom himself.

Cassy's son Henry is another white-looking boy sold into slavery. Henry condenses into one child's body the horrors of corporal discipline evidenced on Topsy's flesh and the incongruity of white bondage at play in Harry's performance. Sentimental discipline is useless with this child. Rather than a means by which she can control him, Cassy's sympathies for her helpless child become a means through which *she* can be manipulated and exploited. Her "master" Butler purchases Cassy's children, making her "as submissive as he desired" (316) when he threatens to sell them. Further, while anxiety on her son's behalf makes Cassy "submissive," she is unable to make Henry submit at all. In fact, when she finally loses both children to slavery, it is in part because her "very bold and high-spirited" (317) son is so undisciplined. Crucially, Henry's misbehavior is *not* amenable to loving maternal discipline. Cassy "tried to make the child respectful . . . but it did no good" (317). As it makes Henry more vulnerable, his disobedience terrifies his mother.

The disciplinary regime under which Henry grows up (until his white father sells his quadroon slave Cassy and their two children) is one deemed appropriate for a white boy, that is, a boy who "had never been brought under, in the least, by any one" (317). Being raised white, then, means being raised outside the specter of corporal punishment, or, in other words, being raised sentimentally. However, Henry's inability to govern himself, to obey his mother or his various "owners," exposes a problem in his sentimental upbringing as an apparently white child; it has left him "unbroken." Lack of self-control is Henry's inheritance from his white father, whom the story reveals to be unfaithful to his wife, susceptible to gambling, and cowardly. The failure of sentiment to "break" this "white" boy's temper and teach him self-governance is resolved by his new interpellation as a "black" boy and the intervention of corporal punishment. The "high-spirited" independence essential to white citizenship must be uprooted in a future slave, who will be governed by others. In this formulation, Stowe includes gambling, philandering, and cowardliness into the package of white behaviors that come with shelter from physical violence.

In Cassy's last glimpse of Henry, he is torn from her skirts to be flogged for failing to obey a new owner. Although she fears he is being initiated into a life of unremitting corporal punishment, Henry resurfaces in the novel's last pages unharmed by this abuse: "Being a young man of energy, he had escaped, some years before his mother, and been received and educated by friends of the oppressed in the north" (377). Somehow, Henry's abuse as a slave gives him the tools for securing the self-possession his mother never could help him achieve. In a book intent on valorizing maternal power, this tale offers a twist in which brutal punishment provides a needed supplement to Henry's sentimental child rearing at his mother's hands. Bizarrely, enslavement helps Henry become self-reliant, giving him a chance to prove his manhood by escaping to the North and enabling him to avoid adopting his father's unregulated passions or further brutalization as a slave.

Henry's high-spiritedness resembles the tempestuousness of Eva's cousin Henrique St. Clare, who transforms the novel's concern for slave children into an alarm about child "masters." Steeped in the milieu of slave discipline, Henrique becomes "a perfect firecracker" (235) when angry. Shown breaking in his new slave Dodo with frequent, unmerited beatings he imagines as instructive, Henrique befuddles his father, who confesses he and his wife had "given [Henrique] up long ago" (233).

Henrique's childish temper frames an extended debate between Augustine and Alfred St. Clare on models of child rearing and national governance. While Augustine St. Clare advocates a sentimental discipline associated with republicanism and character-building pedagogy, Alfred endorses corporal punishment, linked here to aristocratic governance and elite education. Augustine detects an aristocratic "instructive practice" in the free rein given one boy to beat another, dryly wondering how Henrique will thus learn "the first verse of a republican's catechism, 'All men are born free and equal!'" Alfred counters by pointing out the ludicrous nature of Jefferson's "French sentiment and humbug" in light of slavery, claiming that "it's perfectly ridiculous to have that going the rounds among us, to this day" (233). In invoking Jefferson, the brothers place themselves in the tradition of identifying slavery's harm to white boys. Jefferson, for instance, argues in *Notes on the State of Virginia* that parental "intemperance of passion" toward slaves leaves white children "nursed, educated, and daily exercised in tyranny" and thus "stamped with odious peculiarities."[24] For all three men, the problem of badly raised white children bears, of course, on the future of national governance.

This young man's tyranny over Dodo violently mimics his father's harsh slave discipline. Alfred himself finds the system at fault and plans to send Henrique north for school, "where obedience is more fashionable" (235). If this plan to make Henrique more "fashionable" by adding a superficial layer of republican polish sounds dubious, it's not just Alfred's skeptical tone that makes it so. Augustine, Ophelia, and Alfred himself have all received traditional New England educations, yet remain flummoxed by the challenge of governing children and slaves.

Henrique's overly permissive southern childhood and the plan to send him north so he can receive the trappings of democracy make explicit the implied problem in Henrique's conflicted upbringing. Neither the North nor the South can properly rear a dependent white boy to independent manhood while slavery remains intact. Slavery's repressive model of governance leads inevitably to revolution, threatens Augustine: "Sons trained like your Henrique will be grand guardians of your powder-magazines, . . . so cool and self-possessed! The proverb says, 'They that cannot govern themselves cannot govern others'" (235). Here, St. Clare situates Henrique discursively in what Michael Paul Rogin calls "the American 1848," the moment in which colonial wars in Europe, the Caribbean, and Mexico clearly placed the looming conflict over slavery in the context of global revolution.[25] By turning questions of political governance relentlessly into questions of child rearing, and vice versa, Augustine ties "the American 1848" to the problems of both naughty white boys and their grown-up, naughty, violent selves: slaveholders. This allegory of the nation as an arena for children's miseducation leaves the brothers in a stalemate, and they retreat to a game of backgammon. As much of a disciplinary "puzzler" as Topsy herself, Henrique leaves both men mired in the discursive space of childhood, chewing over conundrums of discipline and governance.

Stowe's use of childhood to explore sentimental control and racial identity looks very different with these children in the foreground. Read together, Harry, Henry, and Henrique unsettle the novel's more familiar scenes of child discipline featuring Topsy, in which a series of white people attempt to foster humanity in one brutalized black child, with success attributed to the white child Eva. Instead, as these children struggle to survive childhood in the slave states, they reveal a pattern of uncanny mimicry of adult behavior, a blurring of racial lines, and a surprising challenge to both corporal and sentimental discipline. Children, as Stowe depicts them repeatedly, confound both the brutalization of enslavement and the quieter coercion of sentimental intimacies.

I conclude by returning to the epicenter of childhood's sentimental power, Eva St. Clare's deathbed scene. Unlike most critics of the novel, Eva herself is not sanguine about her sentimental agency as a child. Correctly intuiting from her father's "dry, hard, tearless manner" as she sickens that he will never overcome his ambivalence about religion and slavery, Eva, as she is dying, tries to supplement her sentimental power to die with an uncharacteristic command—"You must not feel so!" In issuing this injunction, she displays her own version of corporal punishment: "The child sobbed and wept with a violence which alarmed them all" (253). Both sentimental and authoritarian modes of control fail to influence St. Clare, who again labels himself with Topsy's famous descriptor: "wicked" (253). He is much wickeder than Topsy, however, since his flippant promise to "feel any way, do any way" (253) that Eva likes goes unfulfilled; he fails to convert to Christianity and to act against slavery.

Stowe uses St. Clare, and his whole southern household generally, as a space of figurative childishness. Led by "a master who found it easier to indulge than to regulate" (177) and a mistress who is "indolent and childish" (179), the St. Clare slaves are repeatedly described as "grown-up children" (150). Here, childhood, slavery, and disciplinary failure are linked axiomatically. Slaves are magnets for children in St. Clare's view not so much because they often care for their master's children but because of their inherent childishness: "They are a race that children will always cling to and assimilate with" (202). Just as slavery is a universally infantilizing condition, so childhood is a key term in St. Clare's attempts to think through slavery. Traumatized in his "sensitive" childhood by witnessing the abuses of his father's slaves, he himself refuses any definitive course, such as beating his own slaves, educating them, or freeing them (196). St. Clare's pronouncements on the question of slavery combine moral condemnation with incapacity for action, an indeterminacy that is itself relentlessly figured in the text as childish misbehavior. He is "a good-for-nothing, saucy boy" (192), an "undutiful boy" (193), "a mischievous fellow" (207), and he compares himself to the novel's naughtiest child, declaring that "as Topsy says, 'I's so wicked!'" (208).

Ultimately, St. Clare's refusal to be drawn into the drama of childhood feeling and redemption he repeatedly stages between Topsy and Eva unsettles the novel's sentimental model of communication. His mourning for Eva does not inspire change but stagnates in fetishism: "All the interests and hopes of St. Clare's life had unconsciously wound themselves around this child. It was for Eva that he had managed his property; it was for Eva that he had planned the disposal of his time; and, to do this and that for Eva,—to buy, improve, alter, and arrange, or dispose something for her,—had been so long his habit, that now she was gone, there seemed nothing to be thought of, and nothing to be done" (264).

This direct refutation of sentimental logic starkly undermines the efficacy of Eva's death. While sentiment accords commodities a central place in the cultivation of emotions, with mourners treasuring mementos as affective links to the departed, Eva's chief mourner grieves his daughter as a lost impetus for further purchases. Whereas there certainly is something left to "buy, improve, alter, and arrange"—that is, her injunction to free his slaves—mourning leaves St. Clare impotent; "a heavy lethargy of sorrow lay on him,—he could not rise" (264). Here, Stowe's depiction of St. Clare's failure to mourn his own child properly by fulfilling her wishes actually echoes Douglas's reservations about sentiment's teary "feminization of American culture," even to the extent that Stowe describes St. Clare as unmanned, unable to assert adult masculine sentiment.[26] Read this way, Douglas's critique only confirms Stowe's own fears.

But—readers trained in sentimental logic will say—Eva's failure to make her father free his slaves only strengthens the impact of the book on readers who will be galvanized to make their actions as right as their feelings. Perhaps. However, St. Clare's spectacular incapacity to feel or do right, coupled with his frequent comparison to, and interest in, children undermines the novel's faith in the power of children to feel right, or to inspire "right feeling." St. Clare seems to offer what a child offers—a promise of immanent reformability and potential on which he stunningly fails to deliver.

A focus on the children of Uncle Tom's Cabin does in fact offer a different take on that novel's infamous sentimentality. Themselves mimics, survivors, and tyrants, the novel's unruly children appear misplaced on Philip Fisher's list of helpless sentimental objects. Disgusted at her own childhood death's failure to free her father's slaves, the novel's child heroine Eva seems at least as despairing as Ann Douglas of her efficacy as sentimental icon.

However, Stowe can be seen looking for other ways to use Eva's sentimental power. I end with the fate of one lock of Eva's hair, notoriously offered on her deathbed to all she loved. Smuggled onto Simon Legree's plantation by Uncle Tom, twined around the coin young George Shelby gave Tom as a pledge that he would come to buy him back, one lock of Eva's hair gives Legree a "fit of alarm," reminding him of his dead mother (322). Though it fails to rouse Eva's father, her memento causes Legree to think "he felt *that hair* twining around his fingers; and then, that it slid smoothly round his neck, and tightened and tightened, and he could not draw his breath" (327). Once she is dead, Eva's hair—the archetypal emblem of sentimental grief—gains new power, helping drive Legree mad and aiding two of his slaves in their escape.

To some extent, then, even Eva is a naughty child, a figure of resilient mischief rather than pathetic vulnerability. Looking at attempts to discipline children on the color line in *Uncle Tom's Cabin* reveals corporal *and* sentimental discipline as parallel systems of compulsion and coercion, both of which children often resist. These children's complex forms of agency and authorial deployments of both child figures and childishness suggest that Stowe's awareness of the limits of sentimental power and her interest in children's naughtiness and survival were much greater than most readings of her novel suggest. The novel repeatedly depicts children as *both* dependent and resourceful, abused and resilient. Despite her own investment in racist regimes of physical brutality and racial masquerade that inform her depictions of children across and on the color line, Stowe uses children to interrogate the racial logic of antebellum sentiment-driven reform.

Notes

1. Hildegard Hoeller, "From Agony to Ecstasy: The New Studies of American Sentimentality," *ESQ: Journal of the American Renaissance* 52.4 (2006): 367.

2. Hoeller, "From Agony to Ecstasy," 366.

3. June Howard, "Sentiment," in *Keywords for American Cultural Studies*, ed. Bruce Burgett and Glenn Hendler (New York: New York University Press, 2007), 213.

4. Howard, "Sentiment," 214.

5. Howard, "Sentiment," 217.

6. Harriet Beecher Stowe, *Uncle Tom's Cabin: Authoritative Text, Backgrounds and Contexts, Criticism*, ed. Elizabeth Ammons (New York: Norton 1994) 385. Hereafter cited by page number.

7. Philip Fisher, *Hard Facts: Setting and Form in the American Novel* (New York: Oxford University Press, 1985), 99, 122.

8. Ann Douglas, *The Feminization of American Culture* (New York: Knopf, 1977), 254.

9. Anna Mae Duane, "An Infant Nation: Childhood Studies and Early America," *Literature Compass* 2.1 (2005): 3.

10. Douglas, *The Feminization of American Culture*, 254.

11. Nancy Scheper-Hughes and Carolyn Sargent, introduction to *Small Wars: The Cultural Politics of Childhood*, ed. Nancy Scheper-Hughes and Carolyn Sargent (Berkeley: University of California Press, 1998), 1.

12. Caroline F. Levander and Carol J. Singley, introduction to *The American Child: A Cultural Studies Reader*, ed. Caroline F. Levander and Carol J. Singley (New Brunswick, NJ: Rutgers University Press, 2003), 5.

13. Gillian Brown, *The Consent of the Governed: The Lockean Legacy in Early American Literature* (Cambridge, MA: Harvard University Press, 2001), 84.

14. Karen Sánchez-Eppler, *Dependent States: The Child's Part in Nineteenth-Century American Culture* (Chicago: University of Chicago Press, 2005), xxv.

15. Recent scholars of children's literature interrogate a related set of questions about the "impossibility" of children's literature as a genre, asserted by Jacqueline Rose in her 1984 book *The Case of Peter Pan; or, The Impossibility of Children's Fiction* (New York: Macmillan, 1992). Rose's assertion that "the problem of the relationship between adult and child [is]. . . at the heart of the matter" (5) upsets essentialized notions of the "child" in children's fiction—as character, reader, past authorial identity. Robin Bernstein paraphrases Rose's paradox in *PMLA* 126.1 (2011) featuring a cluster of articles on children's literature's "theories and methodologies." Bernstein calls children's literature "the only genre that is written by one group for another group; thus, the genre imagines the category of 'child' through the simultaneous describing and hailing of a category that it is in fact creating" (163). In the same issue, several scholars of children's literature respond to this impossibility through interrogation of children's practices of reading, resisting, and enacting texts (Karen Sánchez-Eppler and Robin Bernstein, also contributors to this volume), engagement with other areas of textual analysis from comparative literature (Emer O'Sullivan and Kiera Vaclavik) to queer theory (Kenneth Kidd), and redefinition and refusals of definitions of "children's literature" itself (Marah Gubar). The final "impossibility" with which several of these scholars grapple echoes the title of this volume: the impossibility of voicing insights or texts that come from the humanities' "children's table." O'Sullivan and Vaclavik propose moving out of the academic "ghetto" in which children's literature has been lodged within comparative literature, and Kidd finds that while "children's literature scholars know their queer theory, queer theorists don't seem to know much about children's literature" (184). Sarah Chinn explores this connection further in her chapter in this volume.

16. Bernard Wishy, *The Child and the Republic: The Dawn of Modern American Child Nurture* (Philadelphia: University of Pennsylvania Press, 1968), 13.

17. Richard H. Brodhead, *Cultures of Letters: Scenes of Reading and Writing in*

Nineteenth-Century American Culture (Chicago: University of Chicago Press, 1993), 16.

18. Brodhead, *Cultures of Letters*, 19.

19. Sánchez-Eppler, *Dependent States*, 74n10, 16.

20. Hortense Spillers, *Black, White, and in Color: Essays on American Literature and Culture* (Chicago: University of Chicago Press, 2003), 185.

21. Far from missing in Foucault's own analysis, the state's investment in biology and race is encapsulated in his work by the term "blood" and intrinsic to his notion of biopower. See *The History of Sexuality: An Introduction* (New York: Vintage, 1980), 149, 143.

22. Shirley Samuels, "Miscegenated America: The Civil War," in *National Imaginaries, American Identities: The Cultural Work of American Iconography*, ed. Larry J. Reynolds and Gordon Hutner (Princeton, NJ: Princeton University Press, 2000), 142.

23. Sarah Meer, *Uncle Tom Mania: Slavery, Minstrelsy, and Transatlantic Culture in the 1850s* (Athens: University of Georgia Press, 2005), 12.

24. Thomas Jefferson, *Notes on the State of Virginia* (Princeton, NJ: Princeton University Press, 2002), 195.

25. Michael Paul Rogin, *Subversive Genealogy: The Politics and Art of Herman Melville* (Berkeley: University of California Press, 1979), 103.

26. Here, we can glimpse the extent to which naughtiness "queers" this novel. Michael Borgstrom reads Adolph as a character who "blurs antebellum culture's discrete borders of identity" ("Passing Over: Setting the Record Straight in *Uncle Tom's Cabin*," *PMLA* 118.5 [2003]: 1294). Adolph's racial and gender liminality challenge the book's identificatory hierarchies, since his effeminacy unsettles "natural" gender divisions and his light skin threatens "the notion of a stable and discernable white identity" (1293). Borgstrom's argument is relevant here in two ways. First, his attention to the marginal energies of Adolph's "ostensibly comedic role as an important commentary on the novel's racial and gender politics" provides a model for the kind of rereading of *Uncle Tom's Cabin* I think Topsy and other naughty children occasion (1290). Second, Adolph's mimicry focuses specifically on St. Clare and contributes to the discourse of childishness that surrounds his master. According to Borgstrom, critics have either ignored Adolph's pronounced mimicry of St. Clare or have described it as "a child's yearning to be an adult" (1294). Adolph's significance, in this incurious critical tradition, rests on the same strategy of containment I see as endemic to the novel: he is made into a child. Adolph's adoption of his master's clothing, his manners, and indeed his very name ("Mr. St. Clare"), are made legible through his demotion to the status of child and thus to "only a hyperbolic, more amusing version of St. Clare" (1294). And, I would argue, that strategy of containing his anxiety-provoking gender, sexual, and racial identification fails for the same reason I have been discussing: because he is naughty.

Minority/Majority

Childhood Studies and Antebellum American Literature

Lesley Ginsberg

The field of antebellum American literature has been radically transformed over the last thirty years by spectacular projects of literary recovery that have in turn redefined the foundational texts of the discipline.[1] A renewed interest in authorship and publication studies is currently reinvigorating the field.[2] Further, a turn toward the transnational has highlighted trans-atlantic literary relationships in the pre–Civil War era and introduced to our understanding of the field a hemispheric component. This has complicated assumptions about the relative exceptionalism of the literatures of the United States and challenged received notions of borders, boundaries, and nationalism.[3] While childhood studies may be seeking a more elevated seat at the academic table—as the title of this volume suggests—scholarship is already beginning the work of reshaping antebellum American literature through the lens of childhood studies.[4] Similar to scholarship that has changed understandings of antebellum American literature, the newly emerging discipline of childhood studies is also poised to rediscover the foundational literatures of antebellum America by showing how the study of those who are known legally as minors invites us to realign theories and conceptions of major literary works. Childhood studies has the potential to disrupt the inherently unstable and airless binary of child/adult and to complicate reductive understandings of what constitutes "children's litera-ture" in antebellum America. Additionally, childhood studies may allow scholars to interrogate the category of the child in antebellum American literature as a locus of power differentials in an era so riven by competing claims for equality and parity with power that it is famous for the threat of disunion. While childhood studies has been defined as "a multidisciplinary field that concerns itself with the nature of childhood experience and with ways cultures construct and have constructed childhood," the field can do more than liberate childhood from cultural limits and recognize childhood as something that may be mapped or "constructed" onto various bodies (whether those bodies are classed, raced, ethnically marked, gendered, or juvenile).[5] As Joan Scott puts it in her illuminating study of the potential of gender theories to transform the study of history, it is Foucault who allows gender to be understood as, in part, "a primary way of signifying relationships of power."[6] By understanding childhood as a way of delineating relations of power, childhood studies allows us to rethink the ubiquitous figure of the child in the literature of antebellum America as a discursive signifier whose meanings are inherently constellated around issues of equality and mediated through pedagogy as a tool of power. This chapter explores how the field of pre–Civil War American literature might be reconfigured by recovering what could be called an antebellum culture of pedagogy that both critiqued and reinforced power relations in the antebellum United States. I also suggest that antebellum America's pervasive culture of pedagogy is inextricably linked to the concept of authorship as it was defined in the era. When viewed through the lens of childhood studies, the boundaries of our understanding of antebellum American print culture shift to reveal the centrality of childhood and a concurrent redefinition of authorship that may contribute to the broadening of current conceptions of nineteenth-century American literature.

Little Eva reading the Bible with Uncle Tom: it is almost impossible to imagine antebellum American literature without recourse to this iconic moment in the best-selling novel of the era. According to James F. O'Gorman, the biographer of Hammatt Billings, who illustrated the novel, the engraving of this scene of reading is "without doubt the most important image of the first edition" and was the scene—one of only six that were illustrated in the first edition—that, "of all Billings's scenes," as Jo-Ann Morgan explains, "most captivated viewers. . . . [giving rise to] all manner of ephemera" memorializing the incident.[7] The prominence of the Bible marks the evangelical nature of the moment and the depiction of physical intimacy sexualizes the relationship between Eva and Tom even as it infantilizes Tom as a novice being taught to read by a child. Yet the scene stands more forcefully as an icon from an era marked by a profound faith in the power of literacy and the potential of pedagogy to transform individuals both spiritually and materially.

Uncle Tom's Cabin was published in the early 1850s, during a period that witnessed the growing significance of what Richard Brodhead calls the "literature of the child."[8] Antebellum print culture was marked by an outpouring of child-rearing guides, schoolbooks, readers, primers, juvenile periodicals, Sunday school stories, "toy books," and teacher-training manuals. Sarah J. Hale's iconic children's poem about the intersections of home and school, "Mary's Lamb," appeared in 1830 in the *Juvenile Miscellany*, edited by children's author Lydia Maria Child. Stowe came of age as an author during this era; her first publication was a pedagogical tract, *A Primary Geography for Children* (1833). Although antebellum print culture's turn toward the literature of the child seems self-evident when these works are viewed as an aggregate, it is the advent of childhood studies that allows us to situate Stowe's novel in relation to an antebellum culture of pedagogy in which education itself was at the core of many of the period's numerous reform movements. Transcendentalism, abolition, advocacy for women's rights, the common-school movement, temperance—all these movements were predicated on an abiding faith in the transformational power of pedagogy. Further, when considered in light of childhood studies, the seeming incongruities between such works as Elizabeth Oakes Smith's sentimental classic "The Sinless Child" (1842) and Hawthorne's *The Scarlet Letter* (1850), featuring the impish Pearl, begin to resolve: both participate in a redefinition of antebellum authorship that includes the literature of the child. Indeed, Anne Lundlin's study of the canonization of children's literature notes that "books were read by a dual audience" of adults and children in the long nineteenth century: "Many of the best-selling novels of the nineteenth century were works we now consider children's literature."[9] Beverly Lyon Clarke's analysis of American children's literature agrees: "The nineteenth century was a time 'when majors wrote for minors.'"[10] Finally, if the proliferation of juvenile literature can be associated with American imperial ambitions, as the works of Karen Sánchez-Eppler, Caroline Levander, and Amy Kaplan suggest, many of the canonical works of the era can be also be situated in terms of minority positions and asymmetrical relations of power that both critiqued yet reinforced U.S. racial, cultural, and territorial borders.[11]

If childhood studies asks us to consider the child as a signifier of relationships of power, then turning to the law can help us understand this function better, since terms and definitions of power are most starkly articulated in U.S. law. An examination of the legal status of the child under antebellum juridical codes reveals definitions of power and citizenship that challenge reductive or essentialist understandings of the child. (See Annette Appell's contribution to this volume, which includes a discussion of figurations of the child in current legal practice.) Legal historian R. Kent Newmeyer has argued that antebellum legal culture in New England—fostered and developed by U.S. Supreme Court justice and Harvard Law professor Joseph Story—was inextricably linked to print culture and its relationship to pedagogy as a source of power.

> The success of Harvard Law School [in the 1830s] can be explained by its ability to generate books and circulate them. . . . Making books exactly suited New England, with its tradition of literacy, its print culture, its belief in education and the converting possibilities of the written and spoken word. . . . What the 1820s and 1830s added, besides faster presses and cheaper paper, was a new sense of urgency about the fate of civilization and a new realization that law was an instrument of both social change and social control.[12]

Newmeyer highlights Story's prolific authorship of legal commentaries. In a chapter titled "Contracts for Hire," Story discusses the relative legal "capacity," or power, of various individuals to enter into legal contracts: "The parties must be competent to contract. . . . Thus, married women, idiots, lunatics, and persons *non compos*, by reason of age, infirmity, or sickness, are unable to contract. Minors, also, are incapable of contracting, unless the contract is clearly for their benefit."[13] Here, the power to enter into contracts for hire is delimited by a definition of such power that frustrates seemingly stable boundaries between married women and minors and the apparently self-evident distinctions between the dependency of childhood and the independence of an adult.

Nancy Isenberg contends that antebellum legal definitions of childhood challenge essentialist notions of the difference between child and adult: although fully grown, married women "were never understood to have achieved full independence or adulthood, because married women, like minors, had their rights circumscribed by the legal guidelines for capacity. In the eyes of the law, female and male children reached adulthood at twenty-one, but women who married were divested of their legal capacity. Women's political status never appeared to change from childhood to adulthood."[14] In *Woman in the Nineteenth Century* (1845), Margaret Fuller exposes the intersections among the legal status of married women, the dependency of the child, and the plight of the slave: "It may well be an Anti-Slavery party that pleads for woman, if we consider merely that . . . if a husband dies without making a will, the wife, instead of taking at once his place as head of the family, inherits only a part of his fortune, often brought him by herself, as if she were a child, or ward only, not an equal partner."[15] As Fuller complains, equality is almost impossible in marriage when "the man looks upon his wife as an adopted child, and places her to the other children in the relation of nurse or governess, rather than of parent."[16]

Fuller's critique of the eternal childhood of married women can be linked to another of antebellum America's perpetual minors—the slave. Thomas Cobb's *An Inquiry into the Law of Negro Slavery in the United States of America* (1858) is in part a legal review of antebellum U.S. slavery law and partly a meditation on slavery from its classical and biblical antecedents forward. In his book, Cobb, a lawyer, describes antebellum U.S. slavery in terms that persistently code the slave as a child, a gesture that allows us to rethink the child as a figure for inequality and the lack of power. In Cobb's terms, slavery is an extension of the antebellum family, with the master serving as paternal guardian for the slave: "The slave is incorporated into and becomes a part of the family. . . . Southern slavery is a patriarchal, social system. The master is the head of the family. Next to his wife and children, he cares for his slaves." For Cobb, the master's role is paternal: he "avenges," "protects," "provides," and "guides." And, as Cobb explains, "in return, he is revered and held as protector and master."[17] Invoking the pseudoscientific racist canards that justified slavery, Cobb asserts that persons of African descent are developmentally doomed to an endless childhood: "Negro children would learn with equal facility with the white, during the first essays in the school-room, but so soon as education reaches the point where reason and judgment and reflection are brought into action, the Caucasian leaves the negro groping hopelessly in the rear."[18] As Lucia Hodgson suggests in this volume, "a childhood studies methodology informed by critical race theory" allows us to interrogate the tragic parallels between Cobb's antebellum proslavery racism and "contemporary myths about African American youth" (45). As an eternal minor, the slave can never be a citizen, though he may serve the state: "Possessing none of the privileges of citizenship, the slave is not bound to any of its duties," though he may "rightfully bear arms in a war under the orders of his master."[19] And, like a child, a slave cannot enter into contracts: "The incapacity of a slave to contract, being a part and consequence of his personal status, extends to every place he may go, so long as he remains a slave."[20] In the words of Frederick Douglass, who complained about slavery to the white working boys of Baltimore in terms that conflate the inability of children to contract for hire with the limitations of slavery, "You will be free as soon as you are twenty-one, *but I am a slave for life!*"[21]

Justice Lemuel Shaw's opinion in *Roberts v. City of Boston* (1849) legally enshrined racial segregation in public schools. Shaw found that the rights of a five-year-old African American child, Sarah Roberts, were not violated by a city regulation that, in Shaw's words, "provides separate schools for colored children."[22] As Shaw acknowledges, "This is a question of power."[23] Shaw is speaking of the power or "the legal authority" of the city to make such decisions; however, his diction highlights the extent to which his decision delimits rights in terms of what Isenberg calls a "two-tier system for equal protection: one that entitled competent male adults to full protection and another that subjected those identified as incapable—women and children—to paternal consideration."[24] Shaw admits that "the great principle, advanced by the learned and eloquent advocate of the plaintiff" (who was abolitionist Charles Sumner) is that "all persons without distinction of age or sex, birth or color, origin or condition, are equal before the law." However, Shaw sees a vast difference between the "principle" of equality and its application to real, living, American persons:

> But, when this great principle comes to be applied to the actual and various conditions of persons in society, it will not warrant the assertion, that men and women are legally clothed with the same civil and political powers, and that children and adults are legally to have the same functions and be subject to the same treatment; but only that the rights of all, as they are settled and regulated by law, are equally entitled to the paternal consideration and protection of the law, for their maintenance and security.[25]

In other words, not only does the law have a "paternal" function but the legal disenfranchising of women is equated with the position of "children"; adult women, children, and "the descendents of Africans" are not actually equal under the law as it is applied to particular cases, nor do these groups have "the same civil and political powers" as white, adult men.[26] The decision suggests the extent to which children were defined as a class constituted by a state of legal dependency on "the paternal consideration and protection of the law," a class that seems to also have included adult women, and persons of African descent. Thus, the antebellum legal definition of childhood understood it as a state of dependency irrespective of essentialist limits, while the opposite of the legal child was understood to be a legal class of persons who had access to unabridged rights, privileges, powers, and political independence.

Like many women writers who actively participated in antebellum projects of reform (most prominently Harriet Beecher Stowe), Elizabeth Oakes Smith first achieved wide literary recognition with a work that speaks simultaneously to the reformation of Calvinist visions of childhood, antebellum conventions of female authorship, and the paradoxes of adult femininity in an age when disenfranchisement rendered women a permanent political minority. In "The Sinless Child" (1842), a narrative poem in which the figure of the child and the specter of adult femininity are both mutually constitutive yet inherently opposed, Oakes Smith reiterates a paradox that haunts so much of women's writing for and about children in an era in which, as Elizabeth Cady Stanton and Lucretia Mott complain, marriage legally forced women into a condition of everlasting nonage, rendering them subject to correction as if a child or a slave: "In the covenant of marriage, she is compelled to promise obedience to her husband, he becoming, to all intents and purposes, her master—the law giving him power to deprive her of her liberty, and to administer chastisement."[27] The sinless Eva in Oakes Smith's poem is the "cherished dream," the "pure ideal birth" of the poet's spirit; as an emblem for the poet, she is a woman-child, the embodiment of "Youth" apostrophized as "thou woman-soul."[28] Eva is initially a child renowned for the purity of her thoughts:

> Exalted thoughts were always hers,
> Some deemed them strange and wild;
> And hence in all the hamlets round,
> Her name of SINLESS CHILD.[29]

Eva's fate is to enter into a spiritual marriage with an unworthy young man; just as she is like a woman as a young girl, she retains her status as a child even as the specter of seduction threatens to mark her as a woman. "Eva opens her child-like eyes" (122) to view Albert, who is about to "steal a kiss"

(120) until he is arrested by Eva's purity. Eva's innocence transfixes Albert, so the seduction is forgotten in the wonder of her purity, a paradoxical innocence that is both "childlike" and a symbol of "womanhood":

> Light thought, light words were all forgot,
> He breathed a holier air,
> He felt the power of womanhood—
> Its purity was there. (123)

Eva dies before the consummation of her spiritual marriage, neatly avoiding the transformation to adulthood, if such a change could ever be enacted given the legal codes that rendered married adult women equivalent to children. Heightening the instability in this poem that frustrates the binaries of life and death, child and adult, Eva's demise—what would be the beginning of her transformation into womanhood—is less an abrupt change than a naturalized disappearance: as the poet glosses, "She ceased to be present— she passed away. . . . Eva is the lost pleiad in the sky of womanhood" (133). As Isenberg reminds us, with "the consistent designation of [living] women as 'civilly dead,'" in death Eva is both a woman and a child; as the poet puts it, she is a "true woman, with woman's love and gentleness, and trust and childlike simplicity" (133).[30] Finally, her reformation of a rake, Albert, has the air of a pedagogical act in which both teacher and pupil are students, underscored by the poet's use of italics:

> Yet *teaching* thus her spirit lone
> Aweary would have knelt,
> And *learned* with child-like reverence,
> Where deeper wisdom dwelt. (128)

Edgar Allan Poe's review of "The Sinless Child" faults Oakes Smith for not having more skill in "what is termed in the school-prospectuses, composition," and he also complains that the narrative headings at the start of each chapter of the poem make it read like a child's pictorial reader: "Every work of art should contain within itself all that is required for its own comprehension. An 'argument' is but another form of the 'This is an ox' subjoined to the portrait of an animal with horns."[31] The language of pedagogy that characterizes Eva's practice not only reforms a rake but also recasts the poem as a teaching tool that seeks to reform the reader.

As Oakes Smith became active in the cause of women's rights, she continued to write for and about children while advocating for the liberties of women and others. Three children's books—*The True Child* (1845), *The Dandelion* (1846), and *The Moss Cup* (1846)—were subsequently reprinted in 1849 and 1853 and remained in circulation. Her 1851 women's rights collection, *Woman and Her Needs*, and her feminist tract of 1852, *Hints on Dress and Beauty*, likewise remained available. Oakes Smith's work invites us to retheorize the position of the woman writer in relation to the writing of childhood in the antebellum era. Further, Oakes Smith's construction of an authorial persona blending the writing of childhood with the call to reform can be understood within larger patterns of antebellum female authorship performed by so many of her sister authors, including Eliza Cabot Follen, Lydia Maria Child, Elizabeth Palmer Peabody, Grace Greenwood, and Harriet Beecher Stowe, all of whom wrote for or about children. Caroline Healey Dall is a striking foil parallel to Oakes Smith as one of the few women with whom Oakes Smith shared the lyceum lecture circuit on the topic of rights for women and as a reform-minded woman who was committed to transformational pedagogies. As Dall puts it in *The College, the Market, and the Court*, published in 1867 but based on lectures that Dall delivered before the start of the Civil War, "No better education do I claim for woman than her entire *self-possession*, the ultimate endowment of all the promise she carries in her nature."[32] Finally, participation in the writing of childhood was more than just a conventional route to literary recognition and pecuniary reward; it enabled antebellum women writers to both reify and expose the contradictions inherent in female-authored reformist writings.

In *Woman and Her Needs*, a compilation of her previously printed opinion pieces in the *New York Tribune* that was published in 1851, Oakes Smith argues that contemporary laws and customs render woman a permanent "minority." Since marriage prevents women from ever attaining a legal or spiritual majority, they are not only shackled by a "pupilage of mind by which our faculties are dwarfed" but also by the oxymoronic perversities of labels such as "baby wives" and "girl mothers, hardly escaped from pantalets."[33] When it comes to financial management, women most often remain minors: "Every true woman should assert her right to pecuniary independence," counsels Oakes Smith. "I have heard hundreds of women say that they would rather go without money than ask for it; they feel mean and childish to have it doled out to them in little sums, and then be obliged to render an account of the expenditure" (46). If, under the law, woman is considered a "child" or an "idiot" how can she competently enter into one of the most important contracts of her life—the marriage contract? "Can she, who is an infant, an idiot [under the law] . . . be capable of entering into a contract involving such tremendous interest?" (49). Oakes Smith asserts that such a marital contract is meaningless without "equality": "The parties should be of age—and no girl should be considered competent to enter into such a contract, unless she has reached her majority in law" (57). Yet the question remained whether it was possible for a married woman to achieve "her majority in law." According to antebellum U.S. Supreme Court justice Joseph Story, a married woman's capacity to be judged a major under the law and enter into contracts depends in part on the laws of the state or territory where the husband has legal residence (his domicile): "If by the law of the place of the domicil of the husband a married woman has a capacity to sue, or to make contract, or to ratify an act, her acts so done will be considered valid every where. On the contrary, if she is deprived of such a capacity by the law of the domicil of her husband, that incapacity exists in relation to all the like acts and contracts."[34] Further, Story rescues the marriage contract from the inherent contradiction that Oakes Smith identifies by claiming that it is different from all other contracts, citing Scottish law: "But it will be observed, that marriage is a contract *sui generis*, and differing, in some respects, from all other contracts; so that the rules of law, which are applicable in expounding and enforcing other contracts, may not apply to this."[35] As Story glosses, the difficulty of breaking the marriage contract also means that it differs from other contracts: "Unlike other contracts, it cannot . . . be dissolved by mutual consent; and it subsists in full force, even although one of the parties should be for ever rendered incapable, as in the case of incurable insanity, or the like, from performing his part of the mutual contract."[36]

As Oakes Smith puts it, "there is something appalling, when I see a mere girl promising at the altar to love, honor and obey, 'til death.'. . . It is the style to prate of 'sweet sixteen,' and talk of the loveliness of girlhood[,] . . . and therefore the woman should not be defrauded of the period; she should not be allowed to step from the baby-house to the marriage altar" (64–65). Oakes Smith complains that "it is not unusual for girls to become married and mothers at sixteen[,] . . . and men seem quite proud of these baby wives" (66). Conventional marital codes, both social and legal, ultimately deprive women of their full humanity, rendering them "little better than *great babies*, to be humored and got along with, or unruly animals, who . . . must be so managed as to be left as little dangerous or troublesome as possible" (86). Her children's fiction that was in circulation concurrently with her feminist pieces can be read as her reflection on the dehumanizing position of women in the antebellum family. In "The Well-Educated Dog," young Charles refuses to put a collar on his dog, Echo. When his mother suggests that Echo might run away without restraint, Charles retorts, "If Echo is mine, he must be mine in his very heart." When his mother calls him "a terrible radical" for harboring such sentiments, Charles replies, "Then I will go it alone, mother. . . . I mean to make a friend of my dog, mother, not a slave."[37] The Indian orphan Inadizzie in "Inadizzie; or, The Wanderer," similarly learns the pleasure of freeing what he loves when he captures a dove to alleviate his loneliness. The dove's anguish in captivity is too much for him to bear, so he "let the white dove depart."[38] Given Oakes Smith's identification of women with "unruly animals," her children's tales may contain metaphors regarding the treatment of women even as Oakes Smith reaches out to the child reader.

Parallels can be drawn between Oakes Smith's career and that of Mary Wollstonecraft's. Both simultaneously produced important calls for the political and social equality of women while writing for children: Wollstonecraft's *Original Stories from Real Life* was first published in 1788 and reprinted in 1791 by the same publisher, Joseph Johnson, who brought out her *Vindication of the Rights of the Woman* one year later. Johnson also published Wollstonecraft's first book, *Thoughts on the Education of Daughters* (1787). Both Oakes Smith and Wollstonecraft were reformers who did not separate the writing of children's literature from larger questions of reform. In her groundbreaking study of Wollstonecraft's writings for children, Mitzi Myers argues that Wollstonecraft succeeds in "dramatizing female authority figures, covertly thematizing female power."[39] Myers shows that Wollstonecraft's writings for and about children were consonant with her own development as an author who not only wrote for both children and adults but who saw both categories of writing as means of developing a progressive vision of female power inside and outside of the home. Myers puts Wollstonecraft's "mother-teachers" at the center of the development of a "new rational pedagogy."[40] Yet where Wollstonecraft focuses on "heroic, even Christlike, matrons," Oakes Smith proffers the saintly child who teaches the mother.[41] In "The Sinless Child," Eva's mother is entirely effaced by the serene spirituality and preternatural wisdom of her daughter. Giving voice to older Calvinist visions of fallen humanity, Eva's mother attempts to teach her daughter:

> Dear Eva! 'tis a world of gloom,
> The grave is dark and drear,
> We scarce begin to taste of life
> Ere death is standing near. (79)

Yet it is the daughter who ultimately instructs the mother:

> Nay mother, everywhere is hid
> A beauty and delight. (80)

Eva corrects her mother's view:

> And did we but our primal state
> Of purity retain,
> We might, as in our Eden days,
> With angels walk again. (81)

Similarly, while *The Dandelion* is dedicated to "the Mothers of Our Country," Oakes Smith is not addressing the omnipotent matrons of early British romantic-era fiction for children written by women. Rather, in the brief dedication of *Poetical Writings*, Oakes Smith invokes mothers "who are willing that nature should develop her sweet work in her own sweet way, without forcing it into precocious development." Recall that it is Charles's mother who wants to collar the dog Echo; it is she who calls little Charles "a terrible radical" for promoting a vision of noncoercive freedom. Instruction in Oakes Smith's literature for children has a deeply romantic sense of reciprocity. Charles's mother doesn't contribute to the Revolutionary era's ideal of the "republican mother" who "placed her learning at her family's service" and was put to work "*instructing*" her "*sons in the principles of liberty and government*."[42] Rather Charles, a son of the antebellum era, instructs his mother regarding the domestic equivalents of freedom and citizenship for women and others.

The terms used by Oakes Smith to signal female disenfranchisement are marked by their insistent reference to the status of the child—a being defined as a minor, to invoke the standard nineteenth-century gloss of the word "minority."[43] As Oakes Smith's language suggests, the tragic paradox of antebellum womanhood was that it rendered women permanent minorities, figures of perpetual discomfort for whom growth and development were unnaturally arrested. Oakes Smith privately protested the loss of identity inherent in nineteenth-century conventions of female subordination by appending "Oakes" to her married name and by legally changing the last names of her four sons to "Oaksmith."[44] In public forums, however, she continued to be haunted by the tension between her deeply feminist critiques—*Hints on Dress and Beauty* is dedicated to the feminist activist Paulina Wright Davis, soon to be editor and publisher of the *Una*—and her more conventional authorial persona, a genial writer for children. Eliza Richards sees this paradox played out in Oakes Smith's Eva, "the figure of a female child who in every other regard is an exaggerated ideal of antebellum femininity."[45] As Richards remarks—in terms that speak to Eva's direct descendent, Stowe's Little Eva—"'The Sinless Child' embarks on the pedagogic enterprise of introducing the public to a model of inventive female authorship by showcasing that model as divine intervention."[46] Though Richards sees a competitiveness in the name Oakes Smith assumed as an author—"That Oakes Smith's pen name is not floral, like many poetesses of her generation, but arboreal suggests a competitive desire to rise above and overshadow all the other pen names"—it is one that links her to an emerging national literary culture grounded in associations of the New World with nature and the power of self-creation, reflected, for instance, in Minnie Myrtle's name and in Hawthorne's addition of a "w" to his name.[47] Thus I would suggest that her moniker also bespeaks an ambivalence about the codes and conventions that circumscribed the authorial persona in the antebellum period.

As Hawthorne's participation in romantic self-making as a means of signaling American authorship suggests, ambivalence about the links between authorial identity and the literature of the child was not limited to women writers in the antebellum era. Although Hawthorne playfully laments the "grievous disinclination to go to school" that characterized his "boyhood," he came of age as a writer at the apex of antebellum New England's development of a culture of pedagogy.[48] From his early work with Samuel Goodrich, better known as the creator of the *Peter Parley*'s series of children's books, magazines, and school readers, to his authorship of children's literature in various forms, Hawthorne as an author was inextricably linked to this pedagogical culture. Hawthorne's marriage into the Peabody family also links him to a trio of sisters (Elizabeth, Mary, and Sophia) who were deeply interested in romantic educational practices. Elizabeth's *Record of A School* (1835), a transcription of the conversations that transpired at Bronson Alcott's radical experiment in education, the Temple School, has been credited by Megan Marshall as launching the transcendentalist movement.[49] Mary taught school, wrote for children, married Horace Mann (the champion of the common-school system), and, with Elizabeth, wrote *Moral Culture of Infancy, and Kindergarten Guide* (1863).[50] Finally, Sophia, Hawthorne's bride, worked briefly at Alcott's Temple School (indeed, her first published illustration was a picture of that school) and illustrated her husband's works for and about children while devoting her life to the service of romantic motherhood (as distinct from republican motherhood).[51] Further, if Hawthorne's habitations in Concord and Brook Farm and his associations with its founders link him to the transcendentalist movement, it may in turn be said that a transformative pedagogy that can be associated with him was at the heart of transcendentalism in its early stages. In addition, nearly all of transcendentalism's key figures were associated with romantic educational innovations. In *Nature* (1836), conventionally considered the movement's "pivotal utterance," Emerson rhapsodizes that "in the woods too, a man casts off his years, as the snake his slough, and at what period soever of life, is always a child. In the woods, is perpetual youth."[52] Emerson gave the dedicatory address when the transcendental Greene Street School erected a new building; Margaret Fuller taught at this school, explicitly modeled on Alcott's, before she went on to lead educational "conversations" as a form of adult pedagogy for women. Thoreau and his brother kept a school briefly in Concord, where the young Louisa May Alcott was in attendance, and *Walden* (1854) would not make sense without the pedagogical metaphors with which it is saturated. One of the few successes of the utopian Brook Farm community, where Hawthorne briefly resided and which became the basis of *The Blithedale Romance* (1852), was its school.

Hawthorne was notoriously skeptical of his transcendental counterparts and the reforms that they espoused; nevertheless, I suggest that his conception of authorship was linked to a larger print culture that included children's literature and that conceived of authorship in pedagogic terms. Children and the family circle figured largely as an imagined audience. Unlike Oakes Smith's sinless Eva, Pearl in *The Scarlet Letter* is tainted by original sin, "the guiltiness to which she owed her being."[53] While Eva is associated with angels, Pearl is associated with less holy aspects of the otherworldly; she is a "little elf," an "airy sprite," and far from angelic: she's "intelligent," "perverse," "malicious," given to "wild, desperate, defiant mood[s]" and occasionally offers a "mocking smile" (91–92). Though Pearl would seem the radical opposite of Eva, perhaps she is her dark double; like Eva, Pearl is both a child yet inherently tainted by womanhood: "All this enmity and passion had Pearl inherited, by inalienable right, out of Hester's heart" (94).

Echoing the language of the Declaration of Independence only to deny the full humanity of Pearl (Hester questions "whether Pearl was a human child" [92]), *The Scarlet Letter* exposes the inherent if not "inherited" alienation of the woman-child; as Deborah Gussman claims, "To be an alien is to be precisely the opposite of a citizen: in American political discourse, citizenship requires self-possession, the state of being unalienated from, of owning one's self."[54] The collective quality of Pearl's character—"in this one child there were many children" (90)—suggests that she represents a class or a caste. Further, her status as a double for her mother—Hester's "impassioned state" is "transmitted to the unborn infant" (91)—links the two as they were linked under antebellum law.

While Hawthorne may have sought to distinguish himself from the popular writers with whom he competed—including women writers—he nevertheless competed with the popular literature of his day on its own terms through his career-long investment in the literature of the child. For Oakes Smith, antebellum America's print culture enabled her to bask in the doubling of child and adult that she would later go to great lengths to decry: "After the publication of the Sinless Child my friends called me Eva, and I was having the delights of authorship without the penalties."[55] Stowe understood the audience for *Uncle Tom's Cabin* as composed, at least in part, of children, whom she addresses directly at the end of the serialized version of the work: "In particular, the dear little children who have followed her [the author's] story have her warmest love." In terms that extend her vision to the scene of pedagogy, Stowe admonishes her child readers: "Never, if you can help it, let a colored child be shut out of school, or treated with neglect and contempt, because of his color." Stowe continues, "Remember the sweet example of little Eva, and try to feel the same regard for all that she did." The last sentence of the serialized version of *Uncle Tom's Cabin*, set off as its own paragraph, explicitly acknowledges the child reader: "Farewell, dear children, till we meet again."[56] Charles Stowe's biography of his mother also highlights the presence of children as consumers of the story: "Gathering her family about her she read what she had written. Her two little ones of ten and twelve years of age broke into convulsions of weeping, one of them saying through his sobs, 'Oh, mamma! slavery is the most cruel thing in the world.'"[57] Stowe's imagined audience thus complicates notions of a separate children's literature in antebellum America that can be clearly distinguished from other kinds of literary works.

As I have attempted to show, conceptions of authorship in the antebellum era are inextricably linked to the literature of the child. Through its understanding of the child as a discursive sign for inequalities of power, childhood studies has the potential to reignite the study of antebellum American literature in terms of the questions about power that it poses and the answers it suggests. Who or what is the antebellum child when that figure is liberated from essentialist definitions? The child becomes a mutable figure, linked to other political and legal minorities. Antebellum obsessions with pedagogy and literacy may be interrogated in terms of power, political and civic. Finally, childhood studies asks us to consider how the ubiquity of the child in antebellum American literature, from high to low, from novels to schoolbooks, both challenges and reinforces antebellum inequalities.

Notes

1. Though providing a thorough account of the changes in the field of antebellum American literature over the last thirty years is beyond the scope of this chapter, a milestone in the field and the way it represents itself was reached with the publication of the *Heath Anthology of American Literature* (1990) and reflected in a forum entitled "What Do We Need to Teach?" published in *American Literature* 65.2 (1993), in which older models of teaching/representing the field are dismissed for focusing almost exclusively on "the Big Eight (Poe, Emerson, Hawthorne, Thoreau, Whitman, Melville, Twain, and James)" (325).

2. Michael Newbury, *Figuring Authorship in Antebellum America* (Stanford, CA: Stanford University Press, 1997); Grantland Rice, *The Transformation of Authorship in America* (Chicago: University of Chicago Press, 1997); Meredith L. McGill, *American Literature and the Culture of Reprinting* (Philadelphia: University of Pennsylvania Press, 2003); Naomi Z. Sofer, *Making the "America of Art"* (Columbus: Ohio State University Press, 2005); Sarah Wadsworth, *In the Company of Books* (Amherst: University of Massachusetts Press, 2006); Susan S. Williams, *Reclaiming Authorship* (Philadelphia: University of Pennsylvania Press, 2006); David Dowling, *Capital Letters* (Iowa City: University of Iowa Press, 2009); James L. Machor, *Reading Fiction in Antebellum America* (Baltimore, MD: Johns Hopkins University Press, 2011).

3. Examples abound; see James L. Giles's *Transatlantic Insurrections* (Philadelphia: University of Pennsylvania Press, 2001), Sarah Meer's *Uncle Tom Mania: Slavery, Minstrelsy, and Transatlantic Culture in the 1850s* (Athens: University of Georgia Press, 2005), Susan Manning and Edward Taylor's edited volume *Transatlantic Literary Studies: A Reader* (Baltimore, MD: Johns Hopkins University Press, 2007), and Kate Flint's *The Transatlantic Indian* (Princeton, NJ: Princeton University Press, 2008).

4. Book-length milestones in the developing relationship between childhood studies and antebellum American literature include Richard H. Brodhead's *Cul-*

tures of Letters (Chicago: University of Chicago Press, 1993), Patricia Crain's *The Story of A* (Stanford, CA: Stanford University Press, 2000), Caroline F. Levander and Carol J. Singley's *The American Child: A Cultural Studies Reader* (New Brunswick, NJ: Rutgers University Press, 2003), Karen Sánchez-Eppler's *Dependent States: The Child's Part in Nineteenth-Century American Culture* (Chicago: University of Chicago Press, 2005), Caroline F. Levander's *Cradle of Liberty: Race, the Child, and National Belonging from Thomas Jefferson to W. E. B. Du Bois* (Durham, NC: Duke University Press, 2006), Monika Elbert's *Enterprising Youth* (New York: Routledge, 2008), Ken Parille's *Boys at Home* (Knoxville: University of Tennessee Press, 2009), and Anna Mae Duane's *Suffering Childhood in Early America* (Athens: University of Georgia Press, 2010).

5. Thomas Travisano, "Of Dialectic and Divided Consciousness: Intersections Between Children's Literature and Childhood Studies," *Children's Literature* 28 (2000): 22–29.

6. Joan W. Scott, "Gender: A Useful Category of Historical Analysis," *American Historical Review* 91.5 (1986): 1069.

7. Jo-Ann Morgan, *Uncle Tom's Cabin as Visual Culture* (Columbia: University of Missouri Press, 2007), 26, 27.

8. Brodhead, *Cultures of Letters*, 18.

9. Anne Lundin, *Constructing the Canon of Children's Literature: Beyond Library Walls and Ivory Towers* (New York: Routledge, 2004), 60.

10. Beverly Lyon Clark, *Kiddie Lit: The Cultural Construction of Children's Literature in America* (Baltimore, MD: Johns Hopkins University Press, 2003), 48.

11. See Sánchez-Eppler, *Dependent States*, 186–232, Levander, *Cradle of Liberty*, 29–77, and Amy Kaplan, *The Anarchy of Empire in the Making of U.S. Culture* (Cambridge, MA: Harvard University Press, 2002).

12. R. Kent Newmeyer, "Harvard Law School, New England Legal Culture, and the Antebellum Origins of American Jurisprudence," *Journal of American History* 74.3 (1987): 822.

13. Joseph Story, *Commentaries on the Conflict of Laws, Foreign and Domestic, in Regard to Contracts, Rights and Remedies, and Especially in Regard to Marriages, Divorces, Wills, Successions, and Judgments* (Boston: Little, Brown, 1846), 255.

14. Nancy Isenberg, *Sex and Citizenship in Antebellum America* (Chapel Hill: University of North Carolina Press, 1998), 23.

15. Margaret Fuller, *Woman in the Nineteenth Century* (New York: Greeley and McElrath, 1845), 21.

16. Fuller, *Woman in the Nineteenth Century*, 59.

17. Thomas R. R. Cobb, *An Inquiry into the Law of Negro Slavery in the United States of America*, vol. 1 (Philadelphia: Johnson, 1858) ccxvii–iii.

18. Cobb, *An Inquiry into the Law of Negro Slavery in the United States of America*, 36.

19. Cobb, *An Inquiry into the Law of Negro Slavery in the United States of America*, 260–61.

20. Cobb, *An Inquiry into the Law of Negro Slavery in the United States of America*, 246.

21. Frederick Douglass, *Narrative of the Life of Frederick Douglass, an American Slave*, in *The Classic Slave Narratives*, ed. Henry Louis Gates (New York: Mentor, 1987), 278.

22. Luther S. Cushing, *Reports of the Cases Argued and Determined in the Supreme Judicial Court of Massachusetts*, vol. 5 (Boston: Little, Brown, 1853), 206.

23. Cushing, *Reports of the Cases Argued and Determined in the Supreme Judicial Court of Massachusetts*, 205.

24. Isenberg, *Sex and Citizenship in Antebellum America*, 33.

25. Cushing, *Reports of the Cases Argued and Determined in the Supreme Judicial Court of Massachusetts*, 206.

26. Cushing, *Reports of the Cases Argued and Determined in the Supreme Judicial Court of Massachusetts*, 206.

27. Elizabeth Cady Stanton and Lucretia Mott, "Declaration of Sentiments," in *Antebellum American Culture: An Interpretive Anthology*, ed. David Brion Davis (Lexington, MA: Heath, 1979), 92.

28. "The Sinless Child" appears in three variants. It was first published in the *Southern Literary Messenger* in January 1842; there, the phrase "woman-soul" doesn't appear in the four stanzas of the opening inscription. When the poem was reprinted in book form in 1843, the inscription was expanded to five stanzas and it contains the phrase, though it is printed with a dash rather than a hyphen: "Thou woman— soul, all tender, meek" (Elizabeth Oakes Smith, *The Sinless Child, and Other Poems*, ed. John Keese [New York: Wiley and Putnam, 1843], 39). Reprinted again in 1846 with a new introduction by Rufus Griswold, this "more complete and elegant edition" (as Griswold puts it in his preface) renders the phrase with a hyphen: "Thou woman-soul, all tender, meek" (Elizabeth Oakes Smith, *The Poetical Writings of Elizabeth Oakes Smith*, 2nd ed. [New York: J. S. Redfield, 1846], 16).

29. Oakes Smith, "The Sinless Child," in *The Sinless Child, and Other Poems*, 50. Hereafter cited by page number.

30. Isenberg, *Sex and Citizenship in Antebellum America*, 105.

31. Edgar Allan Poe, review of *The Poetical Writings of Elizabeth Oakes Smith*, by Elizabeth Oakes Smith, *Godey's Lady's Book*, December 1845, 133. See http://www .eapoe.org/works/criticsm/smitheo.htm.

32. Caroline H. Dall, *The College, the Market, and the Court; or, Woman's Relation to Education, Labor, and Law* (Boston: Lee and Shepard, 1867) 126.

33. Elizabeth Oakes Smith, *Woman and Her Needs* (New York: Fowler and Wells, 1851), 26, 42. Hereafter cited by page number.

34. Story, *Commentaries on the Conflict of Laws*, 91.

35. Story, *Commentaries on the Conflict of Laws*, 194.

36. Story, *Commentaries on the Conflict of Laws*, 195.

37. Elizabeth Oakes Smith, "The Well-Educated Dog," in *The Dandelion* (New York: Saxton and Miles, 1846), 27–28.

38. Elizabeth Oakes Smith, "Inadizzie; or, The Wanderer," in *The Moss Cup* (Buffalo, NY: George H. Derby, 1849), 114.

39. Mitzi Myers, "Impeccable Governesses, Rational Dames, and Moral Mothers: Mary Wollstonecraft and the Female Tradition in Georgian Children's Books," *Children's Literature* 14 (1986): 34.

40. Myers, "Impeccable Governesses, Rational Dames, and Moral Mothers," 44.

41. Myers "Impeccable Governesses, Rational Dames, and Moral Mothers," 50.

42. Linda Kerber, *Women of the Republic: Intellect and Ideology in Revolutionary America* (New York: Norton, 1986), 228, 229.

43. See Noah Webster, *A Dictionary for Primary Schools* (New York: Huntington and Savage, 1833), 182.

44. Joy Wiltenburg, "Excerpts from the Diary of Elizabeth Oakes Smith," *Signs* 9.3 (1984): 535.

45. Eliza Richards, *Gender and the Poetics of Reception in Poe's Circle* (Cambridge: Cambridge University Press, 2004), 157.

46. Richards, *Gender and the Poetics of Reception in Poe's Circle*, 158.

47. Richards, *Gender and the Poetics of Reception in Poe's Circle*, 152.

48. Nathaniel Hawthorne, "I Was Born in the Town of Salem," in *Miscellaneous Prose and Verse*, vol. 23 of *The Centenary Edition of the Works of Nathaniel Hawthorne*, 23 vols., ed. William Charvat et al. (Columbus: Ohio State University Press, 1994), 379.

49. Megan Marshall, *The Peabody Sisters: Three Women Who Ignited American Romanticism* (Boston: Houghton, 2005), 314.

50. Though *Moral Culture of Infancy and Kindergarten Guide* was published in 1863, Marshall suggests that large parts of it were lifted from letters that Mary wrote in the late 1830s (*The Peabody Sisters*, 494–95n152).

51. The illustration (of Alcott's School) appears on the first page of the second volume of Alcott's *Conversations with Children on the Gospels* (1837).

52. Miller, introduction, to *The Transcendentalists: An Anthology* (Cambridge: Cambridge University Press, 1978), 4, 26.

53. Hawthorne, *The Scarlet Letter*, vol. 1 of *The Centenary Edition of the Works of Nathaniel Hawthorne* (Columbus: Ohio State University Press, 1978), 90. Hereafter cited by page number.

54. Deborah Gussman, "Inalienable Rights: Fictions of Political Identity in *Hobomok* and *The Scarlet Letter*," *College Literature* 22.2 (1995): 72.

55. Qtd. in Richards, *Gender and the Poetics of Reception in Poe's Circle*, 164.

56. Harriet Beecher Stowe, "Uncle Tom's Cabin; or, Life Among the Lowly," chap. 44, *National Era*, April 1, 1852, 53.

57. Charles Edward Stowe, *Life of Harriet Beecher Stowe* (London: Low, Marston, Searle, and Rivington, 1889), 148–49.

The Architectures of Childhood

Roy Kozlovsky

> But we're children, people's belongings.
> —Elizabeth Bowen, *A House in Paris*

The metaphor of the "children's table" alludes to the familiar architecture of the everyday, where the ambiguous status of the child is literally inscribed into the choreography of domestic space. How then does the scholarly focus on the child challenge or inform current approaches to the study of architecture? And conversely, what can the study of the material culture of childhood contribute to the discipline of childhood studies? This chapter explores the prospects of bringing together these two academic disciplines to open a critical space for engaging core issues facing the humanities. The motivation for studying the "architecture of childhood" resides in the context of modernity itself, as one of its central tenets is a belief in the critical role of childhood in forming the private, biographical self and in the importance of childhood to the making and imagining of nations and collectives. As a result, the architecture of childhood embodies the utopian premises and internal contradictions of what was promised to be "the century of the child," which was aligned with a parallel transformative architectural project, that of the modernization of everyday living environments by modern architecture.

The examination of the spaces of childhood has been traditionally shaped by the different methods and preoccupations of architectural and childhood studies. In the "design-centered" perspective, environments designed for children are often interpreted in relation to other buildings designed by the same architect or are grouped with other contemporary projects to allow for discussion of issues that architectural discourse has autonomy with respect to, such as authorship, technique, or style. In these studies, what is of prime importance is the architectural merit of the object. Even in studies of building typologies specific to children, such as schools or playgrounds, the objects of analysis are chosen primarily for their monumental status as exemplars of an architectural approach at the expense of the ordinary.[1]

In child-centered studies, be they histories of play, education, or childhood in general, these environments receive the status of documents. In *Centuries of Childhood,* the founding text of the field of childhood studies, Philippe Ariès includes a section on the everyday architecture of the home to support his claim that the nuclear, child-centered family is a modern invention.[2] In studies of educational history, the architectural object, the school, is explored as a document of educational and governmental policy, an approach that consequently fails to account for the more architectural aspects of childhood environments.

A subject matter that brings the two fields of inquiry together is their shared investment in analyzing institutions through the theoretical framework of space, power, and knowledge, as part of the "spatial" turn in the social sciences and the humanities. The theoretical work of Michel Foucault, Pierre Bourdieu, and Henri Lefebvre makes space an agent in fashioning important aspects of human life such as selfhood, social relationships, and ideology. Exemplary in this respect is Foucault's *Discipline and Punish* (1975), which examines space as a social practice capable of transmitting regimes of power and knowledge. Foucault draws on the architecture of the school, together with the prison, barrack, and factory, to account for the disciplinary regime of power, which "proceeds from the distribution of individuals in space."[3] The discourse of spatiality has been especially productive for uncovering asymmetrical power relations and tactics used to modify or restrict human behavior with respect to the fashioning of a subject, themes that inevitably arise in connection with children, since, as the sociologist Nikolas Rose suggests, "childhood is the most intensively governed sector of personal existence."[4] One type of architectural scholarship that is indebted to Foucault is the comparative study of building typologies. Thomas Markus's *Building and Power: Freedom and Control in the Origins of Modern Building Types* (1993) explores the school building type as a site for "the production of character" by examining the ways in which human interactions are regulated through partitioning and circulation. One of the limitations of this method that analyzes the layouts of buildings as diagrams of power is that it excludes the possibility of negotiation or resistance by those who come under their sway. Building on Pierre Bourdieu's spatial concept of habitus, which defines the subject as an active agent in fashioning its identity in relation to a field of forces, the sociologist Kim Rasmussen makes an analytical distinction between "spaces for children" and "children's spaces" to highlight the tension between the intentions of authorities for children as they are inscribed in spaces such as playgrounds or schools and how children perceive and appropriate these spaces as legitimate social actors and agents.[5] Rasmussen uses space to map the social construction and performance of gender roles and age hierarchies, in fact redirecting methodologies developed by feminist critique and postcolonial discourse toward the study of childhood.

In addition to scholarship that addresses the theme of power, there is an emerging body of work that explores the aesthetic and material properties of childhood environments as cultural products that encode cultural beliefs about children. Seminal to this line of inquiry is the interdisciplinary collaboration between Ning de Coninck-Smith, a historian of childhood, and Marta Gutman, an architectural historian. In *Designing Modern Childhoods*, which they coedited, they bring together scholarship that examines the reciprocal relations between the design of material objects and human subjects. The material culture of childhood is interpreted as encoding in forms the modern project of realizing the ideal of "good and happy childhood" as a lived experience.[6] This perspective suggests that the study of the aesthetic dimension of the architecture of childhood would be enriched if more attention were given to the specific function of aesthetics in relation to children. Catherine Burke, whose research is focused on the intersection of architecture and pedagogy, contends that "an examination of the visual culture of the school involves bringing into focus, perhaps for the first time, the significance of detailed characteristics of schooling such as the intricate, regulated and ritualized choreography of the body."[7]

Informed by the relevance of space and design to the analysis of power and subjectivity, this chapter focuses on a specific historical moment in which the architecture of childhood became significant to architectural discourse, that of postwar reconstruction in England. There is no other period in architectural history in which buildings and environments designed for children were as important to architectural theory. In contrast to the contemporary period, in which the most significant building type is the museum, the seminal buildings for postwar European architectural discourse were schools, orphanages, child-centered housing estates, and playgrounds. The United States remained an exception to this trend, as the principal building types for architectural speculation were the office building and the suburban house.[8] The aim of this inquiry is to identify the forms of knowledge and modes of power concerning children that permitted these spaces to become significant to British architectural discourse in the first place. Building on the sociologist Nikolas Rose's account in *Governing the Soul* of the British postwar mode of power that shaped the subjective existence of people, I suggest that postwar architectural space was structured according to a novel way of exercising power that was not perceived as coercive, since it operated through creative, self-initiated activities that incited subjects to express their interiority and make it visible to observation and intervention. This technique of power was devised as a response to the perceived failure of the liberal conception of citizenship, previously linked with educational and play practices emphasizing "discipline" and "fair play." What follows is a mapping of the spatial aspects of this regime of power in the two building types most associated with the architecture of childhood, playgrounds and schools, and an account of the consequences of this line of research for architectural history and childhood studies.

The institution of the playground is exceptionally suitable for analyzing this mode of power, since play itself has been constructed in humanist thought as an autonomous realm of freedom and pleasure: in the words of play theorist Roger Caillois, "A game which one would be forced to play would at once cease being play."[9] At the same time, modernity has conceptualized play quasi-scientifically as an innate biological instinct that serves an important function in human development. Modernity has also utilized children's propensity to play to achieve various educational and social goals, including the prevention of juvenile delinquency and "social disorganization." In Anglo-Saxon culture in particular, play also became associated with citizenship, first as an embodiment of the liberal ideal of "fair play" and then, with the rise of the welfare state, as the internalization of the requirement to be an active, free, and responsible citizen. Hence the playground provides fertile grounds for exploring the role of childhood environments as subject-forming technologies.

An illuminating case belonging to the postwar period is the adventure playground. Unlike the conventional playground with its four S's (slide, swing, seesaw, and sandbox), it has no readymade play equipment; rather, it is up to the participants to introduce content and meaning through their self-initiated activity. While the familiar playground with its permanent fixtures incites mostly kinetic modes of pleasure, the open-ended, flexible adventure playground engages the child through the pleasure of making, cooperating, and even destroying. Architectural accounts of playground design such as Lady Allen of Hurtwood's *Planning for Play* (1968) or Susan Solomon's *American Playgrounds: Revitalizing Community Space* (2005) construct a narrative of evolutionary progress from the mechanical, equipment-based playground to the imaginative, participatory play of the adventure playground, which is understood to better reflect the true nature of the playing child and to better respond to his or her needs.

This section seeks to problematize this modernist narrative and its essentialization of free play as responding to a biological need by situating the history of the adventure playground within the political context of postwar reconstruction and by situating its employment of flexibility, agency, and freedom in relation to the postwar model of citizenship as theorized by Rose. This context also explains the substantial difference in appearance and play practices between the original adventure playground and the form it took in the United States when the concept was Americanized in the late 1960s.

The adventure playground originated in the writings of the Danish landscape architect Carl Theodor Sørensen in 1931 and was first realized during World War II in Emdrup, Copenhagen. That the idea came out of a landscape discourse rather than a pedagogical one is indicative of the specialization of playground design as a branch of landscape architecture. This development had a contradictory influence on the form, layout, and meaning of the playground. To use Walter Benjamin's distinction between the "plaything" and the "playing," "playing" being "real, living play," one line of development entailed formally aligning playground design practices with the modernist aesthetics of abstraction, which is the approach the artist Isamu Noguchi and the architect Aldo van Eyck took.[10] The alternative functional approach initiated by Sørensen sought to transform the "playing" by providing children with the agency to invent the playground. If the modernist imperative was to make play environments "imaginative," it followed that the imagination at play should be that of the child, not the designer. The

Danish experiment might have remained a local curiosity had it not been embraced by Lady Allen of Hurtwood, a landscape architect, children rights activist, and founder of the World Organization for Early Childhood Education. Allen popularized the idea in England with her 1946 *Picture Post* essay "Why Not Use Our Bomb Sites Like This?" As the title suggests, what was unique about the English appropriation of this libertarian model of play was that the playgrounds were built on bombed sites, as a conscious strategy for rehabilitating England's damaged cities. This association between playgrounds and war damage is incompatible with our contemporary belief that childhood ought to be sheltered from violence and destruction, but at the time, it was considered curative. George Burden, the chairman of the first junk playground in England, which was opened on the site of a bombed church in 1948, explained the rationale of building playgrounds on sites of destruction (see fig. 1): "Playgrounds such as ours set in a district which has suffered much during the war can lead a child away from the tolerance and approval of that destruction which is associated with the war. The child of nine or ten makes few moral judgments. . . . It lies in our power to assist him in choosing what is socially desirable and morally right."[11] This curative and

Figure 1. "Junk Playgrounds," *Times Educational Supplement*, June 5, 1948. Courtesy of the *Times Educational Supplement*.

pedagogical use of playgrounds (Burden was a psychiatric social worker) provides insight into that period's conception of citizenship and reveals the techniques of power operating in the playground, which allows the revision of design-centered accounts of the adventure playground movement.

The idea that the wounds inflicted by violence could be healed by returning to the scene of destruction is indebted to the work of the pioneer of art therapy, Marie Paneth, which developed independently from the Danish experiment. From 1942 to 1943 Paneth managed a play center in Paddington for slum children who were too violent to be evacuated. Paneth dealt with extreme manifestations of aggression by following the "nonresistance line." The rationale behind her refusal to punish aggressive behavior was twofold: Paneth interpreted the violence directed toward her as the transference of aggression addressed to others, since according to psychoanalytic theory, the root cause of delinquency and one's attitude to society resided in traumatic childhood experiences brought about by punitive parents. Observing rather than suppressing destructive play provided the social worker with indirect knowledge of the pathologies of the home. Secondly, refusal to condemn or judge worked as a strategy for gaining the child's trust. Paneth allowed children to act out their aggression until they reached catharsis and became, in her words, "sick of their own method" and could "start life at the new place with rule and order."[12] In *Branch Street*, Paneth proposed a new type of play center that would provide slum children with a bombed site and building materials from which they could build a home for themselves: "It is a damaged bit. Its very existence is a reminder of damage and destruction. A sore spot and harmful to all of us. But it could . . . have a very healing effect if one were allowed to build upon the very spot where damage has been done."[13] The political meaning of her proposal is revealed in her concluding statement that slum conditions provided the recruiting grounds for fascism: "We should also remember that the horde which Hitler employed to carry out his first acts of aggression—murdering and torturing peaceful citizens—was recruited mainly from desperate Branch Street youths, and that to help the individual means helping Democracy as well."[14] *Branch Street* is an account of using play to build communities on a participatory model of creative citizenship. The act of building playgrounds on bombed sites established a metaphorical correspondence between the reconstruction of the nation and the reconstruction of the damaged self.

In light of Rose's thesis on postwar power, the adventure playground can be seen as an instrument for making the interiority of children observable and governable. This is demonstrated by reading through the reports submitted to playground committees by play leaders: "Today one little girl complained bitterly about her mother who 'has no love for me, she always kicks me out.' We might say that as they have no place to play inside in the happy setting of a home they develop a certain antagonism against the home and later follows boredom and then delinquency."[15] By providing children with a friendly relationship with an amiable adult, the argument goes, we can prevent children's attitude toward society and authority from becoming a projection of their resistance and aggression toward the imperfect parenthood they experience at home. The play leader Jack Lambert reflected that "I succeeded in Welwyn because by that time I had found ways of building in controls without the children recognizing them as such. They felt free."[16] Inciting them to appropriate space and make it their own, "to identify with it, because it would be theirs," was intended to attach children at risk to the social body by providing them with a sense of ownership and agency.[17]

Playground accounts that define play as an autonomous, timeless biological need also fail to disclose its historical specificity as a public, staged event. Playgrounds on bombed sites presented an allegory of reconstructing a new world out of ruins, a world purged of memories of violence and destruction (see fig. 2). These playgrounds exemplify what the historian Tony Judt has identified as the cultural dynamics of active forgetting that accompanied Europe's postwar recovery, "built upon deliberate *mis*-memory—upon forgetting as a way of life."[18] The contemporary primacy of the museum building type reflects Judt's claim that since 1989 "Europe has been constructed instead upon a compensatory surplus of memory: institutionalized public remembering as the very foundation of collective identity."[19] This historical specificity also explains the different meaning this institution assumed across the Atlantic. The first adventure playground in the United States was opened in 1967 at New York's Central Park as part of a broader reform in administering the city's parks initiated by the Lindsay administration. Designed by the architect Richard Dattner, the playground employed imaginative abstract sculptural features that could be used in different, unscripted ways, but it did not provide children with building materials and tools to build their own world as was the practice in Europe: Leonard Lauder, the benefactor who sponsored the playground, explained that "what is appropriate for a bombed-out site in the heart of London is not appropriate for probably the greatest masterpiece of landscape architecture, which is Central Park."[20] This remark makes evident that the English adventure playground, with its privileging of the "playing" over the "plaything," was not the inevitable outcome of a century-long evolutionary progress toward designing playgrounds that better serve the true needs of children but rather a social technology for forging a social democratic model of citizenship out of the ruins of war.

The examination of the spaces of childhood in terms of how they function as components of regimes of power and knowledge entails a revision of the architectural account of postwar architecture and, with it, calls for introducing a different set of questions for architectural history. In the case of the postwar school, such an inquiry brings into focus the construction of subjectivity through spatial and aesthetic practices pertaining to the child's body.

Postwar architectural culture in England has been defined by the polemical opposition between two seminal projects: the schools built by the Hertfordshire County Council (beginning in 1947) and Alison and Peter Smithson's secondary modern school at Hunstanton (1950–54). The Hertfordshire schools, the first to implement modernist notions of prefabrication and system architecture in public buildings, stood for a socially responsible, antimonumental approach, while Hunstanton became identified with the formalist approach: the editor of the *Architects' Journal* wrote that it "seems to ignore the children for which it was built, [and thus] it is hard to define it as *architecture* at all. It is a formalist structure which will please only the architects, and a small coterie concerned more with satisfying their personal design sense than with achieving a humanist, functional, architecture."[21] Subsequent historical accounts of postwar architecture replicate this ideological opposition. For Andrew Saint, because the Hertfordshire schools were built for children and addressed their needs, they exemplify the modernist mission of "making buildings of real benefit to society."[22] In contrast, Reyner Banham criticized the Hertfordshire approach as the self-righteous imposition of "form follows curriculum," a reference to its alignment with progressive child-centered pedagogy, resulting in bureaucratic buildings that lacked architectural character.[23] While Saint criticized Hunstanton's "unapologetic image-mongering," Banham hailed it as the first New Brutalist building in his historical account of that movement and singled out its affinities with Mies van der Rohe's work in Chicago.[24] This debate reenacts the fundamental ideological opposition between "autonomy" and "commitment" that structured postwar theoretical debates.[25] Since the debate took place in relation to school buildings, placing the child at the center of historical inquiry allows us to shift the focus from concerns such as style, authorship, or ideology that architecture has autonomy over to issues of governmentality and power. The school can thus be examined as a *document* of social history, one that exemplifies the spatial practices and social relations embedded in the institution of the school, and as a *monument* of a creative aesthetic practice directed toward affecting the sensual apparatus of the child through its formal and material properties, following the historian of education Nick Peim's suggestion that in schools, "the techniques that organize space are complemented by technologies that organize time and movement."[26] This section concerns itself with the role of rhythm, harmony, and motion in postwar education and with how those qualities inform architectural design, providing an alternative critical perspective for interpreting postwar architectural discourse.

Historians of the postwar English school have established that its uniqueness was the outcome of a fruitful collaboration between architects and educationalists; in part, educationalists legitimized the investment of public resources in the materiality and aesthetics of the school by claiming that it had a positive educational and behavioral impact on the child. The pedagogue Molly Harrison explained to architects that "no one who has much contact with children would deny that they are very strongly influenced by their immediate environment. In a pleasant, harmonious and appropriate building they tend to behave in a much more civilized manner and actually become better balanced and more sensitive than they do if they grow up in an ugly, ill planned or merely neutral environment."[27] Unique to the postwar period, pedagogical aesthetics were based on a biological concept of growth as potentiality: Harrison defined the purpose of progressive education as providing "the best opportunities for growth and to remove hampering influences."[28] To that end, she suggested that the building itself be conceived as a living, growing organism. The aesthetics of growth were conceptualized as a rhythmic, fluctuating process in time and space, an understanding that was indebted to the educational philosophy of Alfred North Whitehead. In "The Aims of Education" from 1916, Whitehead defined the aims of education as the stimulation and guidance of the self-development of the individual in response to a changing external environment. Arguing against the dominant model of education as a linear process of growth, Whitehead reasoned that the learning process has a "rhythm," that it is cyclic in nature: "Life is essentially periodic. . . . That is why I have chosen the term 'rhythmic,' as meaning essentially the conveyance of difference within a framework of repetition."[29]

Whitehead defined these cycles as the stages of romance, precision, and generalization. At the stage of romance, the subject is stirred by desire to learn, as "there can be no mental development without interest." The stage of precision introduces exactness and technique; the stage of generalization is aimed at the enjoyment of culture and intellectual activity, or what Whitehead called "the art of life."[30] Whitehead suggested that every educational activity was to be performed aesthetically, with "style," which he defined as "the fashioning of power, the restraint of power."

For Whitehead's generation, aesthetic education was part of a humanist endeavor of enrichment. The postwar generation redefined its politics as a technique for realizing a peaceful society. In *Education through Art* (1943) the polymath art critic and educational philosopher Herbert Read located the causes for the two world wars in repressive educational practices, claiming that "the secret of our collective ills is to be traced to the suppression of spontaneous creative ability in the individual."[31] Read considered bodily motion as a potent medium for communication and self-expression and suggested that the most important aspect of school design was to provide environments that ensured "freedom of movement. The senses are only educated by endless action . . . and action requires space."[32] Finally, Read sought to habituate children in harmony by reviving the Platonic conception of aesthetic education: "All grace and harmony in life—which form the moral basis of the human soul itself—are determined by aesthetic feelings, by the perception of rhythm and harmony in music and games."[33]

This statement figured prominently in postwar school building manuals and might have informed, together with Rudolf Wittkower's study of Renaissance harmonic theory in *Architecture Principles in the Age of Humanism*, the revival of classical design principles in buildings such as Hunstanton.[34]

These diverse ideas on rhythm and movement were incorporated into English educational policy during the period of postwar reconstruction through an educational pamphlet titled *Story of a School* (1949), which narrated the experimental introduction of Rudolph Laban's dance method at a blighted school in Birmingham during the war (see fig. 2). Laban's expressive yet abstract vocabulary of motion appeared to arise from the body's own rhythm, and it allowed amateur dancers to "discover" their authentic self and make it visible to others. Timid movement was attributed to a "fear of freedom," a concept developed by Erich Fromm and popularized by Read. The task of education was to liberate subjects from such fear in order to "enliven the contact between the self and the world." This process of making children receptive to experience was sequenced according to Whitehead's cyclic model of education. Initially, the child's body was engaged in repetitive, rhythmic movements. Next, the child was encouraged to express the self through motion. Finally, through the staging of conflict in drama classes, children released internal aggression and became socialized.

An education based on cycles of repetition and dramatic openings required teachers to adjust instruction to accommodate the changing subjective state of the individual student: "One child, maybe, would reach this saturation point very quickly in colour, but could go on very much longer before reaching that point using clay. . . . If we kept the child's interest, concentration and imagination at work, there would develop this self-discipline which would carry him through a greater period of time before he reached saturation point."[35]

The physical education manual *Moving and Growing* from 1952 integrated this experimental use of movement, along with the mode of observation that it entails, into England's educational curriculum. It criticized the reliance on the drill for physical exercise classes and sought to replace it with individualized movement, on the grounds that it "gives a better opportunity for the development of self-discipline than mass movement, which demands little more than passive obedience."[36] Aside from its political symbolism, free movement was considered more productive as an instrument of knowledge, as it allowed the teacher "to see the difference between individuals and to observe the pace set by the children for themselves, the enterprise of one child and the repetitiveness of another, or the fatigue and listlessness which, under a uniform régime, may go unnoticed."[37] Following Whitehead's conception of aesthetic education, the manual disseminated Laban's "grammatical movement" to render children's spontaneous motion harmonic and graceful in the hope of shaping the manner in which English children performed everyday chores and interacted with each other. But in what may appear to be a contradiction to the ideal of harmonic grace

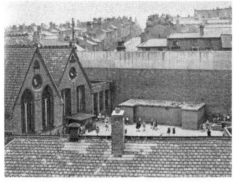

Outside . . .

Figure 2. Illustration from
Story of a School captioned as
"Outside . . . Inside."

. . . Inside.

Figure 3. Photograph from *Moving and
Growing* illustrating a section titled
"Movement as an Art."

promoted by Read, it also sought to intensify the expressivity of movement. *Moving and Growing* associated movement with the archaic "need felt by people to come to terms with their exciting experiences and to put them into shape or pattern of their own creation."[38] This Dionysian conception of movement, expressed in dramatic photographs (see fig. 3), provided the future citizen with an expressive language with which to fashion an energetic ideal of the self and forge communal attachments based on shared, embodied sentiments.

To conclude the exposition of the educational significance of movement and link it back to architectural practice, it is of significance that the HM inspector of schools during reconstruction, Christian Schiller, who supported the Hertfordshire child-centered approach to school building and was personally acquainted with the experiment at Birmingham, considered space and time as key educational categories. Schiller developed a conceptual distinction between personal space (subjective space in which the child moves and explores) and common space (the space the child share with others), and between personal time (the child's own perception of duration) and common time (the objective time of the clock and school routine). According to Schiller, the task of the educationalist was to synchronize the child's subjective perception of time-space with how these categories operate in the external world. Following Whitehead, he conceptualized movement as having a rhythmic pattern, since "almost from birth the mind-body behaves easily in a rhythm." Using terms similar to Read's, he located physical education within the psychological discourse of social reconstruction: "Awareness and command of time and space . . . is a major problem for on its solution depends the growth of balanced men and women who can contribute creatively to civilization."[39]

These techniques for choreographing the body informed the ways in which architects designed schools. To adjust the layout of the school to the definition of the child as a growing organism, architects began to think of space itself in terms of cycles of immersion as experienced by the subject. In the words of the Hertfordshire architect David Medd: "To a child the floor can be home sweet home, or the Atlantic Ocean. I want a tiny space in which I can be quiet and undisturbed with only a handful of people; . . . I want a chair on which I can balance and experiment; I want a chair in which I can curl up with a good book."[40]

This subjective conception of space corresponds with the notion of educational rhythm made of cycles of concentration and relaxation, openness (the ocean), and inwardness (the home). Even seemingly technical aspects of school design, such as lighting, were designed according to the understanding of experience as a process in time. Architects conceptualized the eye as a living muscle that requires its own cycle of concentration and relaxation—a view that stood in opposition to the mechanical conception of the eye as a camera-like apparatus. They incorporated this organic understanding into the design of schools by adding variety, which invigorated the visual perception that otherwise might become desensitized. Medd associated such vibrant light quality with the experience of being alive: "This play and movement of light and shade brings life to our interiors. As the sun and clouds move, so does everything in a room move a little. It is important in education that we do not make people indifferent and insensitive to this manifestation of life."[41]

Postwar architects rethought the school in terms of its sensorial impact and orchestrated the experience of space and time in a rhythmic manner, since it appeared to correspond with the underlying physiological and biological laws that govern "life." This practice allows us to differentiate the architecture of the English school from its American counterpart: Medd, who studied American school design firsthand in the 1950s, used the Hillsdale High School in San Mateo (1955) as an example for how even seemingly purely technical aspects such as the integration of environmental technology in buildings are related to different conceptions of the subject, the child: "Here we have a factory floor with a hermetically sealed perimeter and regular disposition of heat, light, ventilation and services over the whole equal height ceiling area. Within this you have standard partitions which are movable. . . . I hope to make clear that it is, in my opinion, not the kind of flexibility which I believe English education is now demanding."[42]

Schools such as Hillsdale employed neutral and uniform lighting, acoustics, and ventilation to facilitate the use of flexible partitions to accommodate different and changing programs required by progressive educational methods. To Medd, the American approach to technology was shaped by the logic of scientific rationality, in which optimal, universal conditions are achieved by blocking out the unstable variable of the "outside." The difference between English and American design practices is thus located in a different understanding of the role of the senses in education and of the relationship between interiority and exteriority, which allowed English architects to resist the pull of technology toward optimization and homogenization.

Once aesthetic concepts such as harmony, rhythm, and variety are contextualized within the welfare state's mode of power, it becomes possible to interpret school architecture once again as monuments. Exemplary in this respect is the Hallfield primary school, designed by Lindsey Drake and Denys Lasdun in 1952 (see fig. 4). It was heralded at the time as a synthesis of the Hertfordshire and Hunstanton positions but has not been included in customary accounts of architectural history because it did not conform to the terms of the form-function debate. Its animated layout represents education as a dramatic process of rhythmic growth through interaction with the environment. In adapting itself to the site by folding and changing its form to preserve the existing mature trees, while the earth is moved in response to its curves, it manifested Whitehead's definition of education as the "achievement of varied activity . . . in the face of its actual environment."[43] In its oscillation between the subjective states of openness and inwardness, the school brought into equilibrium the opposing claims of rhythmic repetition and dramatic epiphany. Its pattern of circulation rendered motion self-conscious, as there are always two paths for reaching a classroom, either though a meandering corridor or through a series of intimate outdoor spaces. In part, this is a practical alternative to the long corridor that educationalists condemned as being "institutional" and stunting the emotional growth of the child. But such an arrangement also invigorated the senses by exposing the child to the outdoors. In its design, Hallfield embodied Read's maxim that "the school in its structure and appearance should be an agent, however unconscious in its application, of aesthetic education."[44] The linking of architectural design with the techniques of motion and emotion problematizes the standard account of postwar architecture by reframing the opposition between Hunstanton and Hertfordshire as related to different regimes of knowledge, power, and citizenship. In addition, it expands the notion of the architectural object, transforming it from a document of asymmetrical, disciplinarian relations of power into a monument of a regime of activation and sensory saturation through vivid, time-sensitive environments. Such an aesthetic apparatus could only have been implemented for children whose needs were most readily conceptualized in biological terms of development and growth.

The theoretical interest in the spatial, material, and visual aspects of the sites where childhood is enacted brings into focus key issues that engage humanist thought: the definition of the subject as an active agent and the conception of the community as it is defined by placing the child at the center of

Figure 4. Hallfield Primary School, Bishop's Bridge Road, Paddington, London. Lasdun Archive / RIBA Library Photographs Collection, London.

its affective sentiments. The postwar architecture of childhood in England may be used as a critical mirror for reflecting on current practices and notions of childhood and citizenship. For better or worse, state intervention in shaping subjectivity is seen as infringement on individual rights, and child rearing is increasingly privatized, as parents are made responsible for preparing their children to succeed in a competitive economy. Especially in the United States, the task of shaping of childhood has been left to market forces that define the child as a consumer endowed with agency to make lifestyle choices, with the result that childhood is no longer guided by a single force or project. This development informs the shaping of contemporary environments for children, which seem to flourish in the virtual, pluralist spaces of mass electronic media, at the expense of the civic spaces of childhood envisioned by modern architects. It is symptomatic of our times that children's play is no longer associated with a positive model of citizenship, only with its negation, as can be seen in the collective anxiety over bullying and cyber-play. The decline of public spaces for transforming children into citizens bears out Neil Postman's thesis of the "disappearance of childhood."[45] Childhood as a lived experience is undergoing massive transformation. To the many challenges it raises, one can add that of developing an alternative interpretive framework for conceptualizing the visual, spatial, and social aspects of this new, technologically mediated childhood.

Notes

1. Mark Dudek's *Architecture of Schools: The New Learning Environments* (2000) and Susan Solomon's *American Playgrounds: Revitalizing Community Space* (2005) exemplify the 'monumental' approach.

2. Philippe Ariès, *Centuries of Childhood: A Social History of Family Life* (New York: Vintage, 1962), 390–404.

3. Michel Foucault, *Discipline and Punish: The Birth of the Prison* (New York: Vintage, 1995), 141.

4. Nikolas Rose, *Governing the Soul: The Shaping of the Private Self* (London: Routledge, 1990), 121.

5. Kim Rasmussen, "Places for Children—Children's Places," *Childhood* 11.2 (2004), 155–73.

6. Marta Gutman and Ning de Coninck-Smith, introduction to *Designing Modern Childhoods: History, Space, and the Material Culture of Children*, ed. Marta Gutman and Ning de Coninck-Smith (New Brunswick, NJ: Rutgers University Press, 2008), 13.

7. Catherine Burke, "Containing the School Child: Architectures and Pedagogies," *Paedagogica Historica* 4.4–5 (2005): 492.

8. The more decentralized nature of its school building program and a different wartime experience are not the only factors that gave rise to American exceptionalism in this regard. It can also be attributed to the absence of the "population problem" that haunted European planners. The Swedish, British, and French welfare states developed child-centered social policies (including child allowances and universal health care) to address the threat of population decline due to diminishing fertility rates, whereas the United States could rely on its immigration policy.

9. Roger Caillois, *Man, Play, and Games* (Chicago: University of Illinois Press, 2001), 6.

10. Walter Benjamin, "The Cultural History of Toys," in *Selected Writings: 1927–1934*, ed. Michael W. Jennings, Gary Smith, and Howard Eiland (Cambridge, MA: Harvard University Press, 1999), 115. Noguchi's unrealized Play Mountain (1933) established the playground as a sculptural landscape. Van Eyck designed more than seven hundred playgrounds in Amsterdam from 1947 to 1978, most of them utilizing the formal language of de Stijl. See *Aldo van Eyck: The Playgrounds and the City*, ed. Liane Lefaivre and Ingeborg de Roode (Rotterdam: NAi Publishers, 2002).

11. George Burden, "The Junk Playground: An Educational Adjunct and an Antidote to Delinquency," *The Friend*, December 3, 1948, 1029.

12. Marie Paneth, *Branch Street: A Sociological Study* (London: Allen and Unwin, 1944), 35. Paneth was influenced by August Aichhorn, an associate of Anna Freud who introduced psychoanalysis into the institutional treatment of delinquents. Aichhorn allowed his subjects to act out their aggressiveness to the point of explosion, since "when this point came, the aggression changed its character. The outbreaks of rage against each other were no longer genuine, but were acted out for our benefit" (August Aichhorn, *Wayward Youth* [London: Imago, 1951], 175).

13. Paneth, *Branch Street*, 120.

14. Paneth, *Branch Street*, 120. A reviewer doubted that Paneth's principle of freedom and autonomy was desirable for the slum population, who, after all, "wanted a leader whom they could follow" ("Town Life at Its Worst: Social Problems of the Immediate Future," *Times Educational Supplement*, July 29, 1944, 362). This and other reviews of the book make evident that the play of unruly children was interpreted during the war through a discourse on citizenship.

15. Peter C. W. Gutkind, "Report to Clydesdale Road Playground Committee," May 13, 1952, MSS 121/AP/3/2/7, Modern Records Centre, University of Warwick, Coventry, UK.

16. Jack Lambert, *Adventure Playgrounds: A Personal Account of a Play-leader's Work* (London: Jonathan Cape, 1974), 65.

17. Lambert, *Adventure Playgrounds*, 56.

18. Tony Judt, *Postwar: A History of Europe since 1945* (New York: Penguin, 2005), 829.

19. Judt, *Postwar*, 829.

20. Michael Gotkin, "The Politics of Play," in *Preserving Modern Landscape Architecture*, ed. Charles A. Birnbaum (Cambridge, MA: Spacemaker Press, 1999), 67.

21. Colin Boyne, "The New Brutalism," *Architects' Journal*, September 16, 1954, 336.

22. Andrew Saint, *Towards a Social Architecture: The Role of School Building in Post-War England* (New Haven, CT: Yale University Press, 1987), viii.

23. Reyner Banham, "The Architecture of the English School," *History of Education Quarterly* 21.2 (1981): 191.

24. Reyner Banham, *The New Brutalism: Ethics or Aesthetics?* (New York: Reinhold, 1966), 19–20.

25. Theodor Adorno, "Commitment," *New Left Review* 87–88 (1974): 75–89.

26. Nick Peim, "Towards a Social Ecology of the Modern School: Reflections on Histories of the Governmental Environment of Schooling," *Paedagogica Historica* 4.4–5 (2005): 629.

27. Molly Harrison, "The Educational Background," *Architects' Journal*, May 20, 1948, 457. Harrison pioneered museum educational programs at the Geffrye Museum.

28. Harrison, "The Educational Background," 457.

29. Alfred North Whitehead, "The Aims of Education," in *The Aims of Education and Other Essays* (New York: Free Press, 1967), 17.

30. Whitehead, "The Aims of Education," 39.

31. Herbert Read, *Education through Art* (New York: Pantheon, 1945), 202.

32. Read, *Education through Art*, 292.

33. Qtd. in Alfred Roth, *The New School* (Zurich: Girsberger, 1950), 213.

34. Rudolf Wittkower's study, which included a chapter on Palladio's use of harmonic musical ratios in his villas, appeared in 1949. Both the Smithsons and Banham acknowledged its influence on Hunstanton's design. See Banham, "The New Brutalism," 14. As members of the Independent Group, the Smithsons were also familiar with Herbert Read, who founded the ICA.

35. A. L. Stone, *Story of a School*, Ministry of Education pamphlet no. 14 (London: HMSO, 1949), 9.

36. Ministry of Education, *Moving and Growing: Physical Education in the Primary School*, pt. 1, Ministry of Education pamphlet no. 24 (London: HMSO, 1952), 42.

37. Ministry of Education, *Moving and Growing*, 39.

38. Ministry of Education, *Moving and Growing*, 103.

39. Christian Schiller, "Time and Space on a Summer's Day," transcript of a lecture delivered at Lady Nabel College of Physical Education, Wentworth Woodhouse, Rotherham, Yorks, Institute of Education Schiller Archive, DC/CS/0/1/(1).

40. David Medd, "People in Schools: An Attitude to Design," *RIBA Journal* 75 (June 1968), 266.

41. Medd, "People in Schools," 268.

42. Medd, "People in Schools," 264.

43. Whitehead, "Aims of Education," 39.

44. Read, *Education through Art*, 291.

45. While not subscribing to Postman's technological determinism, his much-criticized thesis of the end of childhood is confirmed by the decline of the importance of the architecture of childhood. See his *The Disappearance of Childhood* (New York: Vintage, 1994), 131.

PART THREE

Childhood Studies and
the Queer Subject

This section occupies a fissure in childhood studies that the field is working to bridge between social constructionism—a central insight of childhood studies icon Philippe Ariès and a key tenet of humanities scholarship—and social science's emphasis on biologically determined development. Our first two contributions by Sarah Chinn and Susan Honeyman pick up the theme of educational control ably introduced in section 2 and explore the work of disciplining children's habits of love and attachment. They do so by focusing on heteronormative control over children's gender and sexuality or, to be more precise, the social insistence that children cannot be considered anything other than sexually innocent. The two different methodologies they employ in the process produce a fascinating conversation about the questions of access and authenticity that continue to absorb childhood studies scholars and that form a particular set of problems for those interested in studying children's gender and sexuality.

Chinn's chapter begins with a retroactive assertion of childhood agency: an activist's placard reading "I was a lesbian child." She goes on to ask "what it might mean to say that sentence." Do the lessons that childhood studies has taught us about the constructedness of childhood render statements like "I was a lesbian child" a claim to "a kind of essentialism that both childhood studies and queer studies have assiduously attempted to avoid?" As Kenneth Kidd reminds us, the work of Lee Edelman and Lauren Berlant contend that the child's symbolic role as an emblem of reproduction and compulsory heterosexuality effectively renders the idea of a "lesbian child" an impossibility. On this view, Kidd suggests, "at best, protogay childhood must be forged out of a decidedly heternormative institution."[1] Chinn acknowledges such limitations but argues nonetheless that the very idea of a lesbian child or a gender-nonconforming child defies existing structures in a way that "might . . . help us think about childhood differently, as a welter of desires and self-identifications" (150). While Chinn provides some exciting theoretical models of these possibilities, she remains firmly tethered to the real-world activism that opened her discussion. Perhaps most important, she never loses sight of the potential pitfalls facing adults, even the best-intentioned adults, who assume the voice of children's subjectivity.

Honeyman offers another way of thinking through how children experience—and resist—gender discipline by exploring the different modalities of gender identification that children's literature offers and the ways young audiences for books featuring androgynous, cross-dressing, or otherwise "queer" figures can function as "resisting readers," finding identification and affirmation in stories that are often intended to warn children of the dangers of nonconformity. In so doing, she provides yet another line of inquiry into the question of how to interrogate the relationship between adult intention and children's experiences and responses. As Marah Gubar has recently discussed, there seems to be no resolution of the scholarly question as to whether or not children's literature is "possible"—or, to be more precise, the question of how, if at all, children's literature can provide any insight into the thoughts and desires of actual children. This debate, in turn, is fueled by another line of questioning: How do children read and interpret adult-authored literature in the first place? How do we, as scholars, read both the books and the children at whom they are aimed?[2]

Carol Singley's chapter provides yet another way to think about the work of policing affection as she examines canonical nineteenth-century literature in an effort to chart emerging ideas about the constitution of a "normal" family through, or in spite of, adoption. As David Eng has argued convincingly, adoption confronts both adults and children with "an interlocking set of gender, racial, national, political, economic, and cultural questions."[3] Singley examines these questions as they emerged in the culture of sentiment. Like Chinn and Honeyman, Singley advocates rethinking the boundaries of normality and broadening definitions of what constitutes natural development. As she points out, adoption "de-essentializes race, ethnicity, and nationality by separating them from notions of the family as a unit formed and maintained through biology" (185). Using Hawthorne's short story "A Gentle Boy" as a prism through which to explore evolving ideas about parenting, family, and religious discipline, Singley argues that a child-centered adoption studies offers "new ways to think about origins, domestic affiliation, nurture, and social rights and responsibilities." She ultimately asks how a historically informed understanding of the symbolic role of the adopted child in the nineteenth century can help us to better understand—and, if necessary, critique—the discourses surrounding both domestic and transnational adoption that proliferate in both literary and social scientific discourses today. Ultimately, these three chapters create a web of methodological possibilities for bridging the disciplinary gap between the humanities and the sciences, particularly on the question of human development. By ably moving from adult discourse to childhood experience, from nineteenth-century archives to twenty-first-century activism, the chapters leave us with no easy answers but perhaps provide us with better ways to ask vital questions.

Notes

1. Kenneth Kidd, "Queer Theory's Child and Children's Literature Studies," *PMLA* 126.1 (2011): 183. See also Lee Edelman, *No Future: Queer Theory and the Death Drive* (Durham, NC: Duke University Press 2004), and Lauren Berlant, "The Theory of Infantile Citizenship," *Public Culture* 5.3 (1993): 395–410.

2. Marah Gubar, "On Not Defining Children's Literature," *PMLA* 126.1 (2011): 212; Jacqueline Rose *The Case of Peter Pan; or, The Impossibility of Children's Fiction* (Philadelphia: University of Pennsylvania Press, 1984).

3. David Eng, "Transnational Adoption and Queer Diasporas," *Social Text* 21.3 (2003): 3.

"I Was a Lesbian Child"

Queer Thoughts about Childhood Studies

Sarah Chinn

On September 9, 1992, about a dozen members of the newly formed Lesbian Avengers, a "direct action group focused on issues vital to lesbian survival and visibility," gathered outside the entrance to an elementary school in Queens, New York, School District 24. Over the course of that summer debate had raged about the proposed "Rainbow curriculum" for New York City schools, a curriculum plan that discussed and praised the diversity of New York, including the contributions of the city's large and active lesbian and gay communities. District 24 leader Mary Cummins had spearheaded opposition to the Rainbow curriculum, based almost entirely on its inclusion of LGBT people, and the Avengers decided to come to Queens to let parents, teachers, and administrators know what excising lesbians and lesbian lives from the curriculum meant.

The Lesbian Avengers eschewed traditional protest methods such as picket lines and sit-ins, and the Queens action, the inaugural event for the group, was a clear demonstration of this principle. Avengers handed out balloons with the slogan "Teach about Lesbian Lives" to parents and children arriving for the first day of school. They had written an alternative ABC for the kids, which they distributed to anyone who would take it. Most interesting for my purposes here, though, were the T-shirts the protestors wore, which were emblazoned with the message "I was a lesbian child."[1]

In this chapter I want to explore what it might mean to say that sentence. Given childhood studies' focus on the constructedness of childhood and the figure of "the child," doesn't the avowal "I was lesbian child" (or gay child, or bisexual child, or transgender child, and so on) lay claim to a kind of essentialism that both childhood studies and queer studies have assiduously attempted to avoid?[2] In many ways the terms "lesbian" and "child" seem oxymoronic, in that "lesbian" signifies a self-conscious alignment with a set of sexual desires and practices. However, I'd argue "I was a lesbian child" evokes not just sexuality but also a social, political, and cultural identity that intersects but is not fully coterminous with "queer" or "gay." Particularly in its lesbian-feminist iterations—which the Avengers often alluded to in their use of 1970s pop-culture iconography and semi-ironic invocations of separatist politics—"lesbian" takes on an array of meanings: sexual and affective connection with other girls and/or women but also "the rage of all women condensed to a point of explosion," "women reacting positively to other women," and "the end of all oppressive relationships based on male dominance and the compulsion women feel to seek male approval and support."[3] To say "I was a lesbian child" in this context does not deny childhood sexual activity and curiosity; instead, it gives us an interpretive apparatus with which to understand childhood in intimate relation with structures of gender, desire, and power. As such, this model is very different from the traditional one that sees childhood, as Susan Honeyman argues in the following chapter, is "a desirable but temporary release from the undeniable structures of gendered oppression" (171).

How might concepts like a lesbian child or a protogay child or a queer child or a gender-nonconforming child help us think about childhood differently, as a welter of desires and self-identifications? Recently, scholars in LGBT studies have taken up childhood as a serious subject of study, both holding up "the child" to analysis in a queer context and theorizing queer children and the very queerness of childhood itself. But childhood studies does not seem to have returned the favor quite as generously. Indeed, childhood studies as a field has not really engaged with queer theory. Despite its active interrogation of the role of children as gendered, raced, cultural, social, and national actors, scholarship in the field has not focused on the central concerns of queer theory: performativity, the closet, affect, desire (to name a few).[4] In what follows, I trace the ways in which queer theory has integrated the figure of the child into its embrace (even as scholars like Lee Edelman repudiate "the child" as an intrinsically homophobic construction) and, I hope, suggest ways that childhood studies can use the theoretical toolbox of queer theory to deepen and broaden its analysis of the experience of childhood.

Combining queer and childhood studies approaches to thinking about children, childhood, and the figure of the child can help us out of the nature/nurture, born/made debates that so often bedevil discussions of sexual and gendered identities and give us new modes of understanding. Meshing sharply historicized travels in the archive of childhood and theoretically astute analyses of the formation of the self, the partnership of these two fields can provide a richly layered, subtle, queer-loving, child-affirming, antinormative set of analytical frameworks.

The gender-nonconforming child and/or the child who expresses nonnormative sexual desires was a "problem" for early psychoanalysis and sexology (even though, as Susan Honeyman shows, gender nonconformity among girls was a popular theme in children's literature as far back as the mid-nineteenth century). As Lisa Duggan, Lucy Bland, Laura Doan, Chris Waters, and others have shown, both Sigmund Freud and Havelock Ellis, as well as their intellectual descendents, grappled with the origin of homosexuality, both male and female, locating it in heredity, neurosis, corporeal formation, inversion, narcissism, and so on.[5] While these ways of approaching the queer child were profoundly influential throughout the twentieth century and have continued to be even into the twenty-first, I'm more interested here in how queer-positive thinkers have thought about how the pre- or protogay child might be understood ontologically and phenomenologically; that is, what and how queer kids are and how they experience the world around them.

Talking about protogay kids is difficult, not least because we too often conflate sexual desires and orientations with gender expression. This is particularly true of queer writing at the end of the twentieth century, when vocabularies around gender expression and transidentities were less rich than they are today, not least because dominant culture saw gender nonconforming children as queers in the making.[6] In her beautiful and groundbreaking essay "How to Bring Your Kids Up Gay," Eve Sedgwick often does just that, moving between "protogay child" and "effeminate boy," without significantly commenting on the gaps between the two.[7] Likewise, what does the tomboy signify? As Judith Halberstam has argued, tomboyism has a limited shelf life and there are significant restrictions on its expression: it is "punished when it appears to be the sign of extreme male identification (taking a boy's name or refusing girl clothing of any type) and when it threatens to extend beyond childhood and into adolescence."[8] Beginning with Radclyffe Hall's *The Well of Loneliness* (and its roots in the sexology of Richard von Krafft-Ebing and Havelock Ellis), the narrative of the child who is not like the other girls is a mainstay of transgender stories.[9]

I'd like to focus here, though, on the *queer* child in the making, even though the boundaries between "queer" and "trans" can sometimes be fuzzy. At the same time, lesbian and gay adults find the beginnings of their queerness in childhood resistance to gender normativity, an alienation from their bodies or what their bodies were supposed to signify. Robert Reid-Pharr recalls being mistaken for a girl, "my Afro braided down in neat cornrows. Other children would respond cruelly that I was a boy, that it was only my fat body and long hair that so obfuscated my sex" (156). Indeed, Reid-Pharr, while naming himself (and the title of one of his books) a "black gay man," also cross-identifies in some ways with lesbians, an identification that, ironically, allows him to live more comfortably in his "ill-fitting masculinity."[10]

In these narratives, the gender queerness of the protogay child provides access to a truth that is otherwise invisible to both the child and the adults around her or him. In her graphic memoir *Fun Home*, Alison Bechdel creates a clear link between her tomboyish childhood and her lesbian present, ironically claiming the identity of "invert" for herself (and her closeted father), recognizing that it is "imprecise and insufficient, defining the homosexual as a person whose gender expression is at odds with his or her sex. But in the admittedly limited sample comprising my father and me, perhaps it *is* sufficient."[11] Bechdel narrates a life-changing scene in which she, a young girl of four or five on a trip with her father to Philadelphia, sees "a most unsettling sight"—a butch lesbian. "I didn't know," she says, "there were women who wore men's clothes and had men's haircuts. But like a traveler in a foreign country who runs into someone from home—someone they've never spoken to, but know by sight—I recognized her with a surge of joy."[12] Even as she recognizes part of herself in the adult woman, her father warns her off this identification, asking, "Is *that* what you want to look like?" a question to which the only answer (and the answer, of course, Alison must give) is "no."[13]

Bechdel sees her protoqueerness in her resistance to her father's love of ornament, which even the child Alison reads as deception and lies. Her childhood butchness is a form of truth telling, much as Wayne Koestenbaum's youthful love for musical theater and later opera makes room for the undisciplined expression of passion and pleasure that he narrates in *The Queen's Throat*, passion that "exceeds the bounds of acceptable gender behavior."[14] The protoqueer child loves artifice and hates deception with equal measure, loves the possibility of being other than s/he is and hates the lies s/he has to embody in order to be what s/he is supposed to be.

For protoqueer children, identity and identification exist in both contradistinction and interdependence. Is the young Wayne Koestenbaum who is watching *The Sound of Music* and *Mary Poppins* able to distinguish between these modes, asking "Am I in love with Julie Andrews, or do I think I *am* Julie Andrews?"[15] As Michael Moon puts it,

> For how many gay men of my own and the previous generation were our earliest intimations that there might be a gap between our received gender identity and our subjective or "felt" one the consequence not of noticing our own erotic attraction to another boy or man, but of enthusiastically enjoying and identifying with the performative excesses of Maria Montez rather than Jon Hall, or Lana Turner rather than Burt Lancaster, or Jayne Mansfield rather than Mickey Hargitay?[16]

If, as Karen Sánchez-Eppler argues, childhood is "a period of both remarkable freedom and inherent powerlessness, something to be yearned for and to escape," then the protoqueer child is also the überchild, anxiously looking beyond childhood to an identity s/he doesn't yet know and at the same time recognizing that the surrealness of the child's perspective can make space for fantasy and cross-identification that is not necessarily available to adults.[17]

Moreover, lesbian and gay writers look to their own childhoods, their own experiences as pre- or protoqueer kids, to analyze and affirm how their consciousness of difference was not just a deficit but was also a gift that allowed them a degree of distance and knowingness that that difference often forced on them. For a certain kind of (pre)gay kid, this difference even becomes a virtue, a knowledge of "some other place, some other world, magically different from the world of family and school, from a heterosexual everyday every day more banal, and more oppressive."[18] The pain, according to this narrative, rewards its sufferer with an eventual payoff: for Bechdel, it meant the ability to escape from Beech Creek, Pennsylvania; for Koestenbaum a spiritual kinship with both opera divas and the queens who love them; for Halberstam, a way to understand and embrace her masculinity. Indeed, for Michael Moon, protoqueerness is itself a mechanism that can provide the developing gay child with insights not necessarily available to his or her heterosexual counterparts: processes of "uncanny perception and imitation, of initiation and self-initiation, of the gradual recognition of one's own desires and the production and transmission of images and narratives of these desires."[19] Recently, however, queer studies has shifted its attention away from the pre- or protoqueer child to the figure of "the Child" and how it operates within both homophobic and queer-embracing frames. I'd like to focus now on two books that explore "the child" through an explicitly queer frame. While Kathryn Bond Stockton's *The Queer Child* uses the non- and antinormativity that children often so effortlessly embody to think about how sexual and gendered norms are impressed on the young and how they are resisted, Lee Edelman's *No Future* identifies the figure of "the Child" as the prime weapon used against queers, particularly gay men—the future to their hedonistic present, the innocence to their sexual guilt, the ideal to their real (Lacanian and otherwise).

No Future is particularly compelling in a childhood studies context because it does more than historicize or problematize the figure of the child. Rather, it sees "the Child" as a phantasm of heteronormativity, almost wholly unrelated to actual flesh-and-blood children, what they might experience or want. Instead "the Child" is a judgment and a threat disguised as a promise of a brighter, better future in which "our children" will live happier, more productive lives than we could ever hope to. In this interpretation, the Child and the futurity s/he promises is actually deployed as a strategy to foreclose the possibility of a better, happier, more enjoyable *now*. The Child may reap the benefits of this putative future, but we never can, since "the social order exists to preserve for this universalized subject, this phantasmatic Child, a notional freedom more highly valued than the actuality of freedom itself, which might, after all, put at risk the Child to whom such a freedom falls due."[20] In this formulation, it is discursively impossible to repudiate the Child and the future it represents without sounding churlish, selfish, petty, and self-indulgent; that is, all the things that gay men have been accused of being. This kind of "reproductive futurism . . . impose[s] an ideological limit on political discourse as such, preserving in the process the absolute privilege of heteronormativity by rendering unthinkable, by casting outside the political domain, the possibility of a queer resistance to this organizing principle of communal relations."[21] Edelman provokes his readers to think about what it would mean to refuse to "think about the children" or "fight for the children," and he names "queerness" as that impulse that "attains its ethical value" to the extent that it accedes to the negativity that opposes the Child, "accepting its figural status as resistance to the viability of the social while insisting on the inextricability of such resistance from every social structure."[22]

This is pretty strong stuff, and Edelman has exactly the kind of oppositional voice to dish it out. But this refusal of the sentimental goo that can accrete around the rhetoric of "the children" can be instructive and useful for childhood studies. It is not enough, Edelman's work implies, to historicize and contextualize children and childhood. It is not even enough to see how the figure of the child has been deployed in the cause of nation and empire building, in racial hierarchies, in structurations of class and gender.

Edelman's resistance to seeing historicizing as the central principle behind analyses of childhood runs counter in many ways to the practices of childhood studies as a scholarly (inter)discipline. After all, one of the great contributions of childhood studies has been to explore the historically specific, lived experience of childhood alongside the ideological constructions of "the child." This is particularly true for the lives of children in historical moments quite different from our own. For example, Lois Brown's insightful commentary on Susan Paul's early nineteenth-century narrative *Memoir of James Jackson* combines a deep understanding of the conversion narrative—a genre that infused the imaginations of Christian Americans of the period—with an exploration of the life James Jackson (who died when he was not yet seven years old) might have lived in a free black community in the Boston of the early Republic. Underlying Brown's analysis is the careful attention she pays to the texture of a free black child's life in Boston in the first decades of the nineteenth century. But Edelman moves in the opposite direction to this diligently researched, exquisitely materialist analysis. Instead, he wholly abstracts "the Child" into a discursive formation, "not," he points out, "to be confused with the lived experiences of any historical children."[23] The Child, he maintains, in an argument that in many ways intersects with Karen Sánchez-Eppler's work on the cultural meanings of mid-nineteenth-century American childhood, must be protected at all costs. We must all work to ease the way for "the sacred Child": "The Child who might witness lewd or inappropriately intimate behavior; the Child who might find information about dangerous 'lifestyles' on the Internet; the Child who might choose a provocative book from the shelves of the public library; the Child, in short, who might find an enjoyment that would nullify the figural value, itself imposed by adult desire, of the Child as unmarked by the adult's adulterating implication in desire itself."[24]

As Edelman incisively points out, homophobic rhetoric is too often justi-fied by the struggle to protect "our children" from corruption by (knowl-edge of) sexuality of any kind (we're back to the Rainbow curriculum).[25] The most striking part of Edelman's argument, however, is that it does not attempt to rehabilitate queerness as equally concerned about the future, as equally willing to sacrifice freedom and pleasure today "for the sake of the children." Quite the opposite. Edelman embraces the death drive, which re-fuses the future, and instead "insist[s] on the Real of a jouissance that social reality and the futurism have already foreclosed."[26] Edelman's death drive is the psychic equivalent of a T-shirt slogan that was popular among my lesbian peer group in the early 1990s: "I fuck to come, not to conceive" — it rejects narrative and logic, rejects the orderliness of the Lacanian symbolic, and, in Edelman's words, "exposes sexuality's . . . insistence on repetition, its stubborn denial of teleology, its resistance to determinations of mean-ing . . . , and, above all, its rejection of spiritualization through marriage to reproductive futurism."[27] In other words, to the homophobic claim that queerness is antifamily, antichild, and, in the words of Bernard Cardinal Law "has no future and cannot give future to any society," Edelman says, you're damned right. And that's a good thing in a social order in which "we're held in thrall by a future continually deferred by time itself, con-strained to pursue the dream of a day when today and tomorrow are one."[28] Ultimately, Edelman says, "fuck the social order and the Child in whose name we're collectively terrorized."[29]

We're a long way from the grown-up lesbian children of the Lesbian Avengers protest, but I'd like to suggest that Edelman's work can point a way if not forward then at least sideways. What would it mean to think of a child (not to say "the Child") who was not defined by its relationship to fu-turity, who was queer her- or himself? Is the only alternative to the fascism of futurity the death drive? I'd argue that the recent work of Kathryn Bond Stockton and Ann Cvetkovich offer alternative narratives of how child-hood is both a place of queerness and a site in which queerness can flourish and provide valuable solace for the children who claim it. This comfort is not just the knowing sense of superiority that Joseph Litvak describes or the tough-minded stoicism of Alison Bechdel in *Fun Home*. Rather, it is a mode of thinking about queerness and childhood together that depends on neither the nostalgia of/for the protoqueer kid nor the repudiation of the child as a discursive figure nor the homophobic mandate for reproductive futurity.

The tactics that both Stockton and Cvetkovich employ take on the most difficult, most queer-negative narratives about children's relationship to homosexuality and breathe new and queer-positive life into them. Provocatively, Cvetkovich reimagines what it might mean to believe that girls *are* turned into lesbians by negative sexual experiences with men, particularly by sexual abuse by family members. Struck by the high proportion of lesbians among women writing books about recovering from incest and childhood sexual abuse, Cvetkovich wonders "why saying that 'sexual abuse causes homosexuality' [can't] just as easily be based on the assumption that there's something right, rather than something wrong, with being lesbian or gay. As someone who would go so far as to claim lesbianism as one of the *welcome* effects of sexual abuse, I am happy to contemplate the therapeutic process by which sexual abuse turns girls queer."[30] Certainly, as Cvetkovich observes, lesbians are disproportionately represented in the helping professions, and discussions of lesbian social and sexual structures such as butch/femme and sadomasochism often situate themselves as modes of healing from sexual violence. How, then, might lesbianism be a salutary effect of that healing, a queer way out or working through of heteronormative power relations? In this model, the figure of the "lesbian child" is more fuzzy and less knowable, less dependent on the narratives of gender nonconformity and childhood otherness that reach from *The Well of Loneliness* through *Rubyfruit Jungle* to *Female Masculinity*, and more interwoven with possible strategies for pleasure and survival in the face of threat and violence.

Of course, not all girls find their way to lesbianism like this; nor can we necessarily theorize gay male identity as possessing similar healing potential (although the fabulous knowingness Litvak describes can function as a kind of reparative process; to imagine "what would Judy do?" has a power that can fend off all kinds of attacks). What might happen, though, if we combined Lee Edelman's resistance to heteronormative futurity and Ann Cvetkovich's reparative lesbianism? Funnily enough, we end up where I began: with the queer child. But this time with a difference.

As Kathryn Bond Stockton points out, after all, "If you scratch a child, you will find a queer, in the sense of someone 'gay' or just plain strange."[31] Children are weird; they have weird fantasies, and they translate the world through their own bizarre languages. And children do not just grow "up"; they cannot be so effortlessly identified with futurity. As Stockton argues, "There are ways of growing that are not growing up," not least because growth does not end when we have reached our maximum height and sexual maturity and conversely, because our culture insists that children grow without growing up, that they *not* mature in their knowledge of "adult" topics.[32] Stockton offers the model of "growing sideways," a development that can be shared by children and adults and that in many ways is a more accurate representation of how children do develop, moving laterally as much as vertically.

At first, the model of "growing sideways" seems counterintuitive. Isn't children's job to grow *up*? But, as Stockton points out, much of late capitalist society is devoted to preserving the child's innocence, protecting children from knowledge of "adult" concerns like sex, money, and work; that is, to preventing their acquisition of adult knowledge until the last possible moment of adolescence. Growing sideways can be seen as the only logical response to this impulse to delay passing down mature knowledge, since "delay is seen as a friend to the child. Delay is said to be a feature of its growth: children grow by delaying their approach to the realms of sexuality, labor, and harm"—children, according to this logic, can grow up healthily only in a kind of cultural vacuum in which the central elements of adult life are (ideally) wholly absent.[33] The movement against child labor in the early twentieth century argued that work forced children to grow up too fast, to become mechanized, commodified, desensitized, and sexualized before their time, and sought to extend "childhood" into the mid-teens.[34] To be a child, then, is to be in stasis and growing at the same time. The child is "the specter of who we were when there was nothing yet behind us."[35]

Of course, this fantasy is impossible. As soon as children understand the meaning of money, they are obsessively keen to hatch schemes by which they can get their hands on it. And this eagerness finds its way into childhood enactments of all kinds of "adult" activities. One can find in any playground children "buying" and "selling" imaginary ice cream and pizza, playing dead, clapping each other into jail, forcing each other into slavery, and so on. Similarly, the time-honored game of "doctor" and its myriad variations gives the lie to children's desexualization. In other words, children themselves seek out the very experiences that adults attempt to protect them from, creating imaginatively (and often in strange and perverse performances in public spaces) the forbidden realms of commerce and sex forbidden to them: sideways expression indeed.

Ironically, adults use childhood experiences to make sense of their own adult identities. This is particularly true of the child who is invoked by the phrase "I was a gay child." As Stockton points out, in childhood the signs of resistance and difference did not signify to the child as a given sexual orientation that he or she as an adult would embrace. Indeed, to claim "I was a gay/lesbian child" is in some ways to *create* that child retrospectively "both in the form of a ghostly self, and in the form of 'arrested development,'" the accusation long launched at queer people, transformed into the reconstruction of a "once" and "always" gay child self.[36] The protoqueer child "with no established forms to hold itself, or explain itself, in the public, legal field, is like an explanation unavailable to itself in the present tense"; that is this child "can only publicly appear retrospectively"—I *was* a lesbian child— "after one's straight life has died."[37]

If the "gay child" is always a back formation, a retrospective ghost of the gay adult, what makes a queer child? For Stockton, children are queered by forces that counteract the delay into which postcapitalist childhood delivers them: sex, money, violence—anything that children are supposed to be innocent of.[38] Yet they cannot exist outside of these forces, since money, sex, and work are intrinsic to the ultimate process of growing up into heteronormativity. Pace Lee Edelman, then, the social mandate of delay means that children are *not* our future. Rather, we are theirs, creating them *après la lettre* once we, no longer children, can write ourselves into the world of sex and money. Children, in this narrative, merely circulate. Moving sideways they seem a lot like stereotypical queers (or, perhaps, like that queer icon, Marcel Proust or, more critically, Dorian Gray), spending their time doing nothing productive, living in fantasy, parasitically dependent on the efforts of others.

Queerness here turns chronology on its head. Much like current scholars of childhood, Stockton recognizes that we create children in our own image, but queering that narrative means that we have to radically rethink what that image is. In order to protect children from sexual abuse, law enforcement invents "children" on internet chat rooms, thereby articulating a child with sexual desires, "the voice of childhood that the law denies—yet must believe the public, especially parents, feels increasingly endangered by."[39] In this charade, children's desire is ventriloquized by adults in order to entrap adults who desire children (when you start thinking this way, even heteronormativity looks queer). And yet, ironically, children might just heal the experience of actual sexual abuse by parents and familial/familiar adults through sideways movement into queerness.[40]

So what do these insights lend to the practice of childhood studies? Perhaps, in the spirit of queer inquiry, we might reorient this question and ask why these arguments have not been recognized as part of childhood studies to begin with. Certainly, the work of James Kincaid interrogates the sexualization of children in the nineteenth century and in movies, and gender and sexuality are crucial elements in central texts in the field. And scholars in the subfield of children's literature have been actively engaging LGBT topics and queer theory for decades. But one might argue that the signal difference between contemporary childhood studies scholars such as Karen Sánchez-Eppler, James Kincaid, Anna Mae Duane, Paula Fass, and Howard Chudacoff and the scholars in queer studies who have worked on childhood is the theoretical approaches each brings. Childhood studies is resolutely historicized, not to say historical; its goal, more often than not, is to uncover how children and childhood were defined and understood at any given historical moment, to examine how those definitions changed in relationship to social and economic shifts, and implicitly to argue that childhood is a category being continually invented and reinvented (this being the central argument, after all, of Philippe Ariès in *Centuries of Childhood*, the text that inaugurated scholarly study of childhood in the first place).

By contrast, queer approaches to childhood are less invested in history and far more interested in psyche.[41] It's no coincidence that Eve Kosofsky Sedgwick, Michael Moon, Kathryn Bond Stockton, Judith Butler, Ann Cvetkovich, and Lee Edelman (to name but a few) invoke psychoanalytic and poststructural theoretical formations in their readings of the figure of the child—those bodies of knowledge and ideas are the bedrock on which queer studies as a field has long rested. More importantly, while recognizing the historical boundedness of social and cultural categories, these scholars are most interested in questions of desire and self-recognition (in both Freudian and Hegelian senses). Rather than (or, at least, as well as) asking what historical conditions made certain structures of feeling and identity possible for the child, LGBT theorists dive into those structures and identities themselves: how does the queer child *feel*? What makes her life livable or unbearable? What are the psychic outcroppings of homophobia in children who do not conform to gendered and sexual norms? How are gender expressions and sexual desires sometimes coincident, sometimes in glancing conversation, and sometimes not the same thing at all? How is childhood gender expression made to stand in for or retrospectively understood as sexuality, and how are childhood sexual desires not always translatable into adult sexual identities?

Finally, queer theorists are not afraid to be advocates for a more just, livable world for people of all genders and sexualities—a world that without doubt would be a much more pleasant place for children to live as well—and they invite their readers to recognize the ways in which queer lives and queer practices open up possibilities that reproductive heteronormativity too often forecloses. Eve Sedgwick led the way in this kind of analysis, always situating her work in a context that is, as she called it, gay loving; that is, a context that assumes that a world without queer people in it would be infinitely impoverished. For Sedgwick, difference is the bedrock of human experience, an insight garnered from both her immersion in poststructuralist and psychoanalytic theories and her own commitment to honoring the diversity of human desires.[42] Even as antihumanist a critic as Lee Edelman roots his coruscating appraisal of the damage the figure of "the Child" does in a celebration (however sardonic) of gay male sexual self-expression.

I'd be the last to argue that queer theory resists historicizing: one of its lasting contributions has been the argument that sexual identities as we know them are profoundly cultural and historical constructions. However, childhood studies' intense commitment to grounding the study of childhood in historical specificity can lead to an odd lack of ideological critique. Whereas queer theory was launched and has been primarily promoted by queer people, explorations of the meaning of childhood have not been taken up by children themselves but by adults (again, children's literature, which is mostly written by adults but aimed at children, occupies a fascinating middle ground). And, as Kathryn Bond Stockton argues, some of the experience of childhood is lost in the act of retrieving it as an adult. However, while the implicit goal of queer theory and the scholarship of sexuality more generally is expanding sexual liberties, childhood studies seldom articulates a political mission. A historicist approach largely precludes this strategy:

to take historical specificity seriously means that a scholar must withhold judgment—in that way we are transformed into chronological ethnologists, observing the cultural practices of people very different from ourselves, while struggling mightily to sanitize our observations of any comparison with our own values and practices.

Queer theorists have grappled with many of the same questions: as Judith Butler points out, the relationship between sexual and gender expression in specific geographic locales and the language of human rights is complex. However, she counters the claim that "imposing" the discourse of human rights on gender and sexuality is necessarily an outcropping of cultural imperialism from the global North. Instead, she argues that "when we struggle for rights, we are not simply struggling for rights that attach to my person [i.e. liberal individualism], but we are struggling *to be conceived as persons.* . . . If we are struggling not only to be conceived as persons, but to create a social transformation of the very meaning of personhood, then the assertion of rights becomes a way of intervening into the social and political process by which the human is articulated."[43]

Applying this model to children is instructive. To accept the humanity of another is to accept that we can never fully know that other, is to live with the ethical imperative that "lives with its unknowingness about the Other in the face of the Other, since sustaining the bond that the question opens is finally more valuable than knowing in advance what holds us in common, as if we already have all the resources we need to know what defines the human, what its future life might be."[44] In this way, childhood studies might maintain its rigorous historicism but at the same time embrace a less materialist recognition of the unknowability of children (not least because they don't really know themselves). We can recognize the historically and culturally specific narratives that construct "childhood" while also understanding that actual children are and always have been far more mysterious, perverse, incomprehensible, antisocial, productive, and embodied—that is to say *queer*—than our scholarship has given them credit for.

Notes

1. For more information about the Avengers, go to www.lesbianavengers.com, which includes an image of the T-shirt in the "Shaping Avenger Actions" section.

2. A quick word on terminology here. I'll be using the terms "queer studies" and "LGBT studies" fairly interchangeably throughout this discussion. However, there

are differences between the two that have a direct relationship to my analysis. Often, although not always, LGBT studies assumes a knowable subject, the lesbian, gay, bisexual, or transgender person, who is the topic under discussion, and is primarily concerned with thinking about that subject and what it means. Although "queer studies" is often substituted without comment for "LGBT studies," its brief can be quite different: an unmooring of those subject positions that LGBT studies puts into circulation. Queer studies is as interested in structures of sexuality and desire more generally as it is in actual queer *people*. Given the ambivalent relationship between sexuality studies and the study of childhood, sometimes these terms overlap and other times they are in contradistinction to each other. At its most crass, the division is between "born gay" and "made gay" camps (a division in which analyses of childhood play a crucial role), but even when the discussion is more sophisticated and considered, the agendas of queer studies and LGBT studies can diverge. Equally as important, as Eve Sedgwick observes, is that part of "the exciting charge of the very word 'queer' is that it embraces, instead of repudiating, what have for many of us been formative childhood experiences of difference and stigmatization" ("How to Bring Your Kids Up Gay," in *Tendencies* [Durham, NC: Duke University Press, 1993], 157).

3. Radicalesbians, "The Woman-Identified Woman," in *Out of the Closets: Voices of Gay Liberation*, 20th anniversary ed., ed. Karla Jay and Alan Young (New York: New York University Press, 1992), 172; Rita Mae Brown, "Take A Lesbian to Lunch," in *Out of the Closets*, 192; Gay Liberation Front Women, "Lesbians and the Ultimate Liberation of Women," in *Out of the Closets*, 202.

4. Robin Bernstein's chapter in this volume is an important intervention in this field.

5. For example, the website of the National Association for the Research and Therapy of Homosexuality, an organization that claims to help gay men change their sexual orientation, excerpts part of an article titled "The Complex Interaction of Genes and Environment: A Model for Homosexuality" by Jeffrey Satinover, MD, which argues that "the commonplace dynamic in the pre-homosexual boy is not merely the absence of a father—literally or psychologically—but the psychological defense of the boy against his repeatedly disappointing father" (http://www.narth .com/docs/pieces.html). This article, while not explicitly psychoanalytic, is clearly heavily influenced by psychoanalytic givens, such as the role of parents in shaping children's sexual desires and identities. In her *Brain Storm: The Flaws in the Science of Sex Differences* (Cambridge, MA: Harvard University Press, 2010), Rebecca M. Jordan-Young critiques the current enthusiasm for neuroscientific explanations for the formation of sex, gender, and sexual orientation, which seem in large part to have dislodged psychoanalytic rationales in the scientific establishment.

6. In her chapter "Transgender Butch: Butch/FTM Border Wars and the Masculine Continuum" in *Female Masculinity* (Durham, NC: Duke University Press, 1998), Judith Halberstam works through some of the ramifications of the poverty of language at the time with respect to the differences between butch, trans,

masculine, and other gender-nonconforming identities for masculine women and transmen.

7. It bears pointing out that Sedgwick is responding directly to homophobic psychologists who see effeminate behavior in boys as a warning sign of adult homosexuality, which must be remedied at all costs. Moreover, Sedgwick's protectiveness toward feminine boys is rooted in large part in her affection for gay men and her anger at the homophobia and misogyny they experience as boys.

8. Halberstam, *Female Masculinity*, 6.

9. See Jay Prosser's *Second Skins: The Body Narratives of Transsexuality*, particularly chapter 4, for a detailed and insightful discussion of this.

10. Robert Reid-Pharr, *Black Gay Man: Essays* (New York: New York University Press, 2001), 156.

11. Alison Bechdel, *Fun Home: A Family Tragicomic* (New York: Houghton Mifflin Harcourt, 2006), 97.

12. Bechdel, *Fun Home*, 118.

13. Bechdel, *Fun Home*, 118.

14. Wayne Koestenbaum, *The Queen's Throat: Opera, Homosexuality, and the Mystery of Desire* (New York: Vintage, 1994), 147.

15. Koestenbaum, *The Queen's Throat*, 18.

16. Michael Moon, *A Small Boy and Others: Imitation and Initiation in American Culture from Henry James to Andy Warhol* (Durham, NC: Duke University Press, 1998), 86.

17. Karen Sánchez-Eppler, *Dependent States: The Child's Part in Nineteenth-Century American Culture* (Chicago: University of Chicago Press, 2005), xvii.

18. Joseph Litvak, "Strange Gourmet: Taste, Waste, Proust," in *Novel Gazing: Queer Readings in Fiction*, ed. Eve Kosofsky Sedgwick (Durham, NC: Duke University Press, 1997), 76.

19. Moon, *A Small Boy and Others*, 3.

20. Lee Edelman, *No Future: Queer Theory and the Death Drive* (Durham, NC: Duke University Press, 2004), 11.

21. Edelman, *No Future*, 2.

22. Edelman, *No Future*, 3.

23. Edelman, *No Future*, 11.

24. Edelman, *No Future*, 20–21.

25. Kathryn Bond Stockton is also interested in "the so-called contrast between the sacred child—priceless, useless, and expensive . . . —and queer life depicted by conservatives: hedonistic, arrested, and, especially, wasteful" (*The Queer Child; or, Growing Up Sideways in the Twentieth Century* [Durham, NC: Duke University Press, 2009], 48).

26. Edelman, *No Future*, 25.

27. Edelman, *No Future*, 27.

28. Edelman, *No Future*, 30

29. Edelman, *No Future*, 29.

30. Ann Cvetkovich, *An Archive of Feelings: Trauma, Sexuality, and Lesbian Public Cultures* (Durham, NC: Duke University Press, 2003), 90.

31. Stockton, *The Queer Child*, 1.

32. Stockton, *The Queer Child*, 11.

33. Stockton, *The Queer Child*, 11.

34. For a detailed discussion of the rhetoric of the child labor movement, see my *The Invention of Modern Adolescence: The Children of Immigrants in Turn-of-the-Century America* (New Brunswick, NJ: Rutgers University Press, 2009).

35. Stockton, *The Queer Child*, 30.

36. Stockton, *The Queer Child*, 22.

37. Stockton, *The Queer Child*, 158.

38. These forces exist in a hierarchy, however. In this context Stockton asks whether we "as an American society [are] much less troubled by children's pain (for example their economic suffering) than we are troubled by their sexualized pleasure, even though we cite their possible pain as our rationale for delaying their pleasure?" (*The Queer Child*, 62).

39. Stockton, *The Queer Child*, 38.

40. Karen Sánchez-Eppler's brilliant analysis of the stereotypical temperance text's scene of the drunken father crawling into bed with his young daughter takes on extra resonance here, given the high incidence of women in temperance and other political movements who never married and often took up housekeeping with each other.

41. Again, children's literature studies is a crucial exception to this phenomenon. Given that literature for children and young adults so often focuses on fantasy, desire, identification, and exploration, it's not surprising that a number of scholars in children's literature have actively engaged with both childhood studies and queer theory. Ironically, queer theorists have mostly ignored this growing and vibrant field, even though there are many points of connection between them. Kenneth Kidd's essay "Queer Theory's Child and Children's Literature Studies" (*PMLA* 126.1 [2011]: 182–88) makes exactly this argument: "Can children's literature be positioned as *already* a queer theory of sorts . . . ? What if we were to think of children's literature not simply as a field of literature but as a theoretical site in its own right—even, perhaps, as an unconscious of sorts for queer theory? How can queer theory unsettle what we claim to know about children's literature? And how can children's literature unsettle what we claim to know about queer theory?" (186). I thank him for sharing his insights with me.

42. The best example of this can be found in "Axiomatic," the opening chapter of *Epistemology of the Closet* (Berkeley: University of California Press, 1990), which begins its list of axioms: "*Axiom 1: People are different from each other*. It is astonishing how few respectable conceptual tools we have for dealing with this self-evident fact" (22). An acknowledgment of human (bio)diversity is also essential to the field of disability studies. See, for example, Rosemarie Garland-Thomson's "Welcoming the Unbidden: The Case for Conserving Human Bio-Diversity," in *This is What*

Democracy Looks Like: A New Critical Realism for a Post-Seattle World, ed. Amy Schrager Lang and Cecelia Tichi (New Brunswick, NJ: Rutgers University Press, 2006), 77–87.

43. Judith Butler, *Undoing Gender* (New York: Routledge, 2005), 32–33.

44. Butler, *Undoing Gender*, 35.

Trans(cending)gender through Childhood

Susan Honeyman

If one is not born a woman, as Simone de Beauvoir and Monique Wittig so famously argue, then one is not really born a girl or boy either.[1] In fact, one is not necessarily born a child. Ever since Philippe Ariès posited childhood as an invention of modernity, childhood studies has argued for recognizing the state of prolonged protection (and sometimes fetishization) generally ascribed to Western youth as relatively constructed, class bound, and historically varied. Most of the world's young can't afford what many in affluent nations take for granted as universal: early years of total dependence, security, innocence, extended play, and compulsory education. When we start to recognize the adult-serving ways in which youth have (seemingly arbitrarily) been constructed by an essentializing adult consensus, we can then look, as childhood studies does, at why and how we are complicit in a protracted segregation by age that allows us to idealize youth while appeasing our own dissatisfactions with adult social order.

Though the romantic legacy of idealizing youth has for the past thirty years been blasted by skeptical guilt over self-serving nostalgia and over the desiring and wounding of "the child," there are some qualities of romantic childhood that are worthy of preserving, especially the tendency to frustrate sexed and gendered binarisms. Gender, like childhood, is a social imaginary defined by secondary lack (child is not adult, female is not male). Existing solely as relative negations, each has the potential to frustrate the very binary they bring into existence. But unfortunately, the critical trend is to continue binarizing gender even when its binaries have been potentially decentered—treating neuter positions as countergendered rather than as transcending gendering itself.

Joan W. Scott has explained that gender was initially a concept that allowed the vocabulary necessary for recognizing social construction. As a "social category imposed on a sexed body" it "offers a way of differentiating sexual practice from the social roles assigned to women and men."[2] Likewise, childhood has emerged in scholarship as a cultural construct so that the imposition it represents for young people to whom it is applied can be more keenly discussed. Yet gender "refers to but also establishes the meaning of the male/female opposition," and paying attention to the marginalization of childhood reifies adulthood.[3] The very concepts meant to combat essentializing can't seem to entirely avoid essentializing themselves.

Diana Fuss asks, "Can there be such a thing as 'free space' in a strict antiessentialist view?"[4] From one perspective, this is not possible because childhood, along with adolescence for that matter, is one of the most generalized social positions, usually essentialized by those who have long since been adults and cannot speak for the marginalized young with any verifiable accuracy or political neutrality. But from another perspective, which is more relevant to my argument here, it is possible because if we recognize the essentializing inherent even in constructivist views, then we must recognize that our discourse falls silent at its source of focus and that to inhabit that silent social sphere is at least to (knowingly or not) resist the self-deluded but well-meaning attempts of adults to buffer the forces of an ageist hegemony. As Sarah Chinn remarks in her chapter, by undoing binaristic thought, "the figure of the child can help us out of the nature/nurture, born/made debates that so often bedevil discussions of sexual and gendered identities" (151). In many ways, the romantic child prefigured the postmodern "end of gender" as an unproblematic, useful social category.[5] If generalizable, the romantic child could be described as the neuter child. If not representing the *end* of gender, childhood at least makes a free space *before* gendering becomes imaginable.

For centuries, childhood has been vicariously relished (by those frustrated with adulthood) as an opportunity to put the oppressive gendering of sexual maturity temporarily on hold, resulting in figurations that embody the absence of gender. One problem for feminist and postfeminist theory has been the seeming necessity of recognizing (and thus heteronormatively binarizing) gender in order to understand gendered oppression. But in resurrecting the neuter child from a romantic past, childhood studies, complementing transgender and queer studies, can theorize youth (albeit idealistically) as a position without gender, transcending the pesky essentializing binary of male/femaleness altogether.

Take, for example, Francesco Bonami, who argues In "The Fourth Sex," that

> if we are willing to consider male, female, and homosexual as three categories, three mentally differentiated sexes, then adolescence may be seen as the fourth of these mental states. An utterly particular and sexual state, because it is limited to a precise time span, inside an overwhelming metamorphosis that will eventually thrust the individual into one of the three official sexes, or perhaps into all three, thus preserving an eternally adolescent, oppositional, irreverent and innovative character.[6]

Like Bonami's adolescent on the boundary, the neuter child is a placeholder against gendered adulthood, easily idealized (projected) as embodying transformability. Jody Norton echoes this notion, claiming that "the child does not only long, in some transient way, for the transformation of the real into the imaginary. . . . In fact, the most profound desire of the child is precisely to transform the romantic (the fantastic, the fantasmatic) into the real. That, it seems to me, is the project both of the Wordsworthian and the Lacanian child."[7]

Defined in nonadult terms, the romantic and psychoanalytic child has become the endless repository of adult compensatory fantasy, as David Archard suggests in observing that "the modern child is an innocent incompetent who is not but must become the adult."[8] Rather than standing for a tragically inaccessible solution to adult problems, this ambiguous subject position can host liberatory speculation about future generations and alternative social dynamics. This is the spirit in which childhood studies can take advantage of this free discursive space.

In light of this critical potential, I argue that one of the more persistent but unspoken functions of discursive youth from the late nineteenth century on and into the twenty-first is to serve a genderless ideal. In this light, romantic childhood can be seen as a theoretical precursor to the queer/postmodern end of gender. James Kincaid describes the modern child in the following terms: "This new thing, the modern child, was deployed as a political and philosophical agent, a weapon to adulthood, sophistication, rational moderation, judicious adjustment to the ways of the world. The child was used to deny these virtues, to eliminate them and substitute in their place a set of inversions: innocence, purity, emptiness."[9] Though innocence has become politically suspect as the invention of adult nostalgia, it also allows for progressive speculation. Defined by lack or emptiness, a child can be considered nonadult in the same way Monique Wittig describes a lesbian as "a not-woman, a not-man, a product of society, not a product of nature, for there is no nature in society."[10] Childhood studies posits childhood as a liminal social position through which deconstructing sex, transcending gender, and even achieving social neuter can be performed and fantasized. Inflected through romanticism and psychoanalysis, "innocence became a fulcrum for the postromantic ambiguous construction of sexuality and sexual behavior."[11] Kincaid explains that each movement insisted on and denied child sexuality by theorizing latency: "Freud did tap into one feature of the Romantic child that really was latent: its power."[12] Childhood studies often taps this power, and a parallel tradition of literature permeates the mainstream. Both a denial of sexuality and a potential position of power unfettered by sex roles, presumed asexuality makes genderlessness imaginable.

Leslie Fiedler may have predicted an awareness-to-come of this insistence, denial, and projection when he wrote that "the flight from sexuality led to a literature about children written for the consumption of adults; but the reading of that literature has turned those adults in their own inmost images of themselves into children."[13] The indulgence in an antigender ideal is nothing new in American youth discourse (though it still manifests itself as boy worship in many early incarnations). This gender work is an underlying motive of many professionals in child study and of writers about childhood, who try to grasp the ungraspable child in the image of their own genderless ideals.

It is no surprise that such grasping should often be connected with a simultaneous denial of and resulting insistence on sexual identity. As Jacqueline Rose has explained, "Setting up the child as innocent is not . . . repressing its sexuality—it is above all holding off any possible challenge to our own. . . . What we constantly see in the discussion of children's fiction is how the child can be used to hold off a panic . . . and that sexuality, while it cannot be removed, will eventually take on the forms in which we prefer to recognise and acknowledge each other."[14] Some of the more important and pervasive precedents in American literature are the hoydens and bad boys of the nineteenth century, especially popularized by Mark Twain.[15] Leslie Fiedler has famously noted the androgynous affect of Twain's good bad boy: "Sexually as pure as any milky maiden, he is a rough neck all the same, at once potent and submissive."[16] Fiedler explains the main motive behind such gender blending: "Twain blurred adolescence back into boyhood to avoid confronting the problem of sex; the newer writers, accepting the confusion of childhood and youth, blur both into manhood."[17] Such gender blending has been extensively treated, though more often as gender bending, as a means to expanding social roles. Michelle Ann Abate makes clear, for example, that tomboys are defined in relation to ideals of masculinity, and Kenneth Kidd points out that even the ideal of "androgyny tends to affirm male-female distinction."[18] Though sometimes just another disguised form of boy worship, androgyny can function in American literature as a subversive, ambiguously sexed ideal, but unlike the good bad boy, the neuter figure frustrates the binarization of gender, as does Joan in Twain's *Joan of Arc* (1896).

Although his heroine successfully infiltrates the masculine military through cross-dressing and leadership, Twain highlights Joan's failing attempt to continue transcending gender through adolescence by emphasizing the unusual focus her persecutors put on her male dress once it was no longer considered necessary: "It was shabby work for these grave men to be engaged in; for they well knew one of Joan's reasons for clinging to the male dress was that soldiers of the guard were always present in her room whether she was asleep or awake, and that the male dress was a better protection for her modesty than the other."[19] Such reports on the maid's purity, however, reveal another subtext: that as she enters adulthood (her trials take place when she is seventeen, a time at which her womanhood might be increasingly difficult to overlook, whether virginal or not), Joan no longer fits the young, sexless ideal that might otherwise justify her male attire (one can be androgynously boyish, but not wo/manly). Once an adult, her cry "I would that I were a man" would become too threatening to the gender bifurcation of age-biased heteronormalcy—thus the problematic impossibility of sustained genderlessness that Judy Simon and Shirley Foster amply clarify in *What Katy Read*.[20] The fact that the embodiment of genderlessness is usually exclusive to persons perceived as prepubescent in turn shows how childhood is held up as a desirable but temporary release from the undeniable structures of gendered oppression. A. E. Stone remarks that "the notion that the Maid was believed to have remained a child in body as well as in spirit must have pleased [Twain] and added force to his iterations of her immaculate girlishness."[21] Like many ungendered heroes, she dies young, thus escaping gendered adulthood.

If we follow a constructivist premise of gendering, this escape can be vicariously indulged by conceptualizing childhood as disembodying gender. In her essay "Transchildren and the Discipline of Children's Literature," Jody Norton reminds us that "masculinity is not a matter of anatomy but of meanings" and "femaleness is not a condition of being that begins with a beginning (two chromosomes, say), but rather a becoming that . . . may take an indefinite number of modal shapes."[22] Even at the height of gender rigidity one can see evidence of neuter possibilities in our constructions of youth and in a constructivist approach to youth. While children's literature in the nineteenth century became more firmly established as a separate genre and more divided by gender markets, the gender-free alternative persisted through remaining possibilities for cross-reading, enacting a space free of gendered constraints.

Reflecting the romantic fascination with childhood, the specialized canon allowed for gender subversion, even though at the same time its audience was more intensely bifurcated along lines of gender. As Elizabeth Segal has explained, "It was assumed from the beginning of gender-typed children's books [in the nineteenth century] that girls regularly raided their brother's libraries," and if so, then, even if the fact that "most girls were devouring boys' books" does not mean "the categorizing of books by gender in an attempt to enforce restrictive gender roles" failed, still "the girl reader, no doubt, identified with these enviable heroes as she read, and, theoretically, she could have used them as role models in the dearth of fictional female alternatives to tamed tomboys and saintly sisters."[23] And indeed, sometimes cross-reading wasn't necessary for finding motives for real subversive acts of countergendering or degendering.

DeAnne Blanton and Lauren M. Cook make early cross-dressing heroines more visible in retrospect through their history of real female soldiers in the American Civil War: "The romantic prototype of the Female Warrior Bold was introduced to Sarah Emma Edmonds as a child, when she read the fictional adventure novel *Fanny Campbell, the Female Pirate Captain: A Tale of the Revolution!* That story inspired her to dress as a man in order to escape her overbearing father and his plans to marry her off to an older man."[24] And "flamboyant Loreta Velazquez also read about martial heroines as a child and dreamed of one day emulating the female warriors in her history books. . . . Velazquez boldly settled on no less than Joan of Arc as her personal role model and inspiration."[25] Clearly cross-reading encouraged actual cross-dressing and satisfying countergendered action, which in turn enabled imagined embodiment of sustainable liminality. Even Velazquez's emphasis in interpreting Joan of Arc as a warrior rather than a saint responds to her liminally gendered role in history rather instead of reflecting the feminized spin of her discursive afterlife.

Avi's *The True Confessions of Charlotte Doyle* (1990) approximates a similar effect of such early passing stories for new generations of children—after she's successfully passed as ship's boy, the captain chastises her for setting such an example and for the possible effect her cross-dressing may have on other crew members: "Look at the way you acted! The way you've dressed! It doesn't matter that you are different, Miss Doyle. Don't flatter yourself. The difficulty is that your difference encourages *them* [the ship's crew] to question their places. And mine. The order of things."[26] In her countergendered action Charlotte also makes transcending gender imaginable for the crew and Avi's readers. One particular appeal of boy worship for the girl reader is the opportunity for passing that boyhood presents to the young female, who is in an especially neuterable position cosmetically and socially. Blanton and Cook mention that "for women soldiers, the presence of adolescent boys in the ranks of the Civil War armies provided camouflage for the likewise beardless and high-voiced females. Women unable to pass for full-grown men easily played the part of pubescent boys or young men just emerging from adolescence."[27] Perhaps my idealization of the neuter is biased by my own gender, though Victoria Flanagan shares the view: "There is . . . a sharp disjunction between representations of the male and female cross-dressing experience in children's literature. For females, the cross-dressing experience is liberatory. It exposes the artifice of gender constructions, permitting the female cross-dresser to construct for herself a *unique gendered niche which is not grounded within a single gender category*, but incorporates elements of both."[28] Either way, this overlapping of perceived social definitions might partly explain why romantic American boy worship paired so nicely with an emerging ideal of genderlessness.

Segal writes that "the advent of the 'good bad boy' in the evolving boys' book marked a radical change in what adults expected of children, or, put another way, in what adults defined as the ideal child—ideal boy-child, that is."[29] It was boyhood especially that could be held up as escape from sexuality, responsibility, and other limitations of adulthood. No wonder boy books appealed more broadly, transcending gendered readership. Segal adds, "Whereas in many boys' books, the happy ending is the adolescent 'bad boy' successfully escaping socialization . . . in the girls' book, the protagonist who resists the dictates of genteel femininity must be 'tamed,' her will broken to accept a submissive and sedentary role."[30] Many revisionist fictions redress this difference for young readers, like Pam Muñoz Ryan's *Riding Freedom* (1998), in which protagonist Charlotte sheds her female identity both by rejecting the social role assigned to women and by treating female identity as if it were physically negatable: "With a trembling had, she picked up the scissors and cut off a hank of hair. . . . When Charlotte stood up, she was surprised at how light-headed she felt, as if those braids had been holding her fast to the ground."[31] She not only successfully passes, becoming a stagecoach driver, but she is able to vote. A doctor informs her that passing is common in the West and that women rely on it freely when necessary for their safety.[32] The audience is left with the impression that gender, as a social fiction, is easily cast off by one's embodying a neuter self: "Charlotte was acting, dressing, and talking like a first-rate stage driver, so in folks' eyes, that's what she was."[33]

Cultural androgyny vicariously practiced through transreading may have turned boy worship into girl power. According to Segal, "Though girls . . . could be prevented from joining boys' games and lively exploits, it was harder to keep them from accompanying their brothers on vicarious adventures through the reading of boys' books. And girls were avid readers of boys' books from the start."[34] But more importantly, it presented an opportunity to embody a liminal position in which girl- or boyhood became inconsequential. In *The Resisting Reader*, Judith Fetterley argues that the necessity of transreading for power "immasculates" girl readers: "Intellectually male, sexually female, one is in effect no one, nowhere, immasculated."[35] But one could also see such female readers as more flexible in their ability to adopt other readerly personas—as emasculated, gaining more than they give up in transreading patriarchal literature.[36] In fact, Segal says that "because girls experience less pressure than boys to assume same-sex typed preferences [in reading], they tend to be more *bicultural* than boys."[37] In other words, a patriarchal slant may produce masculinized reading biases, but the resulting gender neutrality benefits female cross-readers by giving them greater gender flexibility.

In *The End of Gender: A Psychological Autopsy*, Shari Thurer explains that in fact "today's young people ... can be aggressively androgynous," citing awareness of the constructedness of gender as a cause: "The categories with which the child identifies are constructed categories, without any essence so, theoretically speaking, transgressing them is both possible and obvious, anyone's prerogative."[38] Even if we don't agree that such awareness is necessarily conscious, surely in a post-Lacanian age we can agree on a subject's polymorphous qualities before *méconnaissance* sets in.

Consider as evidence this four-year-old's vampire version of Cinderella:

Once upon a time a baby cat was born. And she was very small. And since her family was very poor, she decided to run away into a dark, dark woods. And he got lost into a dark, dark woods. . . . The moon went behind a cloud, and when it came out again, the little boy turn into a VAMPIRE! (screams). . . . Cinderella's little boy, and now she's a vampire. And then the Cinderella-vampire smelled—saw a boy and a girl, and some other girls, and he swooped up in the sky saying, "I which one I should eat first?" Then he swooped down and he ATE 'EM! Then he blew up.[39]

Such flexibility may help to overcome the very hurdles that necessitated it. Norton sets transreading as an important countergendering standard: "We can intervene in the reproductive cycle of transphobia through strategies of transreading," which "may involve as simple a move as locating a male identity in a female body (for example, the practice of casting female actresses in the role of *Peter Pan*), or drawing attention to alternatively gendered beings like fairies, who are not always represented as clearly either masculine or feminine."[40] One alternative to gendering is *neither* masculine nor feminine, rejecting both. Juvenile literature is full of such neutered flexibility.

Perhaps the first radical American example comes from L. Frank Baum's *The Marvelous Land of Oz* (1904), in which the main character, Tip, transforms entirely with the help of the wizard's and Mombi's spells, embodying male and female positions and ultimately arguing that his identity transcends both. When Glinda first explains that his boyhood has merely been a temporary disguise, Tip insists "I want to stay a boy, and travel. . . . I don't want to be a girl!"[41] Once transformed back into the Princess Ozma, she tells her friends, "I hope none of you will care less for me than you did before. I'm just the same Tip, you know," to which Pumpkinhead tellingly adds,

"Only you're different!"[42] Tip represents the neuter self as expressed against a society that imposes gendered difference. "Michael Patrick Hearn and Michael O. Riley have stressed," Beverly Lyon Clark notes, "that Baum started his second Oz book . . . with the intention of turning it into a musical comedy. The final gender transformation of the main character echoes the theatrical pantomime tradition associated with the Principal Boy, who is really— is ultimately revealed as—a woman."[43] But Tip is made a boy so that he can escape from danger (and perhaps mockery), and he is only changed to the girl Ozma when she is safe and ready to rule. One could argue, then, that Tip's transcendence still favors gender as necessary and maleness as safe.

A drawback of such moments is the very discursivity that makes them possible and of course, impossible (or merely discursive). Even when convincing, these moments are temporary, something Judith Fetterley makes clear when she claims that in Sherwood Anderson's "I Want to Know Why," "the fantasy of the successful evasion of adulthood becomes the nightmare of being unable to grow up, and this failure is clearly linked to a vision of what it means to be male, which is in turn linked to a fear of sexuality. . . . The boy's resistance to growing up is clearly defined as a reluctance to grow up *male*, and the source of this reluctance is linked to his culture's attitudes toward women."[44] This explains the ambivalence of Peter Pan, the prototype of eternal, sexless childhood: "In the popular imagination, following the propensity of the second half of the twentieth century to idealize the young, resist physical change, and undervalue old age, Barrie's hero has been associated almost exclusively with eternal youth."[45] The desexed namesake of the satyr-god Pan, Peter reflects the adult-serving cult of childhood's denial of youth sexuality (as it only reminds the less young of coming age and death). His sexlessness leaves him heartless but immortal, much to the frustration of Wendy's romantic impulses. James Kincaid argues that " Peter is youth and joy, and she is age and death. . . . Wendy shows us that real monsters have warm bosoms."[46] She also highlights through contrast that boyhood might be used as a retreat from adulthood. If boy worship appeals to woman-fearing men, it could equally appeal to girls wishing to avoid the traps of being a Wendy.[47] And in making the transreading identifications necessary to achieve such insights, the reader just might recognize the uselessness of gender itself.

Of course, some have simplistically conflated undermining gender with corrupting youth. An interesting example is the homoerotic interpretation of sexual ambiguity in the girly good-but-still-bad-boy, which Fredric Wertham famously decried in his homophobic rant against superhero-sidekick comics: "Pederasty means the erotic relationship between a mature man and a young boy. . . . The Batman type of story helps to fixate homoerotic tendencies by suggesting the form of an adolescent-with-adult or Ganymede-Zeus type of love relationship. In the Batman type of comic such a relationship is depicted to children before they can even read."[48] Perry Moore openly mocks this now-clichéd critique while at the same time creating a heartfelt heroic romance from its formula in *Hero* (2007), a YA novel in which Thom, a young gay superhero, fantasizes about becoming Uberman's sidekick but ultimately experiences first love with a young hero of the people. Helping to steer his confusion is the "Hero Fantasy Worship Web site," which Thom enjoys more than surfing porn because "I don't know anyone who turns my crank more than Uberman, and it's not just the body. Honest. The guy is the paragon of everything a man should aspire to be—the perfect hero."[49] Moore's subversive parody of Wertham's reactionary criticism also draws attention to the impossible sexuality of superhero sidekicks. Like the genetic girl/transgender boy Joan of Arc (as idealized by Mark Twain) and the ethereal sexless Peter Pan of Edwardian England, the superhero sidekick represents an idealized escape from rigidly gendered adulthood. And other YA writers have severed gender from sex and sexuality even more—take, for example, Meagan Brothers's cross-dressing Johnny in *Debbie Harry Sings in French*, who tires of people assuming he's gay just because he competes as a drag Debbie Harry: "Sometimes I wish I could be gentle and beautiful and not be called a queer. . . . So what's wrong with putting on a dress every once in a while?"[50]

Psychologist June Singer writes that "from puberty through the childbearing years, sex and gender have traditionally tended to be more closely related . . . than they were in early childhood."[51] This process of gradual relinquishment to gendering is brought into close focus by juvenile publishing, especially in the LGBT subcanon of YA fiction. In Julie Ann Peters's *Luna* (2004), Liam/Luna's sister is babysitting and thinks, "As I resnapped Tyler's onesie, it struck me how ordinary these kids were. . . . You'd never mistake Mirelle for a boy, or Cody for a girl. Tyler was still a baby, *so he didn't count.* If you dressed Ty in frilly clothes, people would probably coo over him and call him a 'pretty little girl.'"[52] The impossible appeal of not having gender matter is more important than people guessing one's correct gender. The reader is encouraged to value the cultural ambiguity of a baby's social genderlessness even more than an ability to pass.

Growing up under threat of future gender expectations, children are in an ideal position to be aware of but also removed from the increasingly contrasting gendered spheres awaiting them. The narrator of *Luna* realizes that there exist different reasons and repercussions for passing (i.e., frustrating binaries of sex, gender, and orientation) depending on genetic sex: "The gender scales didn't extend equidistant in both directions. For example, if you were a girl you could be off-the-scale feminine and that'd be fine, but if you acted or felt just a little too masculine, you were a dyke. Same for guys. Mucho macho, fine. Soft and gentle, fag."[53] To express oneself by differentiating gender oppositionally is fine, but straying toward the center, having more in common with more people or any gender, threatens the absolutist categories made necessary through the historical depths of heteronormative romance. Liam/Luna's sister comes to see the rigid male/female binary as the real problem: "It's not either or. There are shades of gray to people's gender."[54]

Angela/Grady in Ellen Wittlinger's *Parrotfish* (2007) expresses a conscious resistance to the either/or dilemma of selecting her boy name: "It's a name that could belong to either gender. . . . I like the gray part of it—you know, not black, not white, somewhere in the middle."[55] Perhaps the cross-reader can vicariously transcend gender even more convincingly through the focalization of *Parrotfish*, which is narrated by a transgendering teen who keenly feels the clashing socialization that surrounds his/her body: "Where would I be on the gender football field? . . . On the fifty-yard line? And if I was in the middle, what did that mean? That I was both male and female or neither? Or something else altogether?"[56] As social constructions, the notions of a third or fourth sex, androgyny, or even female masculinity are simply alternate essentialisms, though hopefully more open to difference.[57] Grady sees that the either/or imposition of sexual socialization itself impinges on individuation: "In many places sugar and spice were still considered the opposite of snails and puppy-dog tails. When I decided I was a boy, I realized that if I wanted to pass, I'd have to learn to walk differently, dress differently, basically to act differently than I did as a girl. But why did we need to *act* at all?"[58] But the text seems to suggest that revealing alternate essentialisms as socially imposed enables a continued embracing of a neuter ideal.

Sexual ambiguity is more problematic, of course, than it may seem in some idealistic cultural productions for young people. For example, there is the impact of intersexuality as explored both in terms of gender and sexuality in Lucía Puenzo's *XXY* (2007), the medical rights of intersexed infants, and the genetic roulette of Jeffery Eugenides's *Middlesex* (2002).[59] The case of Kathy Witterick and David Stocker, Canadian parents who've decided not to reveal the biological sex of their infant, Storm, exemplifies the fine line adults may cross when trying to put off gender—much of the public has responded as if they are merely imposing yet a different adult agenda.[60] But the trope of genderlessness in childhood can enable discursive exploration of identity while circumventing gender. Childhood studies can take advantage of the possibilities for transcending gender, which is why we don't call what we do "boy- and girlhood studies," even though substudies may focus themselves according to gendered subjects. Instead, the field promises to seek out the free social spaces our discourse allows, loosening the rigid bounds and misleading bifurcation of gender.

Notes

1. Particularly apt here is that de Beauvoir's constructivism stressed *becoming*: "One is not born, but rather becomes, a woman. No biological, psychological, or economic fate determines the figure that the human female presents in society" (*The Second Sex*, trans. H. M. Parshley [New York: Random House, 1974], 301. 301). Is childhood gender undone? This is not to deny that gendering can begin on day 1 but to emphasize that when it does, it is, as a process, a movement away from the neuter ideal.

2. Joan W. Scott, "Gender: A Useful Category of Historical Analysis," *American Historical Review* 91.5 (1986): 1056.

3. Scott, "Gender," 1073.

4. Diana Fuss, *Essentially Speaking: Feminism, Nature, and Difference* (New York: Routledge, 1989), 43.

5. See Shari Thurer, *The End of Gender: A Psychological Autopsy* (New York: Routledge, 2005).

6. Francesco Bonami, *The Fourth Sex: Adolescent Extremes*, ed. Francesco Bonami and Raf Simons (Milan: Charta, 2003), 11.

7. Jody Norton, "Transchildren and the Discipline of Children's Literature," *The Lion and the Unicorn* 23.3 (1999): 430.

8. David Archard, *Children: Rights and Childhood* (New York: Routledge, 2004), 50.

9. James Kincaid, *Erotic Innocence: The Culture of Child Molesting* (Durham, NC: Duke University Press, 1998), 15.

10. Monique Wittig, "One Is Not Born a Woman," in *The Straight Mind and Other Essays* (Boston: Beacon Press, 1992), 13.

11. Kincaid, *Erotic Innocence*, 15. For an example of the romantic neuter child, see Goethe's Mignon and Carolyn Steedman's reading of her in *Strange Dislocations: Childhood and the Idea of Human Interiority, 1780–1930* (Cambridge, MA: Harvard University Press, 1995). Steedman adds, "If James Kincaid is right, and the sustained child-watching that Western culture has indulged in over the last two hundred years has rendered the sex of the child irrelevant in the watcher's pursuit of remoteness, beauty and androgyny, then the fictional and dramatic depiction of the poor children of British urban conurbations is certainly a case in point" (114).

12. Kincaid, *Erotic Innocence*, 57.

13. Leslie Fiedler, *Love and Death in the American Novel* (New York: Criterion, 1960), 272.

14. Jacqueline Rose, *The Case of Peter Pan; or, The Impossibility of Children's Fiction* (Philadelphia: University of Pennsylvania Press, 1984), 4.

15. John Cooley writes that "Twain was attracted repeatedly to shifting gender identifications, all of which are notable for role reversals, unconventional gender behavior, cross-dressing or undressing, and androgyny. In Clemens's private life he called for male dress reform and developed a seemingly pedofilial fascination with the schoolgirls he called 'angelfish.' In his tales of heroic maidens and inadequate males, Twain implicitly deconstructs assumptions about gender roles that dominate the thinking of his generation and his earlier fiction" (*Mark Twain's Aquarium: The Samuel Clemens-Angelfish Correspondence, 1905–1910* [Athens: University of Georgia Press, 1991], 38).

16. Fiedler, *Love and Death in the American Novel*, 268.

17. Fiedler, *Love and Death in the American Novel*, 272.

18. Michelle Anne Abate, *Tomboys: A Literary and Cultural History* (Philadelphia: Temple University Press, 2008); Kenneth Kidd, *Making American Boys: Boyology and the Feral Tale* (Minneapolis: University of Minnesota Press, 2004), 188.

19. Mark Twain, *Joan of Arc* (San Francisco: Ignatius Press, 1989), 370.

20. Twain, *Joan of Arc*, 56.

21. Albert E. Stone, "Mark Twain's *Joan of Arc*: The Child as Goddess," *American Literature* 31.1 (1959): 6.

22. Norton, "Transchildren and the Discipline of Children's Literature," 430.

23. Elizabeth Segal, "'As the Twig Is Bent . . .': Gender and Childhood Reading," in *Gender and Reading: Essays on Readers, Texts, and Contexts*, ed. Elizabeth A. Flynn and Patrocinio P. Schweickart (Baltimore, MD: Johns Hopkins University Press, 1986), 176, 177.

24. DeAnne Blanton and Lauren M. Cook, *They Fought Like Demons: Women Soldiers in the Civil War* (New York: Random House, 2003), 42. *Fanny Campbell* is novel by Maturin Murray Ballou that was first published in 1845.

25. Blanton and Cook, *They Fought Like Demons*, 42.

26. Avi, *The True Confessions of Charlotte Doyle* (New York: Orchard Books, 1990), 198–99.

27. Blanton and Cook, *They Fought Like Demons*, 49–50.

28. Victoria Flanagan, "Reframing Masculinity: Female-to-Male Cross-Dressing," in *Ways of Being Male: Representing Masculinities in Children's Literature and Film*, ed. John Stevens (New York: Routledge, 2002), 79, my emphasis.

29. Elizabeth Segal, "'As the Twig Is Bent . . . ,'" 173.

30. Segal, "'As the Twig Is Bent . . . ,'" 172.

31. Pam Muñoz Ryan, *Riding Freedom* (New York: Scholastic, 1998), 41.

32. Ryan, *Riding Freedom*, 94–95.

33. Ryan, *Riding Freedom*, 96.

34. Segal, "'As the Twig Is Bent . . . ,'" 175.

35. Judith Fetterley, *The Resisting Reader: A Feminist Approach to American Fiction* (Bloomington: Indiana University Press, 1978), xxii.

36. "Emasculated" as a twist on the term "immasculated" comes from Corrine Calice.

37. Elizabeth Segal, "'As the Twig Is Bent . . . ,'" 183.

38. Thurer, *The End of Gender*, 6, 126.

39. Elizabeth Tucker, "'Text, Lies, and Videotape': Can Oral Tales Survive?" *Children's Folklore Review* 13.2 (1991): 27–28.

40. Norton, "Transchildren and the Discipline of Children's Literature," 421.

41. L. Frank Baum, *The Marvelous Land of Oz* (New York: Scholastic, 1970), 182–83.

42. Baum, *The Marvelous Land of Oz*, 185.

43. Beverly Lyon Clark, *Kiddie Lit: The Cultural Construction of Children's Literature in America* (Baltimore, MD: Johns Hopkins University Press, 2003), 138.

44. Fetterley, *The Resisting Reader*, 12, 21.

45. Ann Yeoman, *Now or Neverland: Peter Pan and the Myth of Eternal Youth: A Psychological Perspective on a Cultural Icon* (Toronto: Inner City Books, 1998), 15.

46. James Kincaid, *Child-Loving: The Erotic Child and Victorian Culture* (New York: Routledge, 1992), 286.

47. Fredric Wertham, *Seduction of the Innocent* (New York: Rinehart, 1953). Consider Wertham's critique of comics on the basis that "in these stories there are practically no decent, attractive, successful women. A typical female character is the Catwoman, who is vicious and uses a whip. The atmosphere is homosexual and anti-feminine" (191).

48. Wertham, *Seduction of the Innocent*, 189–90.

49. Perry Moore, *Hero* (New York: Hyperion, 2007), 41.

50. Meagan Brothers, *Debbie Harry Sings in French* (New York: Henry Holt, 2008), 191.

51. June Singer, *Androgyny: Toward a New Theory of Sexuality* (New York: Anchor/Doubleday, 1976), 21.

52. Julie Ann Peters, *Luna* (New York: Little, Brown, 2004), 50, my emphasis.

53. Peters, *Luna*, 51.

54. Peters, *Luna*, 69.

55. Ellen Wittlinger, *Parrotfish* (New York: Simon and Schuster, 2007), 6.

56. Wittlinger, *Parrotfish*, 130–31.

57. In *The Resisting Reader*, Halberstam warns against conflating androgyny with female masculinity, male femininity, or any static sexual orientation: "There are likely to be many examples of masculine women in history who had an interest in same-sex sexuality" (57). She also recognizes the asexual limitations of androgyny as a "neither and both" ideal: "Cross-dressing androgyny has distinctly unqueer limits" in its approximation of boyhood and resistance to adulthood (214). My reference to "'alternate essentialisms" here is to strategic essentializing, as described, for example, by Gayatri Spivak.

58. Wittlinger, *Parrotfish*, 131.

59. In *Bodies That Matter* (New York: Routledge, 1993), Judith Butler asks us to "consider the medical interpellation which (the recent emergence of the sonogram notwithstanding) shifts an infant from an 'it' to a 'she' or a 'he.'" "In that naming," she argues, "the girl is 'girled,' brought into the domain of language and kinship through the interpellation of gender. But that 'girling' of the girl does not end there" (7). In fact, it is a process, one that is arbitrarily imposed on intersexed persons: "Subjected to gender, but subjectivated by gender, the 'I' neither precedes nor follows the process of this gendering, but emerges only within and as the matrix of gender relations themselves" (7).

60. Jayme Poisson, "Parents Keep Child's Gender Secret," *Toronto Star*, May 21, 2011.

Childhood Studies and
Literary Adoption

Carol Singley

Representations of adoption abound in nineteenth-century American fiction and have much to tell us not only about formal aspects of plot but also about the construction of cultural narratives of the child, family, and nation—all important sites of inquiry for the field of childhood studies. This chapter explores the ways that childhood studies can affirm the importance of biological and nonbiological kinship as categories of analysis. It also shows how childhood studies can reveal the historical dimensions and limitations of romantic conceptions of childhood. It is grounded in the understanding, now a given in the field, that the child is historically constructed. It argues that the nineteenth-century literary child is a cultural representation that reflects changes in the middle-class family and society and that portrayals of orphaned and homeless children, in particular, respond to social anxieties that representations of adopted children help to assuage.

I wish to sketch a historical as well as literary schematic for interpreting representations of biological and nonbiological kinship in nineteenth-century American fiction and to use these findings to discuss an early short story about adoption by Nathaniel Hawthorne. Hawthorne's story is a precursor of the popular narratives about adoption that began appearing in volume in the 1850s and continued to be published throughout the century. These tales of dislocation and relocation provide insights about contemporary views of children and child rearing as well as offer perspectives on wide-ranging social changes that were affecting the family and middle-class American culture. Much of this literature positions adoption in the context of romantic notions of childhood, in which an innocent, struggling, and sometimes sacrificed child appears alongside sentimentalized portraits of motherhood in a nurturing environment that serves as antidote to a masculinized, commercialized, and urbanized culture.

Nathaniel Hawthorne is a well-known writer of fiction for children as well as adults.[1] Carol Billman notes that in his collections of myths for children, *A Wonder-Book* (1852) and *Tanglewood Tales* (1853), Hawthorne "celebrates the innocence of and possibilities before children in this infant nation."[2] His early short story "The Gentle Boy: A Thrice-Told Tale" (1832) is anomalous in a body of romantic nineteenth-century literature that glorifies the child and its adoptive home. Hawthorne focuses not on felicitous domesticity but on dislocation, shame, and guilt. In so doing, he calls into question the increasingly popular transcendentalist view of idealized childhood. Despite progressive theories that began circulating at this time, Hawthorne understands childhood as morally problematic, if not sinful, and parenting as self-serving, if not destructive.[3] Literary critics interested in representations of the child have increasingly realized the importance of defining characteristics such as class, race, gender, and ethnicity when interrogating representations of childhood. Caroline Levander, in *Cradle of Liberty*, for example, shows the centrality of the child in U.S. debates about race and liberal democracy; Karen Sánchez-Eppler, in *Dependent States*, explains the child as an organizing figure in discourse about social class.[4] In this volume, Susan Honeyman uncovers masculinist biases in ostensibly gender-neutral discourses about youth and asks that childhood studies work to identify social spaces that transcend gender. And Lucia Hodgson shows how the infantilization of the racialized other perpetuates racism and accounts for the late eighteenth- to early nineteenth-century shift from environmentalism to essentialism. Scholars similarly have made sexual orientation and disability a factor in considering diverse portrayals of the child. In this volume, Sarah Chinn uses queer theory to deepen analysis of the "structures of gender, desire, and power" inherent in the experience of childhood (145). However, despite welcome attention to these markers of difference, critics and scholars often tacitly accept genealogy as an organizing principle and mode of thought, ignoring the fact that kinship is as important a category of analysis as is gender, class, or race. Childhood studies shows us that the child's most formative relationships are with the family, and kinship structures play essential roles in setting the terms of personal identity and social belonging. Adoptive kinship, an alternative to genealogical bonds, invites new lines of inquiry in childhood studies.

The power of adoption studies, a subset of childhood studies, to shape questions about constructions of the self is clear in a 2002 issue of *Tulsa Studies in Women's Literature* on the topic. Adoption, Margaret Homans shows, demonstrates the normatizing premises on which the language of parenting is based, challenging fundamental understandings of what it means to have a child "of one's own."[5] Adoption also de-essentializes race, ethnicity, and nationality by separating them from notions of the family as a unit formed and maintained through biology. Adoption of children by single parents or by gay and lesbian parents challenges the heteronormativity associated with bourgeois parenting, just as biracial families formed through adoption break long-standing taboos against intimacy across racial lines. Transnational adoptions deepen questions about global politics, especially colonialism, and raise questions about the exchange not only of love and nurture but also of power and money in setting terms for children's care.[6] Adoption studies plays a central role in the interrogation of children and kinship. It alters basic assumptions that inform research in the humanities, providing new ways to think about origins, domestic affiliation, nurture, and social rights and responsibilities.

Adoption studies is especially relevant at the intersection of American culture and literature. Since Puritan times, writers have linked the family and nation using metaphors of childhood, youth, and development.[7] John Winthrop's foundational 1637 comment that "a family is a little commonwealth, and a commonwealth is a great family" set the tone for American literary and cultural discourse about the relationship of the individual to the family and nation.[8] In Winthrop's view, however, biological kinship is the presumed social norm, differing only in scale from nationhood. Lineage also forms the keystone in Puritan writings that link family and divine salvation. Increase Mather grounds redemption in heredity in the much quoted "God hath seen good to cast the line of Election so, as that it doth . . . for the most part, run through the loins of godly Parents."[9] Scholars note that the Puritans' tendency to exclude children who were not related by birth or who were not considered to be members of the Elect was inherited from the English, who placed high value on bloodline.[10] Despite this emphasis on genealogical continuity as a basis for personal and collective identity, early American writing provides ample evidence of the embrace of adoption, even though the practice did not yet exist in legal form. Puritans regularly practiced a form of temporary adoption called "placing out," in which children lived with adults who were not their biological parents, and Puritan writings repeatedly refer to adoption as emblematic of God's saving grace. Historians of children and the family are divided about the motivations for placing out, interpreting it as result of financial need, a means of securing training or education for children, a strategy for preventing an overly emotional attachment to children, or a way of protecting against intergenerational conflict, including those resulting from inappropriate erotic affections for children. But they are clear about the fluidity of the Puritan household.[11] Childhood studies, in taking note of these exclusionary and inclusionary practices, can help us assess the strength of family bonds across time periods by using attachment to genealogy as a measure.

By the mid-nineteenth century, representations of felicitous adoption were beginning to proliferate in American literature, particularly in domestic fiction.[12] Stories of children without homes are perennially appealing for reasons of plot: an orphan is free to have adventures impossible for a child nestled at home. However, adoption narratives come into being at a moment of changing views of childhood and child rearing and when adoption was legally formulated as a practice that took into account the child's best interest.[13] Adoption narratives also reflect an American enthusiasm about the child's role in the developing nation. Anne MacLeod notes the "nationalism and optimism" that resulted in "extraordinary attention Americans turned upon their children . . . in an effort to ensure that the rising generation would be equal to the challenges and promises of the future."[14] Childhood studies helps us to see how nineteenth-century literary representations of the orphaned and adopted child respond to developments in society as a whole. These include an increasingly sentimental outlook on childhood and an emphasis on nurture to counter a growing materialism, commercialism, and secularism in everyday life, a decrease of paternal authority and a rise of the cult of motherhood, a post-Revolutionary spirit of democratic individualism, and increased demographic mobility.

The literary orphan with its sufferings is aligned with a growing culture of sentimentality that affected American culture in general and childhood in particular. Critical work in the area of childhood and sentimentality is extensive and growing. Elizabeth Dillon writes that "one of the most strik-ing aspects of sentimental discourse" is "the debut of the child as a central literary and popular figure."[15] Ala Alryyes similarly notes a proliferation of children in fiction from the eighteenth century to the nineteenth.[16] Ann Douglas and Jane Tompkins articulate the role of the sacrificial, dying child in what Douglas calls a "feminization" of American culture and Tompkins the "cultural work" of domestic fiction. Karen Sánchez-Eppler focuses on the interplay of broken genealogy and gender with social reform, com-mercial exchange, and feeling in accounts of homeless newsboys.[17] Claudia Nelson traces the "melodrama" of displaced children through the end of the nineteenth century, noting children's roles in manufacturing emotional climates needed for their survival.[18] And Amy Schrager Lang documents the close relationship between literary adoption and class mobility.[19]

The figure of the adopted child taps this wellspring of sentimentality: orphancy evokes sympathy just as adoption validates nurture, a quality in-creasingly valued in child rearing and propounded by religious and social leaders such as Horace Bushnell, author of *Christian Nurture* (1847). In the nineteenth century, nurture became the domain of the mother, who plays a prominent role in popular adoption fiction.[20] This emphasis on maternal power in adoption narratives reflected a decline of patriarchal authority as generations of post-Revolutionary War young people, especially males, left family farms and homesteads to make their way in the world without for-merly requisite paternal approval or sponsorship. The authoritative family associated with the Puritan era, in which the father ruled unquestionably, gave way to a more "democratic family," in which the individual's impor-tance was increasingly recognized, with sons less dependent on traditional transfers of support in the form of land, inheritance, or status.[21] Adoption stories reflect this national mobility on a smaller scale.

Adoption stories gave expression to a romantic sense of possibility synon-ymous, as Bernard Wishy notes, with an increasingly child-centered Ameri-can society.[22] Whereas Calvinism held to a doctrine of innate evil, even in the newborn, and the need for parental control in order to suppress the will of the child, by the 1830s a new awareness of childhood began to unseat this traditional belief and usher in a new era of romantic potential.[23] The accul-turation of children into a new family through adoption further provided opportunity to implement and assess new forms of discipline, which, as Wishy and Richard Brodhead note, involved a move away from punitive, authoritarian models and toward more gentle forms of persuasion that led children to internalize desired forms of behavior.[24] The successfully adopted child, rescued and rehabilitated through the committed nurture of its adoptive parents, reinforced middle-class ideals of functioning, expanding families, in alignment with the growing nation. Adoption stories, which offer a vision of what the individual can accomplish without genealogical supports, reflected the spirit of democratic individualism and increased demographic and social mobility in the nation as whole.

Paradigmatic stories of adoption include Susan Warner's *The Wide, Wide World* (1850) and Susanna Maria Cummins's *The Lamplighter* (1854). These narratives, subsets of the bildungsroman, are highly gendered and follow the pattern outlined by Nina Baym. In these tales, the female protagonist is separated from her birth family, experiences a series of adoptions, and must use her intelligence and resourcefulness to overcome obstacles that come her way. Eventually, through faith, loyalty, or service to others the girl proves her worthiness and is rewarded with a happy home and a socially acceptable marriage.[25] Tales involving boys, in contrast, describe mentors, teachers, or guides who, although they more often than not do not adopt the boy, help him learn skills and develop the resources he needs to succeed in business or venture westward. Models include Horatio Alger's boys in the Ragged Dick series, who achieve self-made success with the occasional help of benefactors, and Louisa May Alcott's Dan Kean in *Little Men* and *Jo's Boys* and Mark Twain's Huckleberry Finn, who resist the domesticating influences of adoption.

First published in 1832 in the *Token* magazine, "The Gentle Boy" anticipates the abundance of adoption fiction published in the 1850s and beyond. However, Hawthorne's historical tale, set in 1656, does not work uniformly to establish the conventions found in these popular adoption narratives. Hawthorne describes a mild-mannered, feminized male child who is adopted, not just assisted, and who derives comfort from nurturing others rather than from striking out on his own.[26] The tale fits neither conventionally gendered category, suggesting that the categories themselves had not yet solidified by 1832. More importantly, "The Gentle Boy" expresses opposition to romantic representations of childhood and nurture, thereby complicating any simplistic pairings of these terms.

Taking a childhood studies approach, we see Hawthorne choosing a Puritan setting that illuminates the Calvinist tradition out of which popular nineteenth-century concepts of childhood eventually developed. We also see Puritan values set in opposition to Quaker ones. In the story, the non-Elect are figured as Quakers, whom the Puritans both exclude and persecute. Hawthorne's historical setting is not only factual but also interpretive, informed by his experiences as a writer, husband, father, descendent of a Salem witch trial judge, and member of a burgeoning nineteenth-century middle class.[27] "The Gentle Boy" thus allows for multiple views of childhood and child rearing—Puritan, Quaker, and romantic. It also admits a personal dimension of childhood recollected. At an early age, Hawthorne experienced losses like those associated with adoption, after his father died and he was moved from one maternal family home to another.[28] Despite caring relatives, he felt the chronic sting of dependency and dislocation, which marriage to Sophia Peabody may have helped to alleviate.[29]

A childhood studies approach to the story shows the workings of evil as well as good in children, the questionable effect of parental nurture, and the resistance to felicitous endings usually found in popular nineteenth-century adoption tales. The religious strife, child abandonment, and deficient parenting in "The Gentle Boy" all contribute to staging a protest against popular representations of families who are first sundered and then reconstructed through adoption. Specifically, Hawthorne's representation of Calvinist theology, with its emphasis on original sin, salvation through grace not works, and limited election, functions as a trope for the unredeemed and unredeemable aspects of childhood. Depicting a child in need but refusing to offer the child the ameliorative conditions that would become the norm in domestic adoption fiction, Hawthorne not only offers a critique of adoption fiction's premises but also demonstrates the importance of genealogical rupture in shaping understandings of family and childhood.

Neither does Hawthorne demonstrate the adopted child's power to save or heal others. In popular domestic fiction, the adopted child gains in faith, confidence, and the ability to serve others. For example, Warner's Ellen Montgomery in *The Wide, Wide World* exhibits compassion toward Aunt Fortune Emerson, befriends the hapless Nancy Vawse, and resists the Marshmans' materiality. Cummins's Gerty Flint in *The Lamplighter* nurses the dying Nan Grant and aligns herself with the sensible Sullivans rather than the fashionable Grahams, all with felicitous results. In contrast, Hawthorne's protagonist, Ilbrahim, reaches out to help heal a wounded child but is viciously attacked (he ultimately dies) as thanks for his efforts. Hawthorne suggests the limited powers of the saved or suffering child, rejecting a sentimental ideal that fueled popular domestic fiction. A childhood studies perspective on his authorial choice reminds us that such ideals are cultural constructions that reflect and promote particular ideologies. Hawthorne is less sanguine than the domestic writers about the future of American childhood and more concerned than they about the burdens of a repressive Calvinist past. Interpreting his representations through the lens of childhood studies reinforces the understanding that romantic childhood is a historical construction aligned with optimism and possibility rather than restriction and strife.

"The Gentle Boy"—about a Puritan couple who defies society by adopting a homeless Quaker boy—is written in the tradition of the historical romance, the principal literary genre in the first decades of the nineteenth century. At this time Americans venerated their Puritan forefathers, and the adoption literature of the time did not typically offer romanticized portrayals of children. Rather, adoption signified personal genealogical loss and a clash of cultures and religions, with mixed results for both the individual and the community. For example, in *Hobomok* (1824) by Lydia Maria Child, when the mixed-race child Charles Brown is adopted, his Indian heritage is erased. In Catharine Maria Sedgwick's *Hope Leslie* (1827), Hope's sister, Faith, is adopted by Indians and forever lost to Puritan society. "The Gentle Boy" similarly portrays a conflict that adoption cannot completely resolve. Ilbrahim is a victim of enmity between the Puritan and Quaker sects. Neither saved nor saving, he reflects a view of childhood status as dependent on genealogy rather than on individual resourcefulness or potential. Writing at a time of transition from more Calvinist to romantic sensibilities, Hawthorne describes a combination of good and evil in children, reflects on the ambiguous effect of nurture, and offers an equivocal rather than positive ending to the adoption plot.

Although both Puritan and Quaker faiths were known, as David Fischer notes, for being child-centered, Hawthorne focuses on their repressive or delinquent aspects.[30] The Puritans are too rigid to accept children who are different from them; the Quakers too zealous to attend to their own families. A "throwaway" child in today's parlance, Ilbrahim suffers because neither group is able to rise above its aggressions and fears to secure a safe home for him. The story thus does not reflect the principle of "progress" that Michael Davitt Bell finds typical of American historical romance.[31] Neither does it reify romantic notions of childhood circulating at midcentury. Rather, at the intersection of childhood studies and literary studies, we find that nineteenth-century childhood is a contested site of meaning, with notions of innocence and evil in tension.

Bereft of his parents, the young Ilbrahim is first seen grieving at the scene of his father's execution. Unable to step away from the gruesome site, he is lost and at risk of death himself. The kind-hearted Tobias Pearson takes the boy home, but the rescue is fraught with difficulty because Ilbrahim is a Quaker, to whom Puritan doors are closed. Hawthorne's portrayal of the adoptive process does not feature the Puritan practice of "placing out." Hawthorne makes no mention of this felicitous form of temporary adoption because in the society he depicts, religious intolerance trumps considerations of child welfare. The Puritans were dismissive of children who were not in their ranks even though they frequently took in orphaned children of members of their congregation in an effort to help the children and to emulate through their act of benevolence their heavenly father's spiritual adoption of them. Hawthorne underlines their suspicion of outsiders in "The Gentle Boy" with his depiction of enmity toward the Quakers.

An ominous tone likewise imbues Hawthorne's description of Tobias and Dorothy Pearson, who reside on the margins of the Puritan community, a "gloomy" four miles from town.[32] Suspected of being too "worldly" and motivated by material rather than spiritual gain, they are condemned by superstitious Puritans, who attribute the death of the Pearsons' children to the couple's "supposed impurity of motive" (75). Loneliness motivates Tobias's decision to adopt Ilbrahim. He follows the boy's "mournful" cry as if following an inner guidance, exhibiting at this early juncture qualities that later align him with the Quaker faith (70). However, Ilbrahim is not a likeable child. Tobias recoils and drops the boy's hand "as if he were touching a loathsome reptile" (72) when he learns that Ilbrahim is a Quaker. Having absorbed the "religious prejudice" of the Puritans, Tobias has trouble performing the sort of redemption common to nineteenth-century adoption narratives. Only with resolve does he vow not to forsake Ilbrahim "whatever the risk" and to "be kind to him, as if he were his own child." "Look up," he tells the child, "there is our home" (73–74).

In the nineteenth century, as the grip of patriarchal Calvinism waned and the pace of commercial and industrial development increased, women became the emotional and spiritual anchors for the family and nation.[33] Hawthorne reflects this decline in patriarchal authority and rise in maternal prominence, along with their effect on the child, with his depictions of Dorothy and Catherine, Ilbrahim's adoptive and birth mothers. Through his portraits of the two mothers, he critiques certain maternal practices and demonstrates the necessity of nurture to child development. Ilbrahim's adoptive mother, Dorothy Pearson, who is one of the "engaging, natural, affectionate, but unintellectual women of the Heart," comes "very close to Hawthorne's ideal" of motherhood, as Millicent Bell notes.[34] She exhibits kindness that is in keeping with the motherly affection found in popular domestic fiction. She gently asks Ilbrahim, "Have you a mother?" and seeing "tears burst forth from his full heart" in sentimental longing for the mother who has abandoned him, she promises to be a mother to him, prepares his bed, and hears his evening prayer (74). Pious and tender, she feels a "pensive gladness" (75) when she settles him for first night's sleep.

Dorothy contrasts with Catherine, whom Hawthorne finds deficient because she neglects her maternal duties. The Quakers would have been supportive of Catherine's decision to follow her inner calling and proselytize rather than raise her child, but Hawthorne depicts the damage done to children by such self-interest. Catherine's religious fanaticism oversteps the bounds of Christian piety and domesticity he associates with women at midcentury. At the church where Catherine delivers a sermon that rivals the Puritan one, Ilbrahim recognizes his mother and comes forward to join her, whereupon "the indulgences of natural love had . . . made her know how far she had strayed from duty" (82), but the moment of recognition is fleeting, and the scene ends with Catherine admitting maternal responsibility without amending her ways. Having once abandoned Ilbrahim to proselytize her faith, she relinquishes him a second time, saying, "I have ill performed a mother's part by thee in life, and now I leave thee no inheritance but woe and shame" (82).

Ilbrahim seems at first to be a model, quintessentially good child in the sentimental tradition. He bears his trials admirably with beauty and "winning manners" (76), but unlike the sacrificial child of sentimental fiction, he is unable to win over his detractors or positively affect his environment. He is a partially constructed romantic ideal; adoption incompletely accomplishes his renovation. Within a week or two of living with Tobias and Dorothy, he appears to be benefiting from his new home and accepting the Pearsons as his parents. He evinces the behaviors associated with successful adoption; that is, he begins to seem "native in the New England cottage," and his demeanor becomes more childlike, with "an airy gayety" that, like "a domesticated sunbeam" (86), brightens his gloomy adoptive home. He performs tasks expected of an adopted literary child: he brings his new parents solace and hope. The adoption does not fully do its work, however. Ilbrahim still bears the imprint of his roots: "The disordered imaginations of both his father and mother had perhaps propagated a certain unhealthiness in the mind of the boy" (86). He yields to "moments of deep depression" (87). He has absorbed the Quaker and Puritan conflict.

Hawthorne thematizes hurt rather than healing. When a Puritan boy with a "dark and stubborn nature" is injured and brought to the Pearson home for care, Ilbrahim lavishes attention on the convalescent, entertaining him with imaginative stories and devoting himself to the boy's recuperation (89). His good deeds are not reciprocated, however. When children gather to play and target Ilbrahim with curses and blows, the boy offers to help, but when Ilbrahim trustingly goes to him for protection, the boy viciously strikes Ilbrahim and beats him. The bully's betrayal, more than the blow itself, debilitates Ilbrahim, turning him into a morose child so taxed in body and spirit that he becomes filled with "brooding" and "grief" (91). Despite Dorothy and Tobias's ministrations, Ilbrahim gradually declines and then dies.

Taking a childhood studies approach to the story, we see that childhood innocence and purity is a romantic notion still under construction at the time Hawthorne writes in 1832. The notion of Ilbrahim's essential goodness is compromised by the strength of Puritan and Quaker conflict and by the harsher conceptions of childhood that those sects represent. "The Gentle Boy" reflects skepticism about romantic views of the child—and of humanity generally. As Millicent Bell writes, "Rousseau had hailed the instinctive virtue of the savage and the child. . . . [But] 'The Gentle Boy' illustrate[s] the truth that good is not instinct within the human breast."[35]

The adopted child appears with increasing frequency in American literature from the mid-nineteenth century onward and embodies qualities valued in the middle-class culture as a whole. Rescued from poverty or homelessness, the adopted child is "saved" in a secular replication of God's redemption of humankind. Ideally, this child then exhibits not only gratitude but also enthusiasm, resourcefulness, and readiness to embrace the fresh start made possible by the adoption. The success of the fictive adoptive placement parallels the optimism associated with a growing middle class and serves as a reminder that there is a "place" for everyone in an expanding nation.

The historical specificity of these concepts of orphancy and adoption are made clear in Hawthorne's tale, which predates the profusion of adoption fiction at midcentury and demonstrates resistance to its tenets. The optimistic endings in this literature imply a positive development in American selfhood; Ilbrahim's death, in contrast, represents "a narrowing or limitation of possibilities in the growth of the American character."[36] Repudiating romantic portrayals of childhood, "The Gentle Boy" focuses not on the benefit of adoptive placement but on the pain of displacement. With its historical portraits of two opposing sects—one rigid and controlling, the other wild and imaginative—it questions the power of the saved, angelic child to chart a middle ground for family and society.

Hawthorne's story ends in sacrifice but not redemption. Dorothy's maternal affection cannot prevent the bully's attack. The executions of the Quakers cease, not because Ilbrahim dies, but because King Charles orders a stay of violence. The Pearson home remains a source of "gloom" rather than cheer (92). Catherine returns in time to hear her son's parting reassurance—"Mourn not, dearest mother. I am happy now" (100)—and her "fierce and vindictive nature was softened" (101), but she is infantilized rather than empowered when she is taken into the Pearson home.

Childhood studies, taking the multiple dimensions of childhood, including historical ones, into its purview, helps us to see the importance of both genealogical and nongenealogical kinship in creating American literary mythologies. In American literature of the nineteenth century, biologically raised children are represented differently from adopted children. The very act of transferring a child from one home to another has widespread social, political, and religious implications. Childhood studies has been tentative in its embrace of adoption studies, sometimes holding to an unnecessarily rigid demarcation between actual adoption and rhetorical figurations of adoption in literature and other media. However, an analysis of the interplay of history, culture, and literature—the very operations that interdisciplinary childhood studies makes possible—can reveal the naturalizing tendencies at work in constructions of kinship and shed new light on the meanings of home, child relocation, and childhood itself.

Notes

1. Jon Stott asserts that "Hawthorne was the first major American author to approach the genre seriously" ("Nathaniel Hawthorne," in *Writers for Children: Critical*

Studies of Major Authors since the Seventeenth Century, ed. Jane M. Bingham [New York: Scribner's, 1988], 282).

Karen Sánchez-Eppler points out that Hawthorne "wrote more pieces directly aimed at a juvenile audience than any other canonical male author of the antebellum period and argues that "Hawthorne's self-presentation as a writer who wishes to make public on the streets of the town or the pages of a book his connection with childhood provides important insights into his conception of authorship" ("Hawthorne and the Writing of Childhood" in *The Cambridge Companion to Nathaniel Hawthorne*, ed. Richard H. Millington [New York: Cambridge University Press 2004], 143). Noting recent attention to Hawthorne's fiction for juveniles, Laura Laffrado observes that searchable databases and digital archives mean that "Hawthorne's works for children can now be more visibly and accurately located within the generic multi-vocality that was employed by many writers in the nineteenth-century United States" ("Hawthorne 2.0" *Nathaniel Hawthorne Review* 36.1 [Spring 2010]: 41). His literature for children is the topic of the Spring 2010 special issue of the *Nathaniel Hawthorne Review*.

2. Carol Billman, "Nathaniel Hawthorne: 'Revolutionizer' of Children's Literature?," *Studies in American Fiction* 10.1 (1982): 113.

3. Lesley Ginsberg takes a similar view. In his *Notebooks*, she notes, Hawthorne "wrestled with a skepticism that opposed the ideal child, while at the same time he maintained a progressive belief in transcendentalist ideologies which stipulated that not only the child but also the parent would be transformed into a finer person through the careful consideration of child-rearing practices" ("The ABCs of *The Scarlet Letter*," *Studies in American Fiction* 29.1 [2001]: 17).

4. Karen Sánchez-Eppler, *Dependent States: The Child's Part in Nineteenth-Century American Culture* (Chicago: University of Chicago, 2005); Caroline F. Levander, *Cradle of Liberty: Race, the Child, and National Belonging from Thomas Jefferson to W. E. B. Du Bois* (Durham, NC: Duke University Press 2006).

5. Margaret Homans, "Adoption and Essentialism." *Tulsa Studies in Women's Literature* 21.2 (2002): 257–74.

6. Homans, "Adoption and Essentialism," 266–269.

7. Caroline F. Levander and Carol J. Singley, introduction to *The American Child: A Cultural Studies Reader*, ed. Caroline F. Levander and Carol J. Singley (New Brunswick, NJ: Rutgers University Press, 2003), 4.

8. John Winthrop, "A Defense of an Order of Court," in *The Puritans in America: A Narrative Anthology*, ed. Alan Heimert and Andrew Delbanco (Cambridge, MA: Harvard University Press 1985), 166.

9. Increase Mather, *Pray for the Rising Generation* (Cambridge, MA: Samuel Green, 1678), 12.

10. See Edmund Sears Morgan, *The Puritan Family: Essays on Religion and Domestic Relations in Seventeenth-Century New England* (Boston: Trustees of the Public Library, 1944).

11. On the reasons for and benefits of placing out, see John Demos, *A Little Com-*

monwealth: Family Life in Plymouth Colony, 2nd ed. (New York: Oxford University Press 2000), Judith S. Graham, *Puritan Family Life: The Diary of Samuel Sewall* (Boston: Northeastern University Press 2000), Alan Macfarlane, *The Family Life of Ralph Josselin, a Seventeenth-Century Clergyman: An Essay in Historical Anthropology* (New York: Norton, 1970), and Morgan, *The Puritan Family*.

12. By the mid-nineteenth century the connection between adoption and salvation is a staple of literary representation: homeless children severed from biological parents are aided or saved by adoptive parents or guardians and in turn help to redeem others. I trace this development in adoption fiction from Puritan times through the end of the nineteenth century in *Adopting America: Childhood, Kinship, and National Identity in Literature.* (New York: Oxford University Press 2011), 5, 16–39. On the relation between adoption fiction and the developing middle class and nation, see 6–10.

13. The Massachusetts Adoption Act was passed in 1851. The United States was the first Western nation to take the child's best interest into account with such legislation; England did not pass a similar law until 1926.

14. Anne Scott MacLeod, *A Moral Tale: Children's Fiction and American Culture, 1820–1860* (Hamden, CT: Archon, 1975), 9.

15. Elizabeth Dillon, *The Gender of Freedom: Fictions of Liberalism and the Literary Public Sphere* (Stanford, CA: Stanford University Press 2004), 204.

16. Ala Alryyes, *Original Subjects: The Child, the Novel, and the Nation* (Cambridge, MA: Harvard University Press, 2001), 119.

17. Sánchez-Eppler, *Dependent States*, 151–85.

18. Nina Baym, *Woman's Fiction: A Guide to Novels by and about Women in America, 1820–1870* (Ithaca, NY: Cornell University Press 1978), 66–91.

19. Amy Schrager Lang, *The Syntax of Class: Writing Inequality in Nineteenth-Century America* (Princeton, NJ: Princeton University Press, 2003), 18–23. On the role of sentiment, see also June Howard, "What Is Sentimentality?," *American Literary History* 11.1 (1999): 63–81. For a call to extend connections with childhood beyond sentimentality, see Gillian Brown, "Child's Play." *Differences* 11.3 (1999): 84.

20. Mary Ryan coined the phrase "empire of the mother" to describe the greater importance women assumed in domestic life, as they were responsible for nurturing the child's spiritual and emotional as well as physical development (*The Empire of the Mother: American Writing about Domesticity, 1830–1860* [New York: Institute for Research in History and Haworth Press, 1982]).

21. Steven Mintz and Susan Kellogg, *Domestic Revolutions: A Social History of American Family Life* (New York: Free Press, 1988), 53–55.

22. Bernard Wishy, *The Child and the Republic: The Dawn of Modern American Child* (Philadelphia: University of Pennsylvania Press, 1968), 32–33.

23. Philip J. Greven, The *Protestant Temperament: Patterns of Child-Rearing, Religious Experience, and the Self in Early America* (Chicago: University of Chicago Press, 1977), 32–43.

24. Wishy, *The Child and the Republic*, 94–114; Richard H. Brodhead, *Cultures of Letters* (Chicago: University of Chicago Press, 1993), 13–47.

25. Baym, *Woman's Fiction*, 11–12.

26. Ken Parille writes that "Ilbrahim falls into the [female] tradition of the nineteenth-century saintly child." He argues Hawthorne makes him a boy rather than a girl so that his "body can undergo a lengthy and heightened [physical] pain" that sentimental culture associated with males rather than females ("Allegories of Childhood Gender: Hawthorne and the Material Boy," *Nathaniel Hawthorne Review* 36.1 [2010]: 129–30). In a similar vein, Anne Trensky notes that Ilbrahim's spiritual quality "draws heavily upon the rhetoric of feminine morality and immateriality" ("The Saintly Child in Nineteenth-Century American Fiction," *Prospects* 1 [October 1975]: 389).

27. See, in particular, Laffrado's observation that tales such as "The Gentle Boy" "become imbricated in a larger context of representations of children and children's worlds in the nineteenth-century United States" ("Hawthorne 2.0," 39–40). On ways that Hawthorne's Puritan texts reflect the customs and structures of an emerging middle class, especially as they affect gender, see Michael T. Gilmore "Hawthorne and the Making of the Middle Class," in *Rethinking Class: Literary Studies and Social Formations*, ed. Wai Chi Dimock and Michael T. Gilmore (New York: Columbia University Press 1994), 215–38. Gillian Brown likewise draws attention to Hawthorne's interest in popular conceptions of childhood and notes his "lifelong literary and personal concern with the how adults treat and affect children" and their particular "attribution of special or salvific powers to children" ("Hawthorne and Children in the Nineteenth Century: Daughters, Flowers, Stories," in *A Historical Guide to Nathaniel Hawthorne*, ed. Larry J. Reynolds [New York: Oxford University Press 2001], 88). See also my description of Hawthorne's middle-class views of childrearing and his ambivalence about the strengths of both biological and adoptive family bonds in *Adopting America*, 65–68.

28. Gloria C. Erlich, *Family Themes and Hawthorne's Fiction* (New Brunswick, NJ: Rutgers University Press 1984), 76.

29. T. Walter Herbert argues that certain features of his relation with Sophia "make it typical of the social arrangements that gave rise to the domestic ideal. The 'cult of domesticity' envisions a self-made man taking to wife an angel, a figure whose religious energies counteract the unreality 'of a being so unconnected' as himself" (*Dearest Beloved: The Hawthornes and the Making of the Middle-Class Family* [Berkeley: University of California Press, 1993], 60). Childhood studies has much to offer on the subject of the reconstruction of childhood through memory.

30. David Fischer, *Albion's Seed: Four British Folkways in America* (New York: Oxford University Press, 1989), 97, 508. Comparing the Puritan community of Andover, researched by Philip Greven in *Four Generations*, with a Quaker community in southeastern Pennsylvania, Barry Levy notes that Quakers, unlike Puritans, considered their children to be innocents rather than guilty sinners. They

kept their children at home longer, treated them with greater affection, and granted them more autonomy to choose a marriage partner than did the Puritans ("'Tender Plants': Quaker Farmers and Children in the Delaware Valley, 1681–1735," in *Colonial America: Essays in Politics and Social Development*, 5th ed., ed. Stanley N. Katz, John M. Murrin, and Douglas Greenburg [Boston: McGraw-Hill, 2001], 241–65).

31. Michael Davitt Bell, *Hawthorne and the Historical Romance of New England*, (Princeton, NJ: Princeton University Press, 1971), 5.

32. Nathaniel Hawthorne, "The Gentle Boy," in *Hawthorne: Selected Tales and Sketches*, 3rd ed., ed. Hyatt H. Waggoner (New York: Holt, Rinehart and Winston, 1950), 70. Hereafter cited by page number.

33. As Herbert points out, "Middle-class mothers employed the power of suffering love in their rearing of children," and the mother's role was elevated to such a level that "a woman's voice" became "the voice of God" (*Dearest Beloved*, 16).

34. Millicent Bell, *Hawthorne's View of the Artist* (Albany: State University of New York Press, 1962), 106.

35. Bell, *Hawthorne's View of the Artist*, 17.

36. Bell, *Hawthorne and the Historical Romance of New England*, 133.

PART FOUR

Childhood Studies

Theory, Practice, Pasts, and Futures

This section thinks critically about how childhood shapes our relationship with the past—personal, cultural, historical—and considers some ways in which the study of children may shape the future of classroom behavior, disciplinary exchange, and the academy's role in larger culture and society. Robin Bernstein's chapter offers an exciting theoretical model for bridging the gap archivists and others have struggled to negotiate between "real" children and adult representations of childhood. Taking on a question that animates much of childhood studies—and many contributions in this collection— Bernstein draws from performance theory to develop a way of thinking about the mutual constitution of rhetorical and historical children, to "narrate the processes" by which rhetorical and historical children "give body to each other." Bernstein's model cannily acknowledges both the controls brought to bear on actual children and the ways in which children can negotiate with and participate in these powerful constructions through performance. For her "childhood is best understood as a legible pattern of behaviors that comes into being *through* bodies." In other words, children and adults are continually improvising on the question of what a child is, and what childhood means through the "collaborative performances, the bodily practices, of people of all ages" (204). By bringing the insights of performance study and childhood studies into conversation, Bernstein illuminates our attachment to childhood as a remnant of a mourned, if often imaginary, past. "Performance, like abstract childhood," she argues, "is always already in the act of disappearing; performance and childhood are both paradoxically present only through their impending absence" (205).

Karen Sánchez-Eppler turns to the archives to illuminate how adults draw on children's work to define childhood itself. Her chapter explores how we carry the past both as history and as childhood by tracing the connections between archival practice and our nostalgia for the origin stories so often located in childhood. If "childhood is ephemeral by nature," she asks, "a stage to be outgrown," then "what can it teach about the tasks of keeping and cataloging?" (215). Ultimately, she suggests, "to think about childhood in the archives is to think about the tensions and collaborations between institutional and personal frames, control, and affection" (221). In so doing, Sánchez-Eppler provides a new way of thinking about the historical excavation of children's lives, as she brings the insights of childhood studies to bear on the assumptions that structure the archive containing remnants of those lives.

Lynne Vallone's chapter seeks to make childhood physically present in the academy by paying particular attention to the work of the classroom and by attending to the voices of students currently at the forefront of childhood studies scholarship. She explores possible futures for the field by digging into both the theory and practice of childhood studies as it is performed at her institution, Rutgers University, currently the only PhD-granting institution in childhood studies in the United States. She takes the collection's theoretical questions—about how to relate the archive to activism, about how to bring the humanities and social sciences into fruitful dialogue, and about how to negotiate the relationship between real and imagined childhoods—and puts them to the test within the work of administration and teaching. Perhaps most intriguing of all, Vallone includes the voices of a new generation of students who (unlike most of us working in the field today) have not only had the opportunity to train explicitly as childhood studies scholars but have had to face the challenge of such training. Being careful to acknowledge the difficulties of the multidisciplinary endeavor she believes childhood studies must be, Vallone ultimately argues that "'doing' childhood studies is a difficult and exhilarating enterprise that requires students and researchers not only to challenge entrenched notions of the dependent, vulnerable child (among other premises) but also to question and perhaps subvert the academy's assumptions about disciplinarity and methodological orthodoxy." Vallone argues, along with many of the authors of this volume, that the full potential of this paradigm-shifting mode of inquiry has still yet to be tapped. The process ahead is both exciting and intimidating—it requires relinquishing our own authority and privilege and our own investment in an adult-centered paradigm. In the end, it requires nothing less than rethinking what it means to be human.

Childhood as Performance

Robin Bernstein

The relationship between young people ("children") and the cultural construct of "childhood" constitutes a central problem in the field of childhood studies.[1] Is childhood a category of historical analysis that produces and manages adult power, as Caroline Levander, Lee Edelman, Kathryn Bond Stockton, Jacqueline Rose, James Kincaid, Anne Higonnet, Carolyn Steedman, and many others have argued? Or do the complicated lives of young people constantly deconstruct and reconstruct the abstract idealizations of childhood, as is suggested by the work of Karin Calvert, Howard P. Chudacoff, and Steven Mintz, among others?[2] Literary scholars who study "the child" conjured in texts as well as historians and social scientists who focus on the lived experiences of young people have reached an unsatisfying détente with a model in which "imagined" childhood shapes the lived experiences of "real" juveniles, who respond by unevenly colluding in or resisting their construction as "children." Childhood, in this model, is abstract and disembodied, while children are tangible and fleshy. The model may declare superficially, with the requisite nod to Judith Butler, that "real" children cannot preexist "imagined" childhood; however, the model persistently suggests that constructed childhood and juvenile humans exist in tension with if not opposition to one another. Because this model embeds opposition into the very foundation of childhood studies, the field has had difficulty accounting for the simultaneity and mutual constitution of children and childhood. The field struggles to narrate the processes by which children and childhood give body to each other.

That act of embodiment—the historical process through which childhood and children coproduce each other—is, I argue, a performance. Childhood is best understood as a legible pattern of behaviors that comes into being *through* bodies of all ages. The process of constructing childhood, of imagining childhood into being, occurs not only in literary and visual texts but in the collaborative performances, the bodily practices, of people of all ages. As this chapter shows, this paradigm clears space for thinking about the simultaneous, mutual construction of childhood and children's bodies as well as adulthood and adults' bodies.

The process by which childhood is performed into being is best described as surrogation, which Joseph R. Roach defines as the process by which "culture reproduces and re-creates itself."[3] Roach notes that the common definitions of performance (including the famous formulation, "repetition with a difference") "assume that performance offers a substitute for something else that preexists it"; a performing body "stands in for an elusive entity that it is not but that it must vainly aspire both to embody and to replace."[4] This practice of standing-in defines surrogation, and the body that stands in is called an "effigy." A performer's body is an effigy, as it bears and brings forth collectively remembered, meaningful gestures and thus surrogates for that which a community has lost. Children often serve as effigies that substitute uncannily for other, presumably adult, bodies and thus produce a surplus of meaning.[5] For example, four-year-old Shirley Temple engaged in surrogation when she adopted Mae West's swagger and purr to play a prostitute in the 1933 short "Polly Tix in Washington."

Children's ability to surrogate adulthood is well noted, often with dismay. Childhood *itself*, however, is best understood as a process of surrogation, an endless attempt to find, fashion, and impel substitutes to fill a void caused by the loss of a half-forgotten original. In this form of surrogation, the lost original doubles on the construction of childhood itself as a process of loss and forgetting. The Wordsworth-influenced romantic and later sentimental child was defined by its experience of being catapulted, through birth, out of God's presence and hurtled toward a lifetime of increasing separation from God. In "Ode: Intimations of Immortality," Wordsworth declares that "heaven lies about us in our infancy!" but immediately laments the loss of that aura: "Shades of the prison-house begin to close / Upon the growing

Boy." That growing boy travels from the light of heaven but remains within its radiance: he "still is Nature's Priest." Only the onset of adulthood blunts the senses to God's light: "At length the Man perceives it die away, / And fade into the light of common day."[6] It's all downhill from the first breath: to grow is to lose sacred childhood innocence, and each day the juvenile human develops, the essential child dies off a little. As Carolyn Steedman has shown, by the twentieth century, childhood became an emblem of a lost past, of a lost self, and of memory itself.[7]

Performance, like abstract childhood, is always already in the act of disappearing; performance and childhood are both paradoxically present only through their impending absence. As Peggy Phelan has influentially argued, live performance disappears as soon as it appears, and for this reason, mourning and loss necessarily infuse performance.[8] The childhood constructed by romantics and sentimentalists, too, is defined by loss and consternated memory. If surrogation is an attempt to "fit satisfactory alternates" into "the cavities created by loss through death and other forms of departure," then, in the case of childhood, that cavity is constructed through the "departure" of growth rather than by death.[9] Both romanticism and sentimentalism constructs the death of a child—emblematized by Little Eva—not as dispossessive but as preservative, as a freezing that paradoxically prevents the essential child quality from ever dying through maturation. Childhood is therefore best understood as an act of surrogation that compensates for losses incurred through growth.

A young person's body is the most frequently used effigy, or vehicle, for that surrogation. Juvenile bodies are not, however, the only effigies that surrogate childhood. Mature bodies can be used to surrogate childhood, as when a defense attorney vividly describes an accused criminal's youth in an effort to stimulate a jury's sympathy. Nonhuman things, too, can surrogate childhood, as is frequently the case with dolls. James Kincaid correctly asserts that any available body (juvenile human, mature human, nonhuman) can be "thrust into the performance" of childhood.[10] For Kincaid, juvenile actors play no special role in the performance of childhood because "any image, body, or being we can hollow out, purify, exalt, abuse, and locate sneakily in a field of desire will do for us as a 'child'"; therefore the "child is not, in itself, anything."[11] However, Kincaid mistakes the possibility of an alienated fit between effigy and surrogation (that is, a body other than a juvenile human's performing "childhood") for absence of a relationship between the actor and the performance. The relationship between effigy and surrogation is flexible and often perverse—not incidental, as in Kincaid's model, but uncanny.

The issue is that of casting. No body—juvenile, adult, or thing—can perfectly surrogate the ideals of childhood. No act of surrogation fully succeeds in restoring the half-remembered, imagined original, but different bodies partially succeed and yet fall short in importantly different ways. Juvenile bodies cast in the surrogation of childhood have the special ability to naturalize childhood, to assert an essential correspondence between childhood and the young human body—that is, to blur any distinction between children and childhood. Nonjuvenile bodies have other uses and abilities, and such effigies are not necessarily miscast in the surrogation of childhood. A visual mismatch between a mature body and a performance of childhood can, for example, redefine a group out of adulthood and define the power associated with that categorization. This was the case when romantic racialists cast adult African Americans as "childlike." In 1844, for example, the abolitionist Reverend Orville Dewey argued that Negro "nature is singularly childlike, affectionate, docile, and patient," and that such "inferiority" was "but an increased appeal to pity and generosity."[12] This casting of "the Negro" as "childlike" was anything but accidental; it strategically sutured abolition to white supremacy. Within such casting, however, a nonjuvenile actor is likely to exert agency in an attempt to undermine or at least complicate the production of meaning; thus the performance may produce multiple and often self-contradictory meanings.

Juvenile, nonjuvenile, and nonhuman bodies serve, then, as imperfectly useful and usefully imperfect effigies in the surrogation of childhood. These three kinds of effigies coordinate with each other, as becomes clear through a close reading of a recent televisual performance. In January 2006, at the twelfth annual Screen Actors Guild Awards Dakota Fanning, a blonde child actress who was then twelve years old, presented Shirley Temple Black with the Screen Actors Guild (SAG) Life Achievement Award. In the televised awards ceremony, Fanning held a Shirley Temple doll and explained that it was "a part of my mom's doll collection when she was my age. The day I was born, it became mine, and has always sat in my room. My mom loved her, I love her, and I know someday, my daughter will, too. . . . I'm the fourth generation in my family who's loved [Shirley Temple's] films and admired her career of generous public service that followed."[13]

Lifetime achievement awards mark longevity; they are by definition that which a child cannot receive. A child therefore seems an odd choice to present such an award. Fanning, however, was uncannily appropriate in her inappropriateness. As a white, blonde, dimpled child actress who excites excessive desire, Fanning refilled Shirley Temple's particular mold of girlhood. By surrogating Shirley Temple blond girlhood, Dakota Fanning gave life to the awardee's greatest past achievement.[14] The speech (scripted, certainly, by a professional writer) repeatedly located Fanning as Shirley Temple's heir: the Shirley Temple doll, Fanning's speech claimed, descended from mother to daughter, and with that effigy Fanning inherited a tradition of performance and four generations' "love." As Temple's blonde surrogate, Fanning made Shirley Temple present in a way that Shirley Temple Black, the adult, could not. Shirley Temple's extraordinary performance of girlhood resounded through Dakota Fanning, and Fanning, in turn, resurrected that bluest eye of girlhood in the pale, never quite sufficient yet always excessive shadow of Shirley Temple Black, who is and always has been brown eyed.

Even as Dakota Fanning gave life to Temple's greatest achievement—the depression-era actress's performance of girlhood—she also marked Temple's greatest failure: the inability to remain a child. Fanning, at the age of twelve, teetered between childhood and adolescence and thus referenced both childhood and its loss. Her costume reflected that liminal status: the dress sported childish bows and a Peter Pan collar, and the tight bodice highlighted Fanning's board-flat chest, but the dress's elegant long sleeves and floor-length skirt (a contrast with Temple's famously short peek-a-boo pinafores) suggested young womanhood. Fanning's scripted references to her own infancy and her imagined future maternity called attention, too, to Fanning's lost babyhood and impending exit from childhood. In but a few years, Fanning literally announced, she would be able to surrogate Shirley Temple no more uncannily than Shirley Temple Black could, and it would be time to bequeath the doll along with the tradition of performance.[15]

The ever-growing juvenile body—Dakota Fanning's or Shirley Temple's—is an unstable and therefore permanently inadequate effigy for childhood. That inadequacy in no way impedes the process of surrogation, which paradoxically *relies* on failure. Shirley Temple's disappearance into Shirley Temple Black necessitated the emergence of someone like Dakota Fanning—much as Shirley Temple substituted for her now-forgotten predecessors, including the child star Cordelia Howard, who originated the stage role of Little Eva.[16]

The process of surrogation is one of repeated attempts at substitution, and these repetitions with differences are necessitated by each iteration's inexact fit with the imagined original. Each ill fit compels yet another performance. The juvenile body is a naturalistic effigy through which to surrogate childhood, but that body continually grows, incrementally and inevitably losing the state of childhood. Therefore the most naturalistic effigy is also, in its very nature, a vexingly inadequate one, and this inadequacy urgently feeds the process of surrogation. A reciprocal action emerges in which the ever-growing and therefore inadequate effigy of the juvenile body continually surrogates childhood but cannot contain that surrogation. The surrogation overflows into other effigies, including nonjuvenile bodies and nonhuman things such as dolls.[17]

At the SAG Awards, three bodies—those of Shirley Temple Black, Dakota Fanning, and the doll—each substituted differently, and differently imperfectly, for Shirley Temple, the award's true recipient (Temple Black's service as Republican dignitary and ambassador to Czechoslovakia and Ghana notwithstanding). Of these three effigies, only one will never grow and therefore never lose childhood. The doll, even more than Fanning or Temple Black, memorialized the doll-like perfection of Shirley Temple herself. The doll retained that which Temple Black lost and that which Fanning displayed herself to be in the act of losing. The doll, juxtaposed with Temple Black, constituted "before and after" shots and thus measured the distance between Shirley Temple and Shirley Temple Black; it, even more than Fanning, emblematized Temple's achievement and Temple Black's failure in the surrogation of childhood.

Throughout her performance at the SAG Awards, Fanning clutched the Shirley Temple doll at the calves and thus duplicated the posture of an actor receiving an Academy Award. Recruited into the role of an Oscar, the doll surrogated not only Shirley Temple but also the sign of virtuoso acting itself. By simultaneously surrogating for Temple, girlhood, and achievement in acting, the doll articulated the performative foundation of girlhood. And as the doll doubled with an Oscar, Fanning stepped into the role of Oscar recipient. Fanning's lines bestowed the Life Achievement Award on Shirley Temple Black, but the girl's posturing body claimed Shirley Temple's legacy—including Temple's Oscar—for herself.[18]

The performance of childhood is sharply racialized. Especially before the civil rights movement, white children had served as effigies in the popular performance of childhood, while children of color, especially African American children, were forcibly excluded from the surrogation of childhood. This vicious exclusion and its psychological effects constitute the central theme of Toni Morrison's novel *The Bluest Eye*, set in 1941. Claudia, Morrison's child narrator, hates Shirley Temple–like blond baby dolls, and she tears them apart in an effort to find that hidden quality that makes the dolls so loveable—a quality, Claudia knows, that she and other black girls are always already disqualified from possessing. The literary critic Ann duCille writes that she, unlike, Claudia, "didn't have the good sense to hate" Shirley Temple. "The truth is," duCille wrote, "much of the time I wanted to be Shirley Temple."[19] In the second quarter of the twentieth century, when duCille was an African American girl of about eight or nine years old, she asked to have her hair set into "ringlets like Shirley Temple's." After a long and painful process, she looked into a mirror and saw a "gap-toothed, black face that looked back at me from beneath a rat's nest of tight, greased coils [that] was anything but cute." DuCille then "understood, as only a child can, that mine was a self-inflicted homeliness, begot of my own betrayal: in attempting to look like the white wunderkind, I succeeded only in making my black difference ridiculous."[20] In other words, DuCille volunteered her own body as an effigy by which to surrogate Shirley Templeness, and the gap between her body and the imagined original only served to make DuCille's body appear, in her own view, "ridiculous." DuCille realized then that Shirley Temple's "adorable perfection—her snow-whiteness—was constructed against my blackness, my racial difference made ridiculous by the stammering and shuffling of the 'little black rascals,' 'darkies,' and 'pickaninnies' who populated her films."[21] These literary and historical girls—the fictional Claudia and the future critic duCille—both understood that the power of Shirley Temple's blond "perfection" derived crucially from its ability to exclude black children, to relegate black children to degraded performances as little rascals or supernumerary "pickaninnies." This racist exclusion of black children from idealized childhood is the flip side of equally racist libel of African American adults as "childlike Negroes."

The political stakes of black children's exclusion from idealized childhood become especially visible in a late nineteenth-century racist print in which nine naked African American toddlers are captioned "alligator bait" (fig. 5). Each of the nine toddlers is photographed in a moment of ugliness: the first from the left pokes his ear, the second glowers, and the fourth cries.

Figure 5. McCrary and Branson, *Alligator Bait*, ca. 1897. International Center of Photography, Daniel Cowin Collection, New York, 1990.

Attention focuses, however, on the fifth toddler, who occupies the center of the photograph. This toddler stands upright, with a protruding stomach contrasting with skinny shoulders and arms. His or her deeply lined face looks fearfully toward something—presumably an alligator—outside the camera's frame. The nonplump body and the lined face combine with the upright stance to suggest adulthood or even old age rather than childhood.

One wonders how hard the anonymous photographer worked to make each of these toddlers appear as unappealing as possible. Late nineteenth-century studio photography of children routinely and reflexively centered on cuteness.[22] By constructing these children as noncute, this posed photograph strains against its own historically located tropes to exclude these toddlers from the visual cues that simultaneously announced "innocence" and "childhood." Through constructed ugliness, the photograph dislocates these juvenile humans from the surrogation of childhood: this photograph frames a white supremacist "joke" by de-childing African American toddlers and recategorizing them as adults, food ("bait"), and animals (that is, as prey).[23] The photograph uses the human bodies of the toddlers as effigies to *resist* surrogating childhood—to *disappear* their toddlerness—in the service of white supremacy. The visible juvenile bodies conspicuously mark the space that adorably innocent toddlers could have occupied; each body, stark against a blank nonbackground, outlines a hole, an absence, an active exclusion from what I have called, elsewhere, racial innocence. The living children photographed are useful to this image's ideological project exactly to the extent that the photograph makes those children's childhood disappear.

Childhood is extraordinarily flexible and pluripotent: childhood can appear and disappear in adult or juvenile bodies, and the call to "protect the children" can add affective weight to any political argument. I have argued here and elsewhere that performance is a key source of these abilities. Performance, like childhood, is a dense engagement of loss and restoration, of remembering through forgetting and forgetting through remembering. Performance does not make children or childhood alone; rather, it is through performance that children and childhood coemerge and co-constitute each other. Acknowledgment of this configuration relieves the perceived opposition between historically located children and textually based childhood; thus performance theory seals a fissure within the foundation of childhood studies.

Notes

1. Portions of this chapter appeared previously in *Racial Innocence: Performing American Childhood from Slavery to Civil Rights* (New York: New York University Press, 2011) and are reprinted with permission of the author and publisher.

2. A few scholars, including Karen Sánchez-Eppler and Mary Niall Mitchell, have successfully argued from both positions simultaneously.

3. Joseph R. Roach, *Cities of the Dead: Circum-Atlantic Performance* (New York: Columbia University Press, 1996), 2.

4. Roach, *Cities of the Dead*, 3.

5. Roach, *Cities of the Dead*, 36.

6. William Wordsworth, "Ode: Intimations of Immortality," in *Selected Poems and Prefaces*, ed. Jack Stillinger (Boston: Houghton Mifflin, 1965), 188.

7. Carolyn Steedman, *Strange Dislocations: Childhood and the Idea of Human Interiority, 1780–1930* (Cambridge, MA: Harvard University Press, 1995).

8. On loss as constitutive of performance, see Peggy Phelan, *Unmarked: The Politics of Performance* (New York: Routledge, 1992), 146–66.

9. Roach, *Cities of the Dead*, 2.

10. James R. Kincaid, *Child-Loving: The Erotic Child and Victorian Culture* (New York: Routledge, 1992), 5.

11. Kincaid, *Child-Loving*, 5.

12. Orville Dewey, *A Discourse on Slavery and the Annexation of Texas* (New York: Charles Francis, 1844), 10. On romantic racialists' configuration of African American adults as childlike, see George M. Fredrickson, *The Black Image in the White Mind: The Debate on Afro-American Character and Destiny, 1817–1914* (New York: Harper and Row, 1971), 97–129, and Sarah N. Roth, "The Mind of a Child: Images of African Americans in Early Juvenile Fiction," *Journal of the Early Republic* 25.1 (2005): 93–95.

13. See www.youtube.com/watch?v=M1cbTpgZGyo.

14. See Roach, *Cities of the Dead*, 78–85, on celebrities as effigies.

15. Other child actors whom James Kincaid locates in Shirley Temple's genealogy of "big-eyed, kissy-lipped blonde" figures include Jackie Coogan, Tatum O'Neal, Ricky Schroeder, Drew Barrymore, and Macaulay Culkin (*Child-Loving*, 369).

16. On Shirley Temple in relation to Little Eva, see Lauren Berlant, *The Female Complaint: The Unfinished Business of Sentimentality in American Culture* (Durham, NC: Duke University Press, 2008), 49–50, 53–54, Patricia Turner, *Ceramic Uncles and Celluloid Mammies: Black Images and their Influence on Culture* (New York: Anchor, 1994), 83, and Jim O'Loughlin, "Articulating *Uncle Tom's Cabin,*" *New Literary History* 31.3 (2000): 586–89. On Cordelia Howard, see my *Racial Innocence*, 113–17, 119–23, and 125–28.

17. I focus on the performance of childhood as it travels among human bodies and nonhuman things, but other scholars consider the porous line between children and animals. See, for example, Lesley Ginsberg, "Of Babies, Beasts, and Bondage: Slavery and the Question of Citizenship in Antebellum American Children's Literature," in *The American Child: A Cultural Studies Reader*, ed. Caroline F. Levander and Carol J. Singley (New Brunswick, NJ: Rutgers University Press, 2003), 85–105.

18. In 1934, the Academy of Motion Picture Arts and Sciences gave Temple a "special Oscar," which the girl reportedly placed "on her shelf next to the rest of her dolls" (Kevin Starr, *The Dream Endures: California Enters the 1940s* [New York: Oxford University Press, 2002], 259).

19. Ann duCille, "The Shirley Temple of My Familiar," *Transition* 73 (1997): 21.

20. duCille, "The Shirley Temple of My Familiar," 21.

21. duCille, "The Shirley Temple of My Familiar," 21.

22. Lori Merish superbly historicizes cuteness in the context of commodity culture. See her "Cuteness and Commodity Aesthetics: Tom Thumb and Shirley Temple," in *Freakery: Cultural Spectacles of the Extraordinary Body*, ed. Rosemarie Garland Thomson (New York: New York University Press, 1996), 185–203.

23. A juvenile simultaneously surrogating both childhood and adulthood sometimes reads as cute, as when Shirley Temple imitates her character's gruff grandfather in *The Little Colonel*. Such potential cuteness disappears in this print, however, through the construction of the toddlers as food and animals.

In the Archives of Childhood

Karen Sánchez-Eppler

In this chapter I argue that the ideas, practices, and institutions of historical preservation reverberate with conceptions of childhood. I find these connections to be mutually illuminating, productive not only for the comparatively new field of childhood studies but also for the many disciplinary and institutional structures through which we have tried to locate origins and to access, understand, preserve, and recall a time that is gone. For scholarship in the humanities the "archival turn" proves to have much in common with the study of childhood: both elaborate the repositories of our cultural and personal pasts. In many ways, for each of us, childhood is the archive, a treasure box of the formative and the forgotten. Yet until the last few decades, both our archives and our childhoods had remained largely undertheorized sites of origin. I strive here to articulate the threads of connection, both theoretical and practical, that weave between them.

I untie the ribbon and open the handmade folder with a needlepoint bouquet of flowers painstakingly stitched onto its canvas cover, revealing a single sheet of paper decorated with drawings of flowers and birds and inscribed with a short poem (fig. 6). The date, 1856, waves on a small banner at the top of the sheet.

TO MY
dear schoolteacher

emblazoned at the bottom explains something of the purpose and provenance of this obviously cherished object. This artifact, labeled "To My Dear

Figure 6. "To My Dear Schoolteacher," manuscript, 1865. Courtesy of the Cotsen Children's Library, Department of Rare Books and Special Collections, Princeton University Library.

Schoolteacher" and referenced in the catalogue of the Cotsen Children's Library at Princeton University as a manuscript that dates to 1856 whose provenance is likely the United States, was acquired and catalogued as an individual item. It did not enter the library's manuscript collection together with other related papers, personal or institutional. Consequently it remains a singular artifact, an odd, child-made thing that has wended its way from some school room to this library's special collections, from child to teacher to who knows how many other familial, commercial, and antiquarian hands before it reached this green library folder and now this chapter. I want to begin with this strange, charming thing as a way to make specific, immediate, tangible, many of the theoretical questions at stake in this project—but I know that the beguiling promise of grasping what is, of course, gone is a prime symptom of the malady Derrida diagnoses as "mal d'archive," the infectious desire to locate and possess origins.[1] The traces of childhood found in archives and special collections may tend toward the ephemeral—the scrap and the scribble as well as the tome—and thus put pressure on the claims and nature of preservation and valuation. What constitutes the trivial as trivial? If childhood is ephemeral by nature—a stage to be outgrown—then what can it teach about the tasks of keeping and cataloging? What Antoinette Burton calls "the radical inaccessibility of the Truth of the past" has long been recognized as the basic condition of historical research.[2] It is that inaccessibility and its attendant yearnings that prompt the search for the evidence of documents and records, as well as the acts of imagination, interpretation, and narration that transform these shreds into the weft and warp of "history."

In childhood studies the insistence on the lost, hollow, absent status of the child, who can only ever enter this scholarly field as a product of adult imagining, something we adults project and shape with our desire and our study, has proved an extremely fruitful rubric for scholars of childhood across a wide range of humanities disciplines. Jacqueline Rose's insistence on the "impossibility of children's fiction" has had the salutary effect of keeping scholars warily attuned to how adult concerns—from sex to money to politics—structure the genre, and despite the claim of possession that the apostrophe may suggest, most scholars of "children's literature" acknowledge that these books don't really belong to children at all.[3] Similarly, Philippe Ariès's account of "the invention of childhood" in the modern era, while frequently critiqued in its particulars, continues to suffuse historical inquiry with an awareness that the "child" studied is as much an idea as a person.[4] "The image we have of childhood now is just that—an image," Anne Higonnet explains, but her account of how childhood is pictured argues not only for the revaluation of childhood as an artistic subject but even more for changes in how society views and treats children.[5] Much of the force of childhood studies as a mode of cultural critique has derived from unmasking the ideological stakes and benefits of evoking childhood, detailing how often and easily the figure of "the semiotically adhesive child" has been wielded in the name of futurity to sanction any and all political projects, including our own scholarly ventures.[6] Children's limited agency affects both institutional practices and historical interpretation: "We [historians] don't have the advantage of children setting their own political agendas," Barbara Beatty and Julia Grant observe. "Most have been set for them by adults, whether familial or official."[7] One thing Higonnet hopes might be learned from recent trends in the photographic depiction of children is the possibility of "valuing children for what they are instead of for what they are not."[8] Archival work in childhood studies should not deny the elusiveness of childhood and the inequalities of power between adult scholar and child object that vexes all work in this field, but it does strive to mitigate that absence, to locate in the historical record the child's voice and aspirations, to find traces of what children "are." In efforts to negotiate the tensions between the discourses of childhood promulgated by adult desires and agendas, on the one hand, and the lived experiences of children, on the other, archival work has proved a potent resource. Yet in claiming this resource it is important to recognize the extent to which similar motivations of nostalgia, desire, fantasy, and power underlie archival practice itself. It is my hope that examining the intersection of archival practice and childhood studies can illuminate the attractions and limitations of both.

In its more precise usage "archive" refers to a state repository of official documents: the records of the courts, the lists compiled by government bureaucracies, and the systems of classification that store and catalogue them are all discrete expressions of power. The creation and maintenance of such records has proved a defining characteristic of the modern state and the plumbing of them the definitive task of social history.[9] These sorts of materials have proved very rich resources for the history of childhood, precisely because state efforts at control, responsibilities for care, and commitment to modernization have so often been designed to protect the young. Thus, for example, in the early years of the twentieth century as the Ottoman Empire began providing salary grants to foundlings and wet-nurses, the records accrued at the Başbakanlık Osmanlı arşivi (the Prime Ministry's Ottoman Archives) make it possible to trace patterns of child abandonment with a remarkable level of detail.[10] Court cases, welfare records, and the reports social workers made for the Massachusetts Society for the Prevention of Cruelty to Children, provide Linda Gordon with an archive of family violence, recording child abuse, neglect, and incest.[11] Ann Laura Stoler's studies of the colonial episteme, and particularly her efforts to trace its "affective states," rest on ministry accounts of educational policies and proposals aimed at the young. The reliance on government records "does not mean that one is wholly bound by concerns of state," Stoler explains, and drawing on court records that betray anxieties about the corrupting influences of native nursemaids and mothers and government reports such as "Government Care for Upbringing and Education on Behalf of the European Population of the Netherland Indies" (the subject heading for one collection of documents in the Nationaal archief), Stoler traces the dynamics of Dutch colonialism through its treatment of children.[12] The prevalence of records of childhood in government archives may offer one measure of how taking responsibility for actual children can legitimize and naturalize the protective authority of the state. Thus it is not surprising that Stoler, one of the most innovative and insightful theorists of archival practice, centers her archival research on the double dependencies of colonialism and childhood. The questions of politics and power at stake in archival work and in childhood studies are often one and the same. Sometimes, indeed, the very production of the archives proves the work of children; as Stoler wryly notes, "'Indo' youths, barred from rising in the civil service ranks, were the scribes who made the system run."[13]

Marlene Manoff, formerly a collections strategist at MIT Libraries, discusses the "inflation of the term 'archives'" and acknowledges that "even librarians and archivists have become somewhat careless in their use of the term," so that it now frequently refers to a wide range of documents and collecting institutions, including, museums, libraries and, of course, "digital archives."[14] It is in this broadening sense of the archive as any space that collects evidence of the past, preserving it for future study, that "To My Dear Schoolteacher" can be considered an archival object. And it is in this sense, too, that the archival character of childhood itself becomes apparent. Of course, for many archivists, librarians, and curators the distinctions between these various sorts of repositories with their very different policies and practices of access and preservation remain crucial. The tensions between the more precise usage of "archive" to denote governmental and administrative records and the more elastic sense of the term as a repository for the stuff of the past, as a figure for psyche and memory, matter, and I return to them throughout this chapter. But I want to start by marking the provocations of their interconnectedness. In *States of Fantasy*, Jacqueline Rose notes that "the word 'state' has a psychological meaning long before its modern-day sense of polity, or rather one which trails beneath the shifting public and political face of the word," and on that basis, she argues that "the private and public attributes of the concept 'state' are not opposites but shadows—outer and inner faces precisely—of each other."[15] The national desires of Zionism that Rose interrogates in this project echo other "Neverlands." The pinning down of shadows also inaugurates *Peter Pan*, the subject of Rose's first book, which is itself very much about fantasies of possession: "If children's fiction builds an image of the child inside the book, it does so in order to secure the child who is outside the book, the one who does not come so easily within its grasp."[16]

Archives, in their promise of material evidence, something to "grasp," offer the historical record as a literal res publica. Carolyn Steedman's witty and provocative characterization of the archival labors of the social historian as an engagement with "dust" simultaneously registers "history in its modern mode [as] just one long exercise of the deep satisfaction of *finding things*" and notes the crucial absence that structures all historical analysis as "the space shaped by what was and now is no more."[17] In her account, the archival turn needs to negotiate the relations between the possibilities and limitations of material evidence, to note both the acts of historical imagination that fill the gap of the missing as well as the wonderful specificity of stuff. In Steedman's scholarship prior to *Dust: The Archive and Cultural History* the "lost object" most poignantly and repeatedly had "come to assume the shape and form of a child," indeed of a particular child, the eight-year-old "Little Watercress Girl," whom Henry Mayhew interviewed near Farringdon in the winter of 1850–51.[18] This seller of watercress, with her precise, matter-of-fact account of family economy and her work-filled days, appears very fleetingly in *Dust*; there is a single passing reference to "a floor scrubbed 'two or three times a week'" that is only resonant to those familiar with Steedman's previous work.[19] But in "The Tidy House," *Landscape for a Good Woman*, "The Watercress Seller," and *Strange Dislocations* the brief transcript of Mayhew's interview with this girl figures, as Steedman acknowledges, as an "obsession."[20] "My own romance," she states, "is that I may find this child, that there is enough evidence in her narrative, that there is enough detail of her life and the life of her household, to trace her, perhaps through census material, or through an as-yet-unfound survey of street trading in Clerkenwell. . . . The Little Watercress Girl is what I want: the past, which is lost and which I cannot have: my own childhood. She is my fantasy child; and in a different way she was Mayhew's fantasy child too."[21] That romance, fantasy, wanting, is offered by Steedman as the rarely visible ground of historical research itself. Her yearning for a census record that would give this girl an address and a name, for some survey to verify her as real, is palpable here, even though clearly none of these archival lists could possibly provide as rich an account of the girl's lived experience as the one Steedman reads from Mayhew's interview. The longing that permeates Steedman's multiple retellings of the watercress seller insists on the deep interconnection between archival work and childhood studies: "Evidence from children, and about children in the past, throws into relief general problems of historical interpretation. History, as a methodology, is concerned with the reconstruction, interpretation, and use of the past, so it may be as well that it has something to say about that past that occupies all of us, whether we are historians or not—the personal past of each individual childhood."[22] In *Dust* Steedman takes a wonderful, contagious, pleasure in laughing at Derrida, but in many ways her own account of archival labors is far more precise and insistent than his in depicting archival research as "an irrepressible desire to return to the origin, a homesickness, a nostalgia for the return to the most archaic place of absolute commencement."[23] Victoria Rosner seeks to uncover the psychological ground of Steedman's work, and there is, of course, a similar psychoanalytic underlay to Derrida's initial delivery of "Archive Fever" at the opening of the Freud Museum in London. I am myself far more interested in the question of what this recognition of the fantasy child as the impetus for archival research can teach us about both archival and childhood studies than I am in tracing any specific personal psychological imperative, but Rosner is surely right to wonder: "When the *material* enters in, can the *mater* be far behind?"[24]

So let us return to the material, to this bit of childhood flotsam saved in a folder in Princeton. In the remainder of this chapter, I focus on this single child-made object, employing its specificity to articulate some of the connections and tensions between childhood and archival work. Andrea Immel, curator of the Cotsen Children's Library at Princeton University, informs me that this manuscript was purchased by Lloyd E. Cotsen in 1995 from Ross Craig, an antiquarian bookseller in Medina, New York. The Cotsens began assembling their remarkable collection of children's literature in the 1960s in order to create a "family library" that would reflect "two parents' desire to find things the family would enjoy reading together," and JoAnne Cotsen sometimes made notes in these early purchases recording her four children's various responses to these books.[25] Thus the Cotsen collection has at its root an interest in what might interest children, and Lloyd Cotsen augmented his historical collection of children's literature with educational toys and things produced by children themselves. As Immel observes, the scholarly and market attention to children's books and things had burgeoned in the 1990s, so that Cotsen's purchase of this and similar manuscripts can be understood as part of a larger "sea change . . . in the status of juvenilia."[26]

Archives hold what has been thought worth collecting. On the most practical level, childhood and most especially child-made things have generally not been deemed significant in this way, and so they tend to land in archives less as the result of intentional acts of preservation than because someone, at some point, did not bother to throw them away. The only situation that seems to prompt the self-conscious collection and archival preservation of childhood artifacts is the heartbreak of an early death. Grief often prompts families to gather and preserve with curatorial care things that conjure a beloved child, and much of the childhood writings in the Cotsen Collection (the Mary Chrystie Papers, Frederick Locke's Scrapbook) were initially preserved by such memorializing gestures, kept as tokens of loss. Yet it can be difficult for adult-centered institutional structures to know what to make of even lovingly cherished traces of childhood. Databases and library catalogues rarely treat age as a category of classification. Gillian Adams observed in 1992 that the MLA bibliography only included 52 entries under "juvenilia"; that number has now expanded to 241, though the list is still largely confined to studies of the childhood writings of Jane Austen and the Brontës.[27] Immel notes that there is not as yet even a taxonomy of the types of children's manuscripts and no guide to the institutions, like the Cotsen, that purposefully collect them, nor to the childhood holdings of the many institutions that have accumulated such materials less intentionally.[28] The housing of the Cotsen collection at a major research university and its continuing, indeed increasing, commitment to procuring writing by children and of cataloguing its holdings in a manner that makes such materials visible and accessible is a rare boon for the study of childhood; it is also, in itself, an instance of how archival practice affirms and produces value.

Records of childhood and records made by children have been housed in archives and library special collections all along, although they have usually been classified in a manner that tends to obscure rather than highlight their presence. Children generally appear in such collections in two ways: first, as already noted, children are tabulated in the records of institutions charged with the protection, punishment, and education of the young, and, second, children's things and writings can be conserved on the fringes of collections of individual or family papers, producing a residue of domestic life that accompanies the valuable work of adults, for whose prominence these materials have been saved. Even the memorial collections of children who have died tend to be contained by these contexts, preserved as the result of institutional roles or family prestige. Thus to think about childhood in the archives is to think about the tensions and collaborations between institutional and personal frames, control and affection. This odd single object, "To My Dear Schoolteacher," does not quite belong under either rubric but instead vividly conflates them. The student who created this sheet initially labeled the page "TO MY DEAR SCHOOL," taking great care to decorate and color each capital letter and centering the words, all traits that imitate typography. As such, the phrase mimics in its appearance the titling practices of books and newspapers, the layout of commercial signs, the names inscribed over the doors of buildings. It is an individual, handmade thing, and one that stresses intimacy and affection in its address, but it draws its aesthetic from the public sphere. Later some hand—a child's? an adult's? we cannot be sure which—corrects this title and makes the page address not an institution but a person, not the "school" but the "schoolteacher." If it is the student who made this correction, it suggests an interest in addressing the "dear" teacher that is stronger than the desire for a tidy presentation. If it is the teacher who inserted this change, it suggests a strict standard of accuracy, a willingness to correct even an expression of fondness. Thus the change in address alters in subtle but substantial ways the status of this gift and the varieties of allegiance and affection that inform its handiwork. Moreover, squiggles at the bottom of the page just below these words appear to hide some additional writing. The letters beneath these penciled swirls are difficult to decipher, but I believe both obliterated lines make the same request "Give me if you can." Who asks? What is wanted? And why is that desire effaced?

The obstacles to sorting out agency and intention exemplified in these acts of correction prove central characteristics both of archival work and of childhood studies. The evidentiary value attributed to the archive largely derives from the sense that what it holds was produced and collected for purposes quite different from those of the scholar: "The Historian who goes to the Archive must always be an unintended reader, will always read what was never intended for his or her eyes," Steedman avers with a certain ironic excess.[29] Arjun Appadurai refers to this attitude toward archives as an ultimately "ethical view" that presumes "the innocence of the archives."[30] Implicit in most work in childhood studies has been an interrogation of the presumptions of childhood innocence, and, similarly, recent theorizing of the archives has argued for a more self-critical, no longer simply innocent, assessment of the processes of preservation and classification. Michel Foucault's account of the archive as "the law of what can be said, the system that governs the appearance of statements as unique events," insists that the archives can never be a neutral container of the past and that the systematization, classification, and design that the archive imposes on the documents it holds is the essence of discursive formation.[31] The point for Steedman, Appadurai, and Stoler as they strive to read not "against" but "along the archival grain" is to make these material and discursive conditions part of the story of archival work. In childhood studies the child's dependent status complicates all efforts to identify childhood agency or to distinguish between desire and obedience.[32] Errors and alterations are such potent nodes of meaning in children's writing, precisely because they so visibly mark moments of choice. But even if we could be certain that it was the student, not the teacher, who made this shift of address, how could we distinguish the desire to dedicate this sheet to the teacher from the desire to evade a reprimand or correction for not having done so? And what sorts of intention suffuse the effaced request "Give me if you can"? Educational policies and practices ensure, as Steedman puts it, that children "take part in the process of their own socialization."[33] Within the institutional strictures of school, and indeed of adult and child power imbalances more generally, and even more within institutional structures where it is inevitably adult acts and decisions that preserve child-made things, any claim of agency or assertion of desire just has to be hedged around with mediations.

Indeed this page raises issues of control and order in every element of its design. The sheet is decorated with drawings of natural things, flowers and birds, but they are arranged with great symmetry, and interspersed with them are numerous ornamental frames, so that there is no illusion that anything has grown or is perched on this page: nature is arranged. Thus the tension between the natural and the constructed that has long been so central to our discourses of childhood are vividly enacted on this sheet of paper. There is nothing surprising about this; conventions are, after all, conventional. But that doesn't mean that they don't have to be learned, and this page bears the marks of this tutelary process.

At the center of the page is a poem, written in careful cursive on hand-drawn lines. The discipline of penmanship, of learning to write neat and straight, is clearly legible in this gift to a teacher.

> In the schoolroom while we stay
> There is work enough to do
> Study Study through the day
> Keep our lessons all in view
> Theres no time to wast or lose
> Every moment we should use
> For the hours are gliding fast
> Soon our schoolday will pass

The pressures of history and loss, of hours fast gliding away, suffuse this poem. "You are nostalgic for childhood whilst it's happening to you" Steedman observes, and this poem speaks of a need to cherish a time the speaker knows will not last.[34] Allison James emphasizes the importance of distinguishing between the "*time of childhood*—the ways in which childhood as a discrete period of the life course is embedded within the social fabric of any particular culture" and "*time for children*," by which she means how time is "experienced by children in their daily lives."[35] Certainly the time this child spent in the production of this gift with its elaborate needlepoint cover, tidy penmanship, and ornate decorations must have been slow and attentive, quite different from the temporal ideas of a fleeting childhood voiced in this poem.

Mayhew's difficulties in understanding the watercress seller largely stem, in Steedman's accounts, from his middle-class nineteenth-century idealization of childhood as a period characterized by play not work. Just as there is a disjunction between experiential and nostalgic engagements with time, there is a gap between the watercress seller's sense of herself and her labor and Mayhew's conceptions of childhood. This poem evidently celebrates the kind of work that Mayhew's idealizations did sanction for children: "Study Study." As something presented to a "dear schoolteacher" and produced with elaborate care, this poem valorizes the work of school, but it also clearly marks it as "work." The poem is well aware of the enormous quantity of things that a child must learn, and in both the evident care taken in forming these letters and the complete absence of punctuation, this page embodies the onerous demands of literacy. A more disgruntled undertow runs beneath the celebratory message of this verse. The reminder that "theres no time to wast" conjures the factory idioms of production, and it is striking that it is this familiar line of reprimand that proves hardest for this student to spell. Such discontent with the work requirements of each day's "stay" in the schoolroom is most potently expressed in the poem's rhymes. "Day" and "stay" surely conjure a "play" that the poem must resist and repress. Even more telling is the flawed rhyme and meter of the final couplet.

This poem is not, in fact, an original composition, but rather a set piece probably taken from Charles Northend's *The Little Speaker, and Juvenile Reader: Being a Collection of Pieces in Prose, Poetry, and Dialogue, Designed for Exercises in Speaking, and for Occasional Reading in Primary Schools.* In Northend's collection the stanza ends with perfect rhyme and cadence, in a line that confirms the nostalgic, celebratory meanings of this poem and evokes the precious, fleeting qualities of childhood:

> For the hours are gliding fast,
> Soon our school-days will be past.[36]

But that is not what the student penned, and although such a nostalgic celebration of school remains evident on this sheet and is appropriate to the occasion of this gift, the line that ends the manuscript shifts temporal modes to raise instead a surreptitious hope that the school bell will ring, and all this work and study will be over: "Soon our schoolday will pass." In this child's copying, the wistful sense of ephemeral school days tugs against the lived experience of the school day as interminable. The main business of not only scriveners but all sorts of clerks, copying was among the most valuable practical skills taught in nineteenth-century schools. Good penmanship and accuracy could assure jobs in the expanding white-collar ranks, and this student's script is generally even and careful. Moreover, copying was an esteemed pedagogical strategy of the period, grounded in a firm belief that not only literacy and job skills but virtue and character were most surely produced through acts of imitation and memorization. "If we commit a piece to memory, we shall be more likely to understand its meaning," one boy explains in a dialogue included in Northend's *Little Speaker*, "and if we all remember it and act accordingly," his friend adds, "we shall do much better than we have done."[37] Confident that copying would inscribe the practiced words in each student's heart and behavior, copybooks and anthologies for declamation always insist that their selected texts are "calculated to have a good moral influence."[38]

The shared desire for origins discernable in the valuing of childhood and of archives privileges the "authentic" and dismisses the copy. I want to suggest, conversely, that a richer assessment of the derivative act of copying may be important to understanding both archival work and childhood studies. This poem may seem less interesting and valuable, now that we know that this child did not compose it, the student's own original thoughts and feelings legible only perhaps in the mistakes—the spelling errors, the missing punctuation, the erroneous last lines. As a text copied from Northend's *Little Speaker*, this page may disappoint in its failure to provide the authentic originality that seems the implicit promise of childhood voice and manuscript form. But surely the reliance on set texts and conventional words to express personal feelings, along with the traditions of schooling sentiments that this entails, is in itself meaningful, the very core of social replication.[39] As a form of labor, clerical work with both its opportunities and its oppressions and anxieties attests to the increasing bureaucratization and urbanization of American life throughout the nineteenth century.[40] The period engaged not only in a large range of pedagogical and clerical practices that depended on copying but also in many social practices that made personal use of conventional texts: employers demanded clerical labor and school imposed the use of copybooks, but friendship and autograph albums invited play and expressed affection through the reproduction of familiar lines as a kind of conventional but still intimate utterance. It was in the mid-nineteenth century too that ready-made valentines and greeting cards proliferated, manifesting the idea that the sending of someone else's words, even commercially procured, might provide the best expression of private feeling.[41]

Copying permeates childhood and imitation is central to the socializing processes of growing-up, and thus there are many ways in which learning to think about copying is an essential task of childhood studies. It is also a crucial feature of archival practice. The long commonplace-book tradition demonstrates how deeply the act of copying has been etched in Western culture not only as a technology of self-expression and self-creation but also as a mechanism of collective memory and cultural preservation.[42] As the examples of the scrivener and the commonplace book hint, the scribal acts of copying that maintained government and other organizational records and that created the first libraries underlie all archival practices and institutions. Emblematic of the foundational nature of the connections between copying, children, and archives is the fact that the preservation of ancient literature depends to a remarkable extent on the plethora of copies of texts produced by Sumero-Babylonian, Egyptian, Greek, and Roman children learning to write.[43] In short, copying proves one of the most authentic aspects of both childhood experience and archival transmission. The functions such copying serve for the individual and for the polity may be quite different, but they bolster each other.

Related to the belief that childhood and archives might grant access to the authentic and original is the conviction that they contain secrets. In *Strange Dislocations* Steedman traces the history of the idea of "the child as interiority, privacy, the deepest place inside: not to be found."[44] Trauma—the sexual abuse, violence, abandonment, and neglect of children—lurks as the secret underside of our sentimental celebrations of childhood. Psychoanalysis has taught us to think of the recollection of childhood as a means of recognizing and so healing past harms. Similarly, the appeal and status of the archives emanate from the conviction that they contain secrets, and especially evil secrets, evidence of the cruelty and deception that the powerful (whether governments or adults) had wished to keep hidden. The ethical postures of archival study rest on the hope that revelation can produce redress. Such associations of the secret with trauma and harm press against a recognition that the discoveries of archival work so often lie in the most everyday stuff of the past. Thomas Osborne describes how the opening of the confidential archives of the KGB, which had promised revelation, produced in its detailed lists of confiscated items and transcripts of endless interrogations less the secrets of totalitarian society than the "pathos of ordinary existence."[45] The Neverland notion of childhood as a secret place of fantasy magic and the psychoanalytic conviction of childhood as the site of secret wounds have both become so

Figure 7. The hidden drawing of a classroom beneath the rose flap of "To My Dear Schoolteacher." Courtesy of the Cotsen Children's Library, Department of Rare Books and Special Collections, Princeton University Library.

ubiquitous as to hardly seem secret at all; by contrast the ordinary, daily experiences of childhood remain elusive, and it may be in discerning these everyday things that the archival work of childhood studies will prove most rewarding. "To My Dear Schoolteacher" has its own secret form that produces the ordinary: the central rose in the design proves to be a flap that opens to reveal a charmingly detailed drawing of the schoolroom itself (fig. 7).

Nineteenth-century American educational administrators and reformers gave much attention to the organization and proper attributes of the schoolhouse, insisting that the right design of this space would play an important role in the production of an enlightened citizenry.[46] The bibliography of nineteenth-century schooling is dominated by these influential proscriptive texts, supplemented with retrospective memoirs by teachers and students, but the evidence of ordinary schoolroom structures, activities, and affect offered by this child's drawing provides a different kind of insight and immediacy.[47] Princeton's manuscript collections do include other instances of nineteenth-century children's accounts of school, such as a collection of essays on set topics by students who attended a one-room school in Wilbraham, Massachusetts. The folder of compositions on "our schoolroom" provides a mass of evidence confirming Henry Barnard's criticisms of the poor condition of most schoolhouses "built at the least possible expense of material and labor."[48] These essays register many of the traumas of schooling, including the dread of corporal punishment, but they also evince a certain fondness and pride and provide great specificity about the ordinary things and culture of schools:

> It has got eight windows. And it got eight maps in it. Xx And there are sixteen blackboards two setters. There are-is a closit where xxx xx teacher puts bad boys And there is one stove and stovepipe is broke but we have got some wire to hold it with if we did not it would over on to us. the color the walls are lite-blue. One table with sixteen dinner pails under it.—Mary Warner

> In the room there are a picture the title is the happy days of Childhood: And there are a motto by miss Florence Clark I will tell you what it is God Bless Our School there is a door witch Goes into the Closet ther is one thing in there that does not show itself very often but when it does show its self pretty severly and that is teachers rawhide.—Annie Brown Wilbraham Mass

> There are 15 boys And most all sizes from 4 ft. and half tall to 5 feet tall. And 7 girls.—Henry Chatfield

> There are two old blackboards which are oiled and are a great deal smoother than the new ones . . . We have seven quiet girls and fifteen noisy troublesome boys . . . The middle door is xx opens xxx into the closet where the teacher puts the naughty boys . . . we learn to read write and cipher and on the whole have many happy days in our schoolroom. [unsigned][49]

The secret drawing in "To My Dear Schoolteacher" includes much similar evidence of the details of school life: the mix of ages and gender in one schoolroom, the role of maps and geography in the curriculum, the practices of recitation, the prominent posting of inspiring mottos, even the trash of crumpled assignments on the floor. Although the teacher's elaborate chair, the abundance of books, the curtained window, the prominent large globe, and the neat rack for bags and bonnets—James Johonnot's manual for country schoolhouses is particularly adamant about the importance of clothes hooks—all represent this school as being in better repair than the Wilbraham school with its broken stovepipe and uneven blackboards.[50] The young artist provides no evidence of "teachers rawhide" or the punishments of a dark closet, but the drawing does convey complex emotions toward this schoolroom scene. Such childhood manuscripts demonstrate the rich potential of archival work to not only provide access to the activities, spaces, and objects of children's lives but also to improve our understanding of the ideas and emotions that structure these ordinary experiences.

The child artist did not complete the title for this drawing of a schoolroom: "THE _____" tops the page. This picture may not have a specific title, but the abundant details of the drawing reflect a wide array of ideas about knowledge, the institutional structures and systems of classification that organize them, and the power dynamics of age, gender, race, and geography they imbue. As institutions dedicated to the preservation and transmission of knowledge, schools and archives are both profoundly implicated in such dynamics. A sign on this classroom wall proclaims with didactic certainty schooling's capacity to distinguish between aspiration and achievement: "I'll Try" or "Has Done." "The politics of knowledge," Stoler explains, "is a methodological commitment to how history's exclusions are secured and made"; the information about and insight into nineteenth-century education expressed in this student's drawing depict the ordinary operation of this politics as the shared ground of childhood studies and archival work.[51]

A new attention to the strategies and systems of classification, a self-conscious awareness of how information is collected, ordered, labeled, and retrieved, has been the defining characteristic of the "archival turn" with its shift from a use of "archive as source" to an interest in "archive as subject" and a focus on "archiving as a process."[52] Classing students by age was a fraught goal of educational reform precisely during the period when this drawing was made. The mixed educational space of the one-room schoolhouse depicted in this drawing was a feature of rural settings well into the twentieth century, but despite this persistence in practice, beginning with the common-school movement it became a prominent assumption of school reform that students ought to be sorted into age-differentiated classes. By the 1840s new schools were being constructed with multiple age-graded classrooms, and in 1856, the year "To My Dear Schoolteacher" was made, John Philbrick published a detailed scheme to disseminate the age-graded system he had developed for the Quincy School, a model that had already been implemented in every grammar school in Boston.[53] Historians of education continue to debate whether these changes should be viewed as a mark of growing sensitivity to the nuances of child development or as an instance of the emerging bureaucratic order of U.S. society and institutions, but either way the increasingly powerful role of age classification in the history of child-hood exemplifies the ways in which childhood studies and archival studies are intertwined in the same discourses, the same politics of knowledge.

The gender mixing of students in this picture reflects other educational trends of the period; the gradual evolution toward coeducation in public schools was generally praised by the same reformers who sought to divide students by age. Indeed the new practice of classifying students by age, and indeed the whole systematizing of education that characterized the era's common-school reforms, was thought to obviate the need for gender di-visions. Still, there are plenty of mid-nineteenth century instances of par-ents or school districts fighting to retain or even create single-sex public schools.[54] The gendering of schoolteaching was also changing during this period. The common-school movement sought to expand schooling but was not marked by a concomitant increase in educational budgets, a situa-tion remedied by the shift to a far cheaper female teaching staff. The school-room depicted in this drawing registers these dynamics as pleasurable. The "naughty boys" described in the essays by Wilbraham students are not in evidence here; if anything the drawing's depiction of the relation between male student and female teacher reflects what Horace Mann lauded as the chivalrous impulse that made school mistresses so effective.[55] The couple formed by the female teacher and the boy ready to recite are the dominant figures of this scene, and the student artist has invested the most detail and care on their depiction. The teacher is clearly far taller than her student, but sitting in her elegant chair she is nearly on eye level with the boy who stands before her, and they stare directly into each other's faces. The boy is positioned near the center of the circle, and his shirt, jacket, red waistcoat, and blue trousers have been drawn with as much precision and attention as her red dress and white collar. The teacher's arms resting on chair and table and the relaxed angle of the boy's stance express comfort, assurance, ease. Besides the large group of sitting children, more quickly drawn, there is one other student standing for recitation in a red dress of her own. She looks smiling at the pair of teacher and boy, but they do not look at her. This trio may also have been copied from Northend's *Little Speaker*, although in the frontispiece of that volume the boy giving his recitation is turned toward the girl, and both she and the standing female teacher look at him (see fig. 8).

Figure 8. The frontispiece to Charles Northend's *The Little Speaker, and Juvenile Reader: Being a Collection of Pieces in Prose, Poetry, and Dialogue, Designed for Exercises in Speaking, and for Occasional Reading, in Primary Schools* (New York: A. S. Barnes and Company, 1853). Author's copy.

Most of the classroom details in Northend's frontispiece differ from those supplied by the child artist, but notions of performance, as well as a triangle of gaze and desire, structure both pictures.

"As an institution," Appadurai argues, the archive "is surely a site of memory. But as a tool, it is an instrument for the refinement of desire."[56] His account of the archive "as an aspiration rather than a recollection" derives from the particular conditions of immigrant archives, consciously produced as a crucial and highly political effort to create a collective identity and collective memory, but it suggests as well the more general ways in which acts of preservation express desire and hope.[57] The giving of the gift to the teacher and the preservation of it testify not only to educational demands but also to emotional bonds. This is a page and a picture that may function now in the archives primarily as a source of historical information, registering such facts as the gender structure of a one-room school in 1856. But the making, giving, and keeping of this object were all loaded with affect, aspiration, and desire. Someone at some point (the artist? the teacher? the person who did the keeping? and when? at the time of creation? or later in

Figure 9. The needlepoint cover and pink ribbon binding of the folder holding "To My Dear Schoolteacher." A lyre is similarly embroidered on the back of this folder. Courtesy of the Cotsen Children's Library, Department of Rare Books and Special Collections, Princeton University Library.

remembrance?) has lightly written the name "John" on the wall, suggesting that this might be a portrait of some specific boy. In any event the gender dynamics of this painted scene and the triangulation of desire for learning and for love that swirls through it are striking, and all the more so because it seems extremely likely that this page was made by a female student—the girl watching at the picture's edge, not the boy in the center. A girl certainly had some hand in this gift since it is virtually unimaginable that the needlepoint cover that contains "To My Dear Schoolteacher" was stitched by a boy (fig. 9). By the 1850s coeducation meant that talented girls could learn most academic subjects together with boys, but the creation of needlepoint bouquets remained a largely female skill.

"Geography became the educational status symbol for American daughters and idealized future mothers," Martin Brückner observes, and the central features of this vignette are the map and globe, schoolroom apparatuses that Henry Barnard and James Johonnot considered indispensible.[58] During the early nineteenth century, both ideals of home decoration and object-based pedagogy set some young women to actually embroidering maps and globes.[59] The circular frame of this drawing presents the schoolroom as a world and positions geographical representations at its center. Geography thus functions in this drawing as the icon of education and knowledge. Questions of power and politics are clearly discernable in this curricular priority; as Brückner explains, "The fantasy and process of colonization and western expansion" played an important role in popularizing geography in American schools.[60] This child artist had access to yellow and green, but a patriotic red, white, and blue predominate. Beginning with Jedidiah Morse's influential textbooks, school curriculums in the United States emphasized American geography, so the prominence in this classroom of a map of Africa rather than America is surprising and suggestive. The map on the wall in the schoolroom of Northend's frontispiece depicts Massachusetts. Teaching children about Africa may evoke missionary activity.[61] Moreover, in 1856, just a few years before the outbreak of the Civil War, for the white students in this schoolroom to be studying Africa surely carries particular and highly charged political connotations.

The complex histories and power dynamics of categories of age, gender, race, geography, and more are thus clearly legible in this ordinary scene. Such systems of classification and their effects are described by Foucault with the resonant phrase "pouvoir-savoir" rendered by his English translators as "power/knowledge": "The longer I continue, the more it seems to me that the formation of discourses and the genealogy of knowledge need to be analyzed, not in terms of types of consciousness, modes of perception and forms of ideology, but in terms of tactics and strategies of power."[62] Foucault's interest centers on the way that knowledge and power prove mutually constitutive, his work charting the inseparable nature of their entanglement. This insight into the relations between power and knowledge permeate the self-conscious analyses of archival studies. So there is a certain frisson, a shock of the uncanny, a collision of history and theory we experience in finding this motto prominently displayed on this schoolroom wall: "KNOWLEDGE IS POWER." It was a common pedagogical strategy to draw on mottoes, as is evident in the more religious saying displayed on the wall of the Wilbraham schoolroom. In a book of advice to teachers, Charles

Northend, whose *Little Speaker* contained the poem copied on this sheet, explains that "short and appropriate mottoes learned by children will be remembered and felt during life" and suggests that "it is well for teachers to have them placed upon the school-room walls or upon the blackboard, and occasionally to make one the subject of conversation or remark." Northend is himself fond of this particular phrase; in "Rules and Maxims for the Teacher," he advises "daily add to your own stack of knowledge, never forgetting that knowledge is power," and he also uses the motto as the heading for his section on scholarship.[63] Richard Brown recognizes such faith in the dissemination of information as a core attribute of the new republic, the very "ideology of liberty [being] tied to the diffusion of knowledge," and notes the broad appeal of "the common saying 'knowledge is power.'"[64] Obviously both the teacher who put this saying on her classroom wall and the student who thought it an important enough aspect of the classroom to choose to reproduce it in this drawing understood it in the simple, unidirectional way that Foucault's work critiques. If the common saying implies that possessing knowledge gives you power, and hence that school lessons will prove enabling for later life, Foucault insists that the very content and nature of knowledge is itself shaped by relationships of power, that childhood, school, these lessons of literacy or geography, cannot be extracted from the mesh of power/knowledge that will discipline and socialize the child. Yet the uncanny inscription of these words on this childhood drawing enacts the very ties between childhood studies and archival practice that I have traced in this chapter, suggesting that in some strange way the child already is or knows the questions we would ask of the archive and the past.

Notes

1. Jacques Derrida, "Archive Fever: A Freudian Impression," trans. Eric Prenowitz, *Diacritics* 25.2 (1995): 9–63.

2. Antoinette Burton, "Thinking Beyond the Boundaries: Empire, Feminism and the Domains of History," *Social History* 26.1 (2001): 67.

3. Jacqueline Rose, *The Case of Peter Pan, or the Impossibility of Children's Fiction* (Philadelphia: University of Pennsylvania Press, 1984); Peter Hunt, *Children's Literature: An Illustrated History* (Oxford: Oxford University Press, 1995).

4. Philippe Ariès, *Centuries of Childhood: A Social History of Family Life* (New York: Vintage, 1962).

5. Anne Higonnet, *Pictures of Innocence: The History and Crisis of Ideal Childhood* (London: Thames and Hudson, 1998), 8.

6. Henry Jenkins, introduction to *The Children's Culture Reader*, ed. Henry Jenkins (New York: New York University Press, 1998), 15.

7. Barbara Beatty and Julia Grant, "Entering into the Fray: Historians of Childhood and Public Policy," *Journal of the History of Childhood and Youth* 3.1 (2010): 113.

8. Higonnet, *Pictures of Innocence*, 224.

9. Burton, "Thinking Beyond the Boundaries," 66–67.

10. Nazan Maksudyan, "Modernization of Welfare or Further Deprivation? State Provisions for Foundlings in the Late Ottoman Empire," *Journal of the History of Childhood and Youth* 2.3 (2009): 361–92.

11. Linda Gordon, *Heroes of Their Own Lives: The Politics and History of Family Violence* (New York: Viking, 1988).

12. Ann Laura Stoler, *Along the Archival Grain: Epistemic Anxieties and Colonial Common Sense* (Princeton, NJ: Princeton University Press, 2009), 295, 348; Ann Laura Stoler, *Race and the Education of Desire: Foucault's History of Sexuality and the Colonial Order of Things* (Durham, NC: Duke University Press, 1995), 161.

13. Ann Laura Stoler, "Colonial Archives and the Arts of Governance," in *Refiguring the Archive*, ed. Carolyn Hamilton, Verne Harris, and Graeme Reid (Cape Town: David Philip, 2002), 91.

14. Marlene Manoff, "Theories of the Archive from Across the Disciplines," *Portal: Libraries and the Academy* 4.1 (2004): 10.

15. Jacqueline Rose, *States of Fantasy* (Oxford: Oxford University Press, 1996), 111, 134.

16. Jacqueline Rose, *The Case of Peter Pan; or, The Impossibility of Children's Fiction* (London: Macmillan, 1984), 2.

17. Carolyn Steedman, *Dust: The Archive and Cultural History* (New Brunswick, NJ: Rutgers University Press, 2002), 10, 154.

18. Carolyn Steedman, *Strange Dislocations: Childhood and the Idea of Human Interiority, 1780–1930* (London: Virago, 1995), 174.

19. Steedman, *Dust*, 119.

20. Carolyn Steedman, "The Watercress Seller," in *Past Tenses: Essays on Writing, Autobiography and History* (London: Rivers Oram, 1992), 194; Steedman, *Strange Dislocations*, 174.

21. Steedman, "The Watercress Seller," 200.

22. Steedman, "The Watercress Seller," 193.

23. Steedman, *Dust*, viii; Derrida, "Archive Fever," 57.

24. Victoria Rosner, "Have You Seen This Child? Carolyn K. Steedman and the Writing of Fantasy Motherhood," *Feminist Studies* 26.1 (2000): 27.

25. Andrea Immel, "Choice Scraps of History: Lloyd E. Cotsen and Modern Children's Book Collecting," in *A Catalogue of the Cotsen Children's Library*, vol. 1, ed. Andrea Immel (Princeton NJ: Princeton University Library, 2000), xxiii.

26. Andrea Immel, "Frederick Lock's Scrapbook: Patterns in the Pictures and Writing in the Margins," *The Lion and the Unicorn* 29.1 (2005): 65.

27. Gillian Adams, "Speaking for Lions," *Children's Literature Association Quar-*

terly 17.4 (1992): 2; Lesley Peterson and Leslie Robertson, "An Annotated Bibliography of Nineteenth-Century Juvenilia," in *The Child Writer from Austen to Woolf*, ed. Christine Alexander and Juliet McMaster (New York: Cambridge University Press, 2005), 269–303.

28. Andrea L. Immel, email correspondence, May 1, 2011.

29. Steedman, *Dust*, 75.

30. Arjun Appadurai, "Archive and Aspiration," in *Information Is Alive: Art and Theory on Archiving and Retrieving Data* (Rotterdam: NAi Publishers, 2003), 15–16.

31. Michel Foucault, *The Archaeology of Knowledge* (New York: Pantheon, 1972), 129.

32. Karen Sánchez-Eppler, *Dependent States: The Child's Part in Nineteenth-Century American Culture* (Chicago: University of Chicago Press, 2005), xxiv–xxv.

33. Carolyn Steedman, "The Tidy House," in *Past Tenses*, 83.

34. Carolyn Steedman, *Landscape for a Good Woman: A Story of Two Lives* (New Brunswick, NJ: Rutgers University Press, 1987), 146.

35. Allison James, "The Temporality of Childhood," in *Theorizing Childhood* (New York: Teachers College Press, 1998), 61, 80. My thanks to Rachel Conrad for inspiring me to think about time.

36. Charles Northend, *The Little Speaker, and Juvenile Reader: Being a Collection of Pieces in Prose, Poetry, and Dialogue, Designed for Exercises in Speaking, and for Occasional Reading, in Primary Schools* (New York: S. A. Rollo, 1859), 77.

37. Northend, *The Little Speaker*, 130.

38. Northend, *The Little Speaker*, 5.

39. Karen Sánchez-Eppler, "Copying and Conversion: An 1824 Friendship Album 'from a Chinese Youth,'" *American Quarterly* 59.2 (2007): 301–2, 318–19.

40. Thomas Augst, *The Clerk's Tale: Young Men and Moral Life in Nineteenth-Century America* (Chicago: University of Chicago Press, 2003).

41. Barry Shank, *A Token of My Affection: Greeting Cards and American Business Culture* (New York: Columbia University Press, 2004).

42. Earle Havens, *Commonplace Books: A History of Manuscripts and Printed Books from Antiquity to the Twentieth Century* (New Haven, CT: Yale University Press, 2001).

43. Gillian Adams, "In the Hands of Children," *The Lion and the Unicorn* 29.1 (2005): 38; Raffaella Cribiore, *Gymnastics of the Mind: Greek Education in Hellenistic and Roman Egypt* (Princeton NJ: Princeton University Press, 2001).

44. Steedman, *Strange Dislocations*, 172.

45. Thomas Osborne, "The Ordinariness of the Archive," *History of the Human Sciences* 12.2 (1999): 125.

46. Henry Barnard, *School Architecture; or, Contributions to the Improvement of School-Houses in the United States* (New York: A. S. Barnes, 1848); Horace Mann, *Lectures and Annual Reports on Education* (Cambridge, MA: Mary T. Mann, 1867); James Johonnot, *Country School-Houses: Containing Elevations, Plans, and Specifications, with Estimates, Directions to Builders, Suggestions as to School Grounds, Furni-*

ture, Apparatus, etc., and a Treatise on School-House Architecture (New York: Ivison and Phinney, 1859); William W. Cutler III, "Cathedral of Culture: The Schoolhouse in American Educational Thought and Practice since 1820," *History of Education Quarterly* 29.1 (1989): 1–40.

47. Barbara Finkelstein, *Governing the Young: Teacher Behavior in Popular Primary Schools in Nineteenth-Century United States* (New York: Falmer Press, 1989).

48. Barnard, *School Architecture*, 39.

49. "Our Schoolroom," Massachusetts Elementary School Student Compositions Collection, 1866–80, box 1, Firestone Library, Princeton University.

50. Johonnot, *Country School-Houses*, 185.

51. Stoler, *Along the Archival Grain*, 877.

52. Stoler, *Along the Archival Grain*, 873; Stoler, "Colonial Archives and the Arts of Governance," 83.

53. Howard P. Chudacoff, *How Old Are You? Age Consciousness in American Culture* (Princeton, NJ: Princeton University Press, 1992), 35–36; Cutler, "Cathedral of Culture," 5.

54. David Tyack and Elisabeth Hansot, *Learning Together: A History of Coeducation in American Public Schools* (New York: Russell Sage Foundation Publications, 1992), 89–91.

55. Carl F. Kaestle and Maris A. Vinovskis, *Education and Social Change in Nineteenth-Century Massachusetts* (New York: Cambridge University Press, 1980), 153; Tyack and Hansot, *Learning Together*, 67.

56. Appadurai, "Archive and Aspiration," 24.

57. Appadurai, "Archive and Aspiration," 16.

58. Martin Brückner, *The Geographic Revolution in Early America: Maps, Literacy, and National Identity* (Chapel Hill: University of North Carolina Press, 2006), 162; Barnard, *School Architecture*, 60; Johonnot, *Country School-Houses*, 192.

59. Martin Brückner provides wonderful examples of such cartographical handiwork in "The Material Map," *Common-Place* 8.3 (2008), www.historycooperative .org/journals/cp/vol-08/no-03/lessons, and in "Maps in the Classroom: Picture Pedagogy, Object Lessons, and the Cult of Cartifacts," paper presented at "Home, School, Play, Work: The Visual and Textual Worlds of Children," Princeton University, February 13–14, 2009.

60. Brückner, *The Geographic Revolution in Early America*, 244.

61. On the symbiotic ties between the education of American children and American missionary activity see my *Dependent States*, 186–220.

62. Michel Foucault, *Power/Knowledge: Selected Interviews and Other Writings, 1972–1977* (New York: Pantheon, 1980), 77.

63. Charles Northend, *The Teacher's Assistant; or, Hints and Methods in School Discipline and Instruction, Being a Series of Familiar Letters to One Entering upon the Teacher's Work* (Boston: Crosby and Nichols, 1859), 350, 300, 322.

64. Richard D. Brown, *Knowledge Is Power: The Diffusion of Information in Early America, 1700–1865* (Oxford: Oxford University Press, 1991), 288, 3.

Doing Childhood Studies

The View from Within

Lynne Vallone

After seventeen years at a university in central Texas, I accepted a position in southern New Jersey. This fact is not so very surprising or even particularly interesting; academics relocate frequently and for a host of reasons. Two things, however, made this move somewhat unusual: I left a conventional, well-established discipline at the center of liberal arts curricula—English—to join a nascent multidisciplinary department in an emergent field, childhood studies. In what follows, I reflect on what this move has meant for me as a scholar of children's literature. I also outline the creation of the Department of Childhood Studies at Rutgers University, Camden, the first PhD-granting department of childhood studies in the nation, which constituted the first steps toward institutionalization of childhood studies within the academy. Most importantly, I relate what doctoral students in the program, the next generation of scholars and practitioners, have to say about their experiences in childhood studies' methods and research as well as their thoughts about the future of childhood studies.

In thinking about possible futures for childhood studies, it makes sense first to ask "Why childhood studies now?" I am not suggesting that the field of childhood studies does not currently exist. There are American programs and departments of childhood studies (Brooklyn College and Eastern Washington University offer BA degrees in childhood studies and children's studies, respectively), as well as European centers and departments (such as the Norwegian Centre for Child Research at the University of Trondheim and the Department of Child Studies at Linköping, Sweden). In addition, various recent conferences (such as the biannual conferences sponsored by the Centre for the Study of Childhood and Youth at Sheffield University), journals (such as *Childhood: A Journal of Global Child Research*, published by Sage Publications since 1993), and proliferating articles and books—including this one—on the topic of childhood studies make it abundantly clear that the field enjoys both a history and an identity. However, the field's potential as an urgent and relevant critical discourse that cuts across disciplines is as yet untapped—particularly in the United States. And I believe that it is worthwhile to question what intersections of academic, cultural, and political trends and, perhaps, current events have encouraged the multidisciplinary field of study and pedagogy we are calling childhood studies to grow.

It is important to note at this juncture that in this country the steps to institutionalize childhood studies have not been taken because the United States has become a particularly child-loving place or because the academy at large has at last realized what it had forgotten to value. No—as cuts to social, health, and educational programs for children, the lack of respect (as evidenced by salary) afforded to schoolteachers and childcare workers, and inadequate paid maternity (let alone paternity) leaves make clear, the United States remains deeply ambivalent about children. For its part, the academy continues to be highly suspicious of any perceived "immaturity" within the ivory tower. Even today it is not unusual for scholars from a wide array of disciplines to have to defend why they have placed children and childhood at the center of their research programs. So, if the growing institutionalization of childhood studies has not been an entirely organic process emerging from a perfect confluence of research and culture, what other powerful forces or events have occurred in recent years to make such an inquiry about the construction of childhood studies salient? Briefly, in my opinion, the reason that childhood studies is making itself felt now has to do with a number of factors: the existence of functional models of interdisciplinary departments and programs such as American studies, gender studies, cultural studies, and visual studies; the gathering of a critical mass of energetic top scholars of childhoods and youth from both the humanities and social sciences; and the burgeoning belief in the importance and viability of linking scholarship to community engagement. Individual scholars have been successful enough and vocal enough and plentiful enough to contemplate, and take, in some cases, the step of bringing discrete disciplines together and, most risky and thrilling of all, of bridging the deep divide between the humanities and social sciences. Childhood studies requires self-confidence, resolve, and commitment from faculty members, administrators, and students—commitment in terms of resources, space, and faculty and graduate student lines, as well as a deep commitment to posing the pressing questions that shape or have shaped the lives of children or their construction and representations, to formulating responses and answers, and to sharing knowledge about children and childhoods broadly.

Although a full-scale discussion of what we mean when we talk about childhood studies—and we will not all mean the same thing when invoking childhood studies—is beyond my purview here, a word about definitions and disciplinarity is in order. Allison James distinguishes "childhood studies" from the disciplinary study of children and childhood.[1] According to James, the distinguishing characteristic is the "new paradigm" for studying children offered by childhood studies, one that attends to the child as a social actor with a voice and that understands "childhood" as a social construction.[2] Given this new paradigm and the emphasis in childhood studies on ethnography (I return to this in attempting some version of this research methodology), where does the sociological/anthropological birthplace of childhood studies leave the humanities? While this is a question better answered in the introduction and some of the other contributions to this volume, I will let it linger as an important issue as we consider childhood studies and the humanities. If multidisciplinarity is essential to this discipline—and I believe that it is—then within childhood studies the humanities must accept and respect the social sciences—if not the sciences— just as the social sciences must accept and welcome some of the insights and theoretical models of literature, history, and philosophy (to name a few germane fields). To do otherwise, to withdraw into disciplinarity, as Allison James comments, "risks diluting the commonalities of interests that have, so far, successfully shaped the emergence of childhood studies."[3]

While childhood studies as discipline has unique qualities, which it is in part my aim here to describe, it also has much in common with other multidisciplinary fields. Certainly, the creation of childhood studies has not been a matter of parthenogenesis but rather a process involving many fathers and mothers; thus, we may look to other interdisciplinary or multidisciplinary fields for models of success. Childhood studies, like American studies and women's studies, draws on the disciplines of history, anthropology, sociology, political science, religion, literature, philosophy, and psychology, among other fields, for methodologies, theories, texts, and research questions that help it explore and understand its object of inquiry, in this case, children and childhoods. Women's studies, which in some institutions may now be found gathered under the umbrella "gender studies" (which includes men's studies, queer studies, and sexuality studies), may provide the best model of a successful multidisciplinary venture with a significant presence in the American academy. Not only are women's studies and gender studies programs and departments well established (according to the 2007 National Women's Studies Association "National Census of Women's and Gender Studies Programs in United States' Institutions of Higher Education," there are 652 women's and gender studies programs at community colleges, colleges, and universities), women's studies shares a number of interests with childhood studies, including an activist perspective and the core goal of bringing the voices and concerns of the previously marginalized to the center of social and scholarly activity.[4] There is much for childhood studies to learn from the success of women's and gender studies in creating multidisciplinary curricula, cultivating buy-in from students, faculty, administrators, and those outside of the academy, organizing conferences, and initiating journals and special issues. Well respected and rigorous, women's and gender studies programs have become mainstream.

Although lacking the participatory or activist piece that helps define women's studies and much of childhood studies, a consideration of the evolution of visual studies, or visual culture studies, a newer multidisciplinary field of interest, has much to offer those interested in building childhood studies, in part because of its vigorous tradition of self-assessment. Visual studies is an interdisciplinary and theoretically sophisticated field that combines traditional disciplines such as art history, literature, history, communication, and studio art with newer fields such as media studies and cultural studies. Some critics, such as James Elkins, feel that visual studies will not reach its potential until it is able to include the hard sciences (especially research that pertains to vision and visuality) in its purview as well. This notion of a very big tent may be of some concern to those who work in childhood studies and who are invested in its growth and sustainability.[5] In an aside found in his chapter on "visual literacy" in his *Visual Studies: A Skeptical Introduction*, Elkins reminds his readers that "images cross boundaries that humanists do not." It may be said that children do as well.[6] Practically from its inception, visual studies scholars have been debating its parameters, constitutive subjects, and best practices. In 2002, W. J. T. Mitchell posed a number of questions that could be asked of any interdisciplinary project, including childhood studies: "Does [visual culture studies] have a specific object of research, or is it a grab-bag of problems left over from respectable, well-established disciplines? If it is a field, what are its boundaries and limiting definitions? Should it be institutionalized as an academic structure, made into a department or given programmatic status, with all the appurtenances of syllabi, textbooks, prerequisites, requirements and degrees?"[7] While there is a definite edge to Mitchell's questions—which seem to entertain the notion that visual studies may be incoherent—persistent self-examination, debate, and slow growth attests to its strength. Marquard Smith calls visual studies a "living methodology" in the preface to *Visual Culture Studies*, a collection of interviews with visual culture studies scholars. In my opinion, this idea, coupled with the uneasy status of visual studies, offers a useful perspective for childhood studies' scholars to consider as our field similarly grows and responds to current pressures on the academy and trends in multidisciplinary study.[8] While visual studies as currently conceived may be considered a "failure" in some quarters, the ability to be flexible and to adapt to new paradigms, technologies, politics, and so forth, bodes well, in my mind, for its staying power.

However useful models may be during a building phase, models are also made to be subverted or altered. Interestingly, the art historian Michael Ann Holly, one of the founders of the American branch of visual studies (the first graduate program in the United States was founded in 1989 at the University of Rochester where she taught at the time), describes visual studies as a field that formed in order to stage a "quiet revolution" against, in particular, art history.[9] Perhaps childhood studies, too, represents revolution, a breaking with tradition and a remaking of disciplinary "culture." On reflection, however, for childhood studies, "revolution" may seem unnecessarily violent or suggestive of obliteration of parent discipline or culture. In fact, the aspects of childhood studies most appealing to me are its energy and relevance—more progression than revolution, perhaps. Certainly I think that the future of childhood studies is very bright or I would not have staked my academic career on its success. While I left my "home" (my home discipline), I did not leave it in order to "grow up" or to gain "independence." I do not envision childhood studies from a teleological perspective as "perfecting" or "completing" inquiry into children and childhood but rather as a kind of bridge between disciplines that enhances the work of discrete disciplines.

In fact, childhood studies has advanced far enough as a field to engage in its own acts of reassessment. Adrian L. James's 2010 article "Competition or Integration? The Next Step in Childhood Studies?" argues that childhood studies is "approaching a crossroads, reaching a point in its history and development when searching questions must be asked about how the field is now perceived and whether there is any longer a shared understanding of what was once a unified project."[10] For James, the need for self-assessment arises from the disconnect or moral imbalance that may be created when comparing the research of those who study victimized children of the global South and developing world and the work of those who study the children of privilege in the West. Should research that concentrates on children's rights in the neediest parts of the world somehow "trump" the work of those who are concerned, for example, with the social and political constructions of childhood? James calls this divide the "plurality vs. singularity debate," in other words, the debate between those who emphasize the idea of multiple childhoods and those who stress the universality of childhood as a social category. James believes that childhood studies may overcome this divide, that it need not imperil the childhood studies project. Using a weaving metaphor to anchor his idea of integration, James describes the "warp" of the fabric of childhood studies (the lengthwise and strongest threads) as "the commonalities of childhood, the stronger analytical and conceptual strands from which the fabric is made and that run through all aspects of the fabric of childhood," and the weft, the shorter threads that interlace with the warp, as the "finer strands that create the detailed patterns that describe the diversities of childhood."[11] James suggests that "such an approach provides a model for recognizing the importance of both macro and micro issues in the analysis and understanding of childhood, rather than insisting on the primacy of either one or the other."[12]

The reader may have noticed that literary constructions of children and childhood appear to be left out of this debate or invisible in the "fabric" of childhood. Or perhaps one might have to turn the fabric over in order to see the "knots" that represent children's literature. What might children's literature—my own corner of childhood studies—learn from childhood studies and vice versa? Various chapters in this volume answer the question I have posed more fully than I am able to here. (See, in particular, Bell's and Singley's contributions.) Yet a number of different scholars, including Richard Flynn, Elizabeth Goodenough, Karen Coats, Nina Christensen,

Kenneth Kidd, and Thomas Tavisano, among others, have begun a vigorous discussion about the productive relationship between children's literature and childhood studies.[13] One point of potential fissure in childhood studies—along with that between the humanities and social sciences—is the same tension that can emerge within childhood studies between those who study living children and those whose research has to do with children and childhood of the past or with images and representations of children or children's culture (in this last category I place children's literature). Within children's literature the analogue may be the tension often described between "child people" and "book people." "Child people" are those critics, librarians, and practitioners who are most interested in pedagogy and the effects of literature on the "real child," while "book people" are those critics who work in literature departments and use theory and criticism to discuss children's literature in contexts other than those that involve children. While many find this distinction specious, there are aspects of truth to the idea that each side harbors suspicion about the "other." A self-avowed "book person," Richard Flynn has suggested that working together benefits everyone, including children: "Contemporary theory about childhood and children's literature has offered a significant and powerful corrective to the dominant educational ideologies that threaten our children's literacy and ability to think. If being a book person means promoting meaningful rather than merely functional literacy, then book people are child people indeed."[14]

One area within the academy in which all people are "child people," that is, working with a population that requires instruction and attention, is pedagogy. Teaching the next generation of scholars and practitioners is an often overlooked aspect of "doing childhood studies," an issue related to my larger point about the importance of listening to what graduate students who are training within childhood studies have to say. My move to a department of childhood studies has meant, in part, a shift in the nature of the courses I teach. To give just one example, soon after my arrival at Rutgers I developed a graduate seminar I called the "Visual and Material Cultures of Childhood," a course in which I drew on aspects of children's literature study I was comfortable with—picture books—yet in which I also stretched myself by including content areas outside of my disciplinary training, such as architecture and the children's clothing industry. By analyzing image and ideology, history and context, the course aimed to provide a deeper understanding of the visual and material cultures of (Western, primarily but not exclusively American) children and their childhood(s) over time. In a necessarily partial examination of such a broad topic, the seminar participants studied the history of children's things (furniture, toys, clothing), built environments and spaces intended for child play or participation, media and artistic representations of children, and visual literacy as manifest in childhood. As material objects indebted to illustration for meaning, picture books represent a unique link between the visual and material cultures of childhood and served as a particular focus of inquiry in the last weeks of the seminar.

The seminar ended with a four-week case study of the picture book as an example of a productive union between the visual and material cultures of childhood. Early on, students were introduced to the concept of *ekphrasis*— simply put, using one art form to describe or represent another. The specific example we discussed was William Carlos William's "Children's Games" as a response to Pieter Bruegel the Elder's painting *Children's Games*. While the critical readings and writings the students would produce over the course of the semester were not meant to be "artistic," I believe that showing how one form may comment on or enhance the understanding of another helps make multidisciplinary thinking and writing as less alienating and scary to students. While in general I am pleased with the seminar (I would tinker with the syllabus, certainly, in any future semester, but the basic outline of the course would probably remain the same), the breadth and depth of "children's material and visual culture" is so vast that no semester-long course—or even year-long course—could actually do justice to the topic. Much has to be left out in terms of the kinds of visual and material culture considered as well as "kinds" of childhood or children. Infants, young children, and adolescents get thrown together, and global childhoods may be given short shrift. Although students in childhood studies take a "theories of childhood studies" course (which covers Bourdieu, Foucault, Sen, de Certeau, among others), those interested in visual and material culture would benefit from a "preseminar" in the work of foundational theorists of material and visual culture that they may not have read within the program, theorists such as Roland Barthes, Bill Brown, and Stuart Hall. The issue of coverage, of breadth and depth of knowledge, recalls the concerns Mitchell raised in thinking about visual culture studies. Is it reasonable to expect there to be a "center" to all branches of childhood studies? Should students' coursework be composed of discrete units of primarily disciplinary-based instruction (certainly easier for the instructor), or should each course be designed to be as multidisciplinary as possible? Does multidisciplinarity in practice require too much of the instructor? Of the students? Here I am thinking primarily of graduate students, but the same questions should be asked of the undergraduate curriculum in childhood studies.

In addition to answering these pressing questions about coursework with concrete proposals and curricula, which is difficult work, what else does it take to create a department of childhood studies? The first and most important ingredient is imagination—the ability to imagine something new and different. Institutionally, not surprisingly, the two most crucial elements that must be in place before a multidisciplinary department may be launched include significant initial and then sustained support from the highest levels—financial support, faculty lines, space, TA/GA lines, and so forth—and faculty buy-in. From an institutional standpoint, it is much easier to augment existing departments and programs rather than start something innovative from scratch, and thus the players involved must be particularly steadfast—if not stubborn—and the commitment to creating the new department—especially one in an emerging field with few direct models to follow—must be especially strong. The Rutgers University department was years in the making, and it relied on consistent efforts in persuading, fundraising, and hiring led by Margaret Marsh, dean of the Camden College of Liberal Arts for support. The Center for Children and Childhood Studies provided an anchor for the department through its proximity and mutual projects and concerns. Its successes in promoting the welfare of the children of Camden, New Jersey, sponsoring lecture series and workshops on issues related to children and youth, fostered a productive atmosphere of inquiry, research, and focus that created the context for the academic wing of childhood studies to flourish. The faculty associates in the center from across the college, whose research interests coalesced around children and childhood, enhanced the department through their courses and, most importantly, through their hard work in conceptualizing the department, particularly in the time before a critical mass of faculty were hired into the department itself.

When the Department of Childhood Studies at Rutgers University, Camden, opened its doors in 2007 it consisted of two senior faculty members and two partial appointments. In academic year 2012–13, there are concrete plans to grow the number of the department's full-time faculty. Between 2007 and 2011, the department hired four additional full-time tenured or tenure-track faculty members (three assistant professors and one full professor) and one half-time faculty member. The disciplines represented by the full-time faculty range across the humanities and social sciences and include anthropology, communications, education, history, literature, and sociology. Faculty with partial appointments in the department hail from nursing, psychology, and religion. In 2012 the department had thirty-seven graduate students enrolled on a full- and part-time basis. The majority of these students were in the doctoral program; the master's level program was much smaller in size. Over four years the undergraduate major has grown very rapidly, and in 2012 we had approximately 150 majors. This is what the department is now; what will childhood studies become in the future?

What does a changing academy (and a changing United States) need from childhood studies now? Certainly I would like to see the greater development of the traditional support systems that discrete as well as multidisciplinary fields such as American studies, cultural studies, and women's studies enjoy in many colleges and universities: for example, additional academic journals that would provide forums for multidisciplinary research on childhood or discipline-specific work that would benefit from reaching a wider audience of scholars, more conferences and symposia that bring scholars together to share work on particular topics or themes related to all aspects of childhood studies research, funding opportunities for graduate students and faculty, and academic positions for our doctoral students who choose the academy as their profession. Of course, I would also like to see a social and political climate shift that resulted in the welfare, rights, and cultures of childhood being taken seriously and in children's needs being addressed in systematic and sustained ways.

In political and policy discussions, actual children are evoked, but are often ignored in fact. In childhood studies, the "body of interest" that seems to me to be lost most frequently is the *student* body. That is, for me, as a former administrator and faculty supervisor in childhood studies, one of the principal obligations in developing a field of inquiry and research is to address the "who" of childhood studies—not only children but also students. Childhood studies is not solely a discipline, a research agenda, or a paradigm; it is also a pedagogical, training, and mentoring field. While faculty members, even those who claim to work within childhood studies, primarily publish and present papers within discipline-specific areas of academic expertise— for obvious reasons—even as they collaborate within a multidisciplinary program, the people who will be required to perform interdisciplinarity or multidisciplinarily—at the foundational level in their coursework and in their research—are the students themselves. One of the greatest challenges of the institutionalization of childhood studies is how to create students not in our own image.

Thus far I have provided a partial understanding the "why" and the "what" of doing childhood studies; now I turn to considering the "who" of childhood studies—doctoral students, in particular. I accepted the invitation to contribute to this volume knowing that anything I might write about "doing childhood studies" would be weakened if it did not include the perspectives of graduate students enrolled in the program. (Any future project such as this one might also include the voices of undergraduate students.) However, as scholars in the social and hard sciences know well, it's not so easy to include student voices in research. Such work constitutes "work with human subjects" and thus is subject to federal laws and university requirements constructed to regulate this research and to protect human subjects from harm. Before I could apply to the Rutgers Institutional Review Board (IRB) for permission to proceed with my research, I had to successfully complete the Rutgers University Human Subjects Compliance Program. After spending some hours reading the material on the website, taking (and passing) the online exam, and receiving notification of certification, I was able to compose my questionnaire, consent form, recruitment poster, and IRB application. I devised a method that permitted the questionnaires to be submitted anonymously (a method designed to encourage the greatest degree of openness in answering the questions) while still allowing for informed consent. Given the voluntary, risk-free, and anonymous nature of the project, my application was eligible for "exempt review" (which does not mean what one might think it means: "exempt review" simply means exempt from *full* IRB review). I carefully wrote and submitted all of my materials and then waited, with some trepidation, for formal IRB approval. Without approval, my study would be doomed to failure, as I could not conduct any research involving the students without it.

With this study, should it be approved, I was hoping to catch up with my students who, as part of their methods coursework, had already completed the same training and had much greater knowledge of the protocols of human subject research. Happily, some three weeks after submitting my materials (which is actually quite speedy given the vast size of Rutgers University), I received my approval and my study number (#E11–496), and I was ready to advertise and encourage participation in the research project. Once again, I had to wait to begin writing, since the students had to be given time to complete the questionnaire (five open-ended questions about their experience within the department and their thoughts on the future of childhood studies). As someone who is used to, mostly, her own procrastination or life events determining the relative speed with which writing projects are conducted and concluded, all of the waiting involved in ethnographic work—of which using a survey is the least involved with human subjects (as compared with interviews or participant observation)—was frustrating indeed. I have a new perspective on ethnographers after this brief foray into one aspect of their methods.

My appreciation of ethnographic data collection is not limited to respect for the effort that must be expended in creating an instrument and organizing consent and retrieval of the responses or for the character building that ensues in exercising patience while waiting for initial approval or for final approval after revisions: after this study and, especially, in observing my colleagues in the social sciences, I have learned to appreciate more fully the kinds of nuanced knowledge generated through narrative reporting and ethnographic inquiry. In this case, my assumptions about the childhood studies project, multidisciplinary research, and the concerns of our students were both challenged and confirmed through the thoughtful answers I received.[15] In addition, the information, the research, is not keyed to my thoughts but to others'. While it will be up to me to synthesize the material I receive, this method of creating new knowledge is collaborative and open ended. The author has much less control in ethnographic research, and this fact caused me some discomfort—one of the themes that emerged from the responses.

As I have suggested, it is all well and good for academics—especially those secure in a tenured or tenure-track job—to extol or "celebrate" multidisciplinarity and quite another thing to be required to perform it in seminars and in a dissertation. One of the recurring themes that emerged from the questionnaires generally as well as in response to a direct question was that multidisciplinary study is both demanding and destabilizing. Many students characterized multidisciplinary work as challenging, "daunting," and "scary." One student finds the seeming unending multiplicity of multidisciplinary work to be its greatest challenge: "Not having a single set of 'core principles' in which to fall back onto. Not having a single of set anything!" Multidisciplinarity asks emerging (and senior) scholars to attend to the methods, theories, ideas, history, and practices of other fields. One student points out that faculty members are not always clear when they invoke multidisciplinarity: "I have seen students and faculty struggle with the meaning and limitations of multi- and interdisciplinary work." Indeed, at times, the idea is more in the air we breathe than firmly pinned down and analyzed; as one student comments, "We have not spent enough time in the classroom problematizing this very idea of a multidisciplinary study."

Students rightly point out that gaining true knowledge—particularly in more than one arena—cannot be rushed. Yet it would be the height of naïveté to ignore the fact that moving right along is what we ask of doctoral students. This disconnect may produce anxiety or alienation. One student states that "I feel that it will take many years of study and practice to accomplish [multidisciplinary research], and to acquire depth of understanding," and another observes that "the multi-disciplinary nature of the program can sometimes produce a 'stranger-in-a-strange land' feeling."

Overwhelmingly, however—and it was pleasant music to this former department administrator's ears—the student responses enumerate the virtues of their struggles in multidisciplinary study and describe them as valuable on the way to attaining their educational and career goals. "Freedom" is a concept that comes up frequently—the freedom to define multidisciplinarity and the freedom to be innovative and independent as a scholar: "I find the freedom to draw upon so many traditions, and also to be innovative, to be the most rewarding aspects of studying multidisciplinarily." Another student comments,

> Rather than prescribing a method of multiple methodologies to be practiced with a strict definition of what Childhood Studies is, my department allows me to do multi-disciplinary work in whatever way I see fit. I've encountered elsewhere rigid definitions of Childhood Studies in statements like, "Any work in Childhood Studies must ultimately have as its goal locating the agency of the child." (Seriously!) Similar definitions exist for multi-disciplinarity [as a term]. As comforting as such definitions may be for their clarity and exactitude, they are obviously constricting, limiting research and knowledge.

Even "discomfort" can be reclaimed by some of these flexible students: "Since being at Rutgers, I've learned that the variety I came for is not only exciting and intellectually stimulating, but also slightly uncomfortable. . . . But this discomfort is one of the greatest advantages to the program and to Childhood Studies. There is something new and vibrant to uncover from being uncomfortable. I am constantly challenged in the way I think and approach a topic."

The students who feel the most able to negotiate the insecurities of multidisciplinary study are those who had felt constrained by traditional programs in the past or whose intellectual curiosity might not have been well served in such departments: "Multidisciplinary study has taught me to ask more nuanced questions that place my materials in a broader historical/cultural context. For example, when I study a literary text, I feel I am able to discuss it more fully by connecting it to other (non-literary) materials/objects. This was not something I was encouraged to do in a traditional English program." "I find the 'surprises' of multi-disciplinary work the most rewarding. You never know what you'll find within disciplines that you are unfamiliar with or what might turn out to be the most important thing from a different field." The multimethods approach is considered by many to enable sophisticated research: "I have training in methods that are used in various disciplines and can adopt as many of these as possible for my own research project as and when the research question demands. This enhances the quality of research since the method is informed by the research question and not the other way round as is often the case in other disciplines."

Yet the divide between theory and praxis is very real to these students, and they offer a cogent view of the difficulties inherent in attempting to bridge that divide when working with or about children and childhoods. For example, one student writes, "While some academic disciplines blend together somewhat easily, 'theory' and 'practice' seem to sit side-by-side rather than blend and at times feel like two separate Childhood Studies. This is the division, it seems to me, that is hardest to cross." Does this divide need to be crossed in order for "true" or "real" multidisciplinarity to ensue? What other models are available? The same student remarks,

> The goal is not so much that everyone in Childhood Studies does multi-disciplinary research, but that everyone studying children and childhood contribute their research, findings or conclusions to a multi-disciplinary pot. This entails a crucial next step: everyone in Childhood Studies reads or hears the research, findings and conclusions contributed by others working in other disciplines. . . . Rather than becoming completely conversant in multiple disciplines, it seems the multi-disciplinary scholar needs to be able to take research from multiple disciplines back to his or her own realm to see how those findings look when seen through the lens of his or her own disciplinary methods and epistemology.

Put simply and elegantly by one student: "It's important to remember that 'multi' is many and not 'every.'"

This idea of communication and collaboration seems to me to represent an ideal childhood studies community—one that may be more easily attempted if not attained—within a department or program devoted to childhood studies rather than in the outside world, as it were. Childhood studies doctoral students are keenly aware of the potential pitfalls of exiting Rutgers University with a degree that may be misunderstood or incomprehensible within the academy at large or in a wider arena. Students express concerns about their future marketability and about the sustainability of the childhood studies experiment. One student remarks, "My goal in this department is to achieve as best I can as a scholar, but after I leave the department, the stakes change. Will my multi-disciplinary background make my work seem well-rounded or just out of focus? Will potential employers see me as diverse or as someone who doesn't 'fit in'?" Given that the field is still so new in the United States, many students wonder how their degree might be received. A clear expression of this fear is evident in one student's remark that "sometimes I feel that I am a jack of all trades but master of none." Here again, as students contemplate their future employment, discomfort enters the conversation: "Childhood Studies scholars will leave the department having to justify not only the quality of their work but, in many cases, . . . its existence." As one student notes, structural limitations to multidisciplinary work exist, and the academy is not especially well set up to acknowledge or reward collaboration across disciplines. As someone who has superintended a tenure case for a junior colleague whose work combines nursing, community health, and psychology, I agree that it takes additional work and some finesse to enable gatekeepers to understand truly multidisciplinary work, yet creating the space for such work and helping it receive its due must number among our highest priorities. While we all do not have to conduct research that reaches so broadly across disciplines, we could be striving to develop the tools and the will that would enable us to assess such work and to benefit from its findings.

The students who answered the questionnaire believe, overwhelmingly, in the pivotal role that childhood studies plays in creating new knowledge: "Childhood Studies tends to advance other fields/disciplines by pointing to how these fields have ignored/downplayed themes of childhood or the experiences of children—in other words, it critiques the 'adultist' tendencies of research and offers more child-centered approaches." Students also indicate a clear sense of pride in actively engaging in creating a new field:

"Being in the only PhD-granting CS program I have come to realize that CS will also be defined by my own research project as a graduate with a degree in Childhood Studies." In answering the question of what advice they might give to others considering childhood studies, the students return again and again to the idea of being at the forefront of something valuable; to engage in this enterprise is to "commit to becoming a 'pioneer'" and to work at "the frontier of a new realm of knowledge production."

This spirit of adventure may be said to underpin childhood studies and the humanities. "Doing" childhood studies is a difficult and exhilarating enterprise that requires students and researchers not only to challenge entrenched notions of the dependent, vulnerable child (among other premises) but also to question and perhaps subvert the academy's assumptions about disciplinarity and methodological orthodoxy. Although adults placed at the "the children's table" may feel that they have been exiled to a social Siberia, the children's table is also a raucous, liminal, and pleasurable space to be, and one where, in this positive formulation, it might be imagined that childhood studies metaphorically resides. The children's table, with its mismatched chairs, awkward placement, and first crack at the drumstick and wishbone, provides a good location from which new ideas can be hatched, friends can be made with far-away relatives, and dreams about future possibilities can be both imagined and launched.

Notes

1. Allison James, "Interdisciplinarity—for Better or Worse," *Children's Geographies* 8.2 (2010): 215.

2. James, "Interdisciplinarity, 215–16. See also Alan Prout, *The Future of Childhood: Towards the Interdisciplinary Study of Children* (Abingdon, UK: Routledge Falmer, 2005), and Alan Prout and Allison James, *Constructing and Reconstructing Childhood: Contemporary Issues in the Sociological Study of Childhood* (London: Falmer, 1990).

3. James, "Interdisciplinarity," 216.

4. Women's studies programs grew especially rapidly in the American academy in the 1970s and 1980s. In 1977, there were a total of 276 women's studies programs. This number grew to 525 by 1989. For more information, see the entire census report: http://082511c.membershipsoftware.org/files/NWSA_CensusonWSProgs.pdf.

5. See James Elkins, *Visual Studies: A Skeptical Introduction* (New York: Routledge, 2003), esp. 159–73.

6. Elkins, *Visual Studies*, 173.

7. Qtd. in Marquard Smith, ed., *Visual Culture Studies* (Los Angeles: Sage, 2008), viii.

8. Elkins, *Visual Studies*, x. For genealogies, definitions, and challenges to visual studies, see both Elkins and Smith (especially the preface and introduction). The 2011 Stone Summer Theory Institute (Chicago), entitled "Farewell to Visual Studies," was meant to debate and assess the relevance, condition, and future of visual studies.

9. Qtd. in "An Interview with Michael Ann Holly," in Margaret Dikovitskaya, *Visual Culture: The Study of the Visual after the Cultural Turn* (Cambridge, MA: MIT Press, 2005), 200.

10. Adrian L. James, "Competition or Integration? The Next Step in Childhood Studies? *Childhood* 17.4 (2010): 485.

11. James, "Competition or Integration?," 492–93.

12. James, "Competition or Integration?," 494.

13. See, for example, Karen S. Coats, "Keepin' It Plural: Children's Studies in the Academy," *Children's Literature Association Quarterly* 26.3 (2001): 140–50, Nina Christensen, "Childhood Revisited: On the Relationship between Childhood Studies and Children's Literature," *Children's Literature Association Quarterly* 28.4 (2003): 230–39, Kenneth Kidd, "Children's Culture, Children's Studies and the Ethnographic Imaginary," *Children's Literature Association Quarterly* 27.3 (2002): 146–55, and Thomas Travisano, "Of Dialectic and Divided Consciousness: Intersections Between Children's Literature and Childhood Studies," *Children's Literature* 28 (2000): 22–29.

14. Richard Flynn, "The Intersection of Children's Literature and Childhood Studies," *Children's Literature Association Quarterly* 22.3 (1997): 145.

15. I received thirteen responses to my voluntary questionnaire. At the time the survey was distributed, Rutgers University had 28 full- and part-time doctoral students in childhood studies, so the response rate represents nearly 50 percent participation.

Contributors

ANNETTE RUTH APPELL is a professor of law at Washington University Law School, where she previously served as the inaugural associate dean of clinical education. Her research centers on childhood, motherhood, and nontraditional families and explores themes of belonging, authority, legitimacy, and connection. Recent publications regarding childhood include "Representing Children Representing What? Critical Reflections on Lawyering for Children" in the *Columbia Human Rights Law Review* and "Controlling for Kin: Ghosts in the Postmodern Family" in the *Wisconsin Journal of Law, Gender and Society*. She is currently completing the sequel to her chapter in this book, tentatively titled "The Political Child."

SOPHIE BELL is an assistant professor at St. John's University in the Institute for Writing Studies. She is interested in the intersections among American literature, education, and culture in nineteenth-century and contemporary contexts and is influenced by scholars working in composition theory, cultural studies, critical pedagogy, critical race theory, feminist theory, postcolonial theory, and childhood studies. She studies antiracist alliances and visions articulated in social arenas from books to schools. Specifically, she has written about literary depictions of interracial contact zones and how antebellum American writers used child figures to articulate responses to massive racial conflicts such as Indian removal and the abolition of slavery. Her doctoral dissertation, titled "Naughty Child: The Racial Politics of Sentimental Discipline in Selected Antebellum Texts," argues that the image of a disobedient child of color—one who refuses to learn from the adults in power around her—became a powerful trope for racial reformers before the Civil War. Her other research on the racial dynamics of language focuses on university student writers whose texts complicate constructions of "whiteness" in secondary and postsecondary educational spaces.

ROBIN BERNSTEIN is an associate professor of African and African American studies and of studies of women, gender, and sexuality at Harvard University. Her book *Racial Innocence: Performing American Childhood from Slavery to Civil Rights* (2011) won the 2012 Outstanding Book Award from the Association for Theatre in Higher Education (ATHE). Bernstein has published essays in *PMLA*, *African American Review*, *J19: The Journal of Nineteenth-Century Americanists*, *Theatre Journal*, *Social Text*, *Modern Drama*, and other journals. Her anthology, *Cast Out: Queer Lives in Theater*, was published by the University of Michigan Press in 2006. Her 2009 article "Dances with Things: Material Culture and the Performance of Race" won ATHE's Outstanding Article in a Journal Award and the Vera Mowry Roberts Award from the American Theatre and Drama Society. Bernstein is currently writing a book titled "Paradoxy: Lesbians and the Everyday Art of the Impossible."

SARAH CHINN teaches in the English Department at Hunter College, CUNY. She is the author of *Technology and the Logic of American Racism: A Cultural History of the Body as Evidence* (2000) and *Inventing Modern Adolescence: The Children of Immigrants in Turn-of-the-Century America* (2009). She's published widely in American studies, queer studies, and disability studies and is currently at work on a manuscript on race, gender, and national identity on the early American stage.

ANNA MAE DUANE is the director of American studies and an associate professor of English at the University of Connecticut, where she teaches courses in American literature, African American studies, and disability studies. She is the author of *Suffering Childhood in Early America: Violence, Race, and the Making of the Child Victim* (2010) and has published essays in *American Literature*, *Studies in American Fiction*, *African American Review*, and *The Cambridge History of the American Novel*. She is currently working on two monographs. The first, "Strange Place Blues," analyzes the intertwined discourses of African colonization and education by tracing the careers of the alumni of the New York African Free School (1787–1833). The second project explores posthuman childhood in speculative fiction.

LESLEY GINSBERG is an associate professor of English and the chair of the Department of English at the University of Colorado, Colorado Springs. She has published articles and book chapters on antebellum American literature, nineteenth-century American women writers, and the literature of the child in journals including *American Literature*, *Studies in American Fiction*, and the *Nathaniel Hawthorne Review* and in edited collections including *American Childhood*, *The Worlds of Children 1620–1900*, and *Enterprising Youth*.

LUCIA HODGSON is an assistant professor of English at Texas A&M University where she teaches courses in American literature and children's literature. She is the founder and faculty convener of Critical Childhood Studies, a working group of the Melbern G. Glasscock Center for Humanities Research. Hodgson began writing about children's issues in 1991 while working for Yale's Edward Zigler Center in Child Development and Social Policy. She is the author of *Raised in Captivity:*

Why America Fails Its Children (1997). She has organized seven panels on childhood studies at national conferences over the past seven years. Her current project concerns child subjectivity and slavery in antebellum American literature. She argues that figurations of childhood in American prose narratives are shaped by foundational questions about who gets to come of age politically in a republic founded on principles of equality and a racialized slave system.

SUSAN HONEYMAN is a professor of English at the University of Nebraska at Kearney, where she teaches children's and adolescents' literature, as well as the graphic novel. She is the author of *Elusive Childhood: Impossible Representations in Modern Fiction* (2005), which addresses the difficulty of fictively representing children, the need for recognizing the extent to which childhood is imposed on children, and the degree to which adults are unaware of the biases they have that limit children. Her second book, *Consuming Agency in Fairy Tales, Childlore, and Folkliterature* (2010), is about consumer culture, food politics, and child agency in popular culture. Honeyman's interests range from Rapunzel's greens to Popeye's spinach, with a lot of folk culture in between. Her work is committed to promoting an interdisciplinary approach to understanding the history and concept of childhood and to incorporating actual child voices whenever possible—as children are usually excluded from self-representation in academia. Her PhD from Wayne State University is in cultural studies, but when Honeyman grows up, she wants to be a real folklorist and child-rights activist.

ROY KOZLOVSKY is an architectural historian whose field of expertise is postwar architecture. He is currently an assistant professor at Northeastern University School of Architecture, Boston, and a senior lecturer at Tel Aviv University School of Architecture. His forthcoming book, *The Architectures of Childhood: Children, Modern Architecture, and Reconstruction in Postwar England* (2013), examines the child-centered infrastructure of the postwar English welfare state.

JAMES MARTEN is a professor and the chair of the History Department at Marquette University and the founding secretary-treasurer and president of the Society for the History of Children and Youth (2012–13). He has written or edited more than a dozen books on the sectional conflict and children's history, including *The Children's Civil War* (1998), *Children and War: A Historical Anthology* (2002), *Childhood and Child Welfare in the Progressive Era: A Brief History with Documents* (2004), *Children in Colonial America* (2006), *Children and Youth in a New Nation* (2009), and *Children and Youth during the Civil War Era* (2012). He is also senior coeditor of the six-volume *Cultural History of Childhood and Family* (2010). *The Children's Civil War* won the Alpha Sigma Nu Jesuit National Book Award for History in 1999 and was named an "Outstanding Academic Book" by *Choice Magazine*. He was appointed to the Organization of American Historians Distinguished Lectureship Program in 2004.

KAREN SÁNCHEZ-EPPLER is a professor of American studies and English at Amherst College. The author of *Touching Liberty: Abolition, Feminism, and the Politics of the Body* (1993) and *Dependent States: The Child's Part in Nineteenth-Century American Culture* (2005), she is currently working on two books, "The Unpublished Republic: Manuscript Cultures of the Mid-Nineteenth Century United States" and "In the Archives of Childhood: Personal and Historical Pasts," a project precipitated by her contribution in this collection. She is one of the founding coeditors of the *Journal of the History of Childhood and Youth.*

CAROL SINGLEY is a professor of English and director of graduate studies at Rutgers University-Camden, where she teaches American literature, childhood studies, and children's literature. She is the author of *Adopting America: Childhood, Kinship, and National Identity in Literature* (2011) and *Edith Wharton: Matters of Mind and Spirit* (1995). She is also the editor or coeditor of six volumes, including *The American Child: A Cultural Studies Reader* (2003) and three on Wharton. Her current work explores literary and cultural constructions of childhood, especially in relation to kinship and adoption.

LYNNE VALLONE is a professor of childhood studies at Rutgers University-Camden, where she teaches graduate and undergraduate courses in children's literature, visual culture, and the practice of childhood studies. She is the author or coeditor of six books, most recently *The Oxford Handbook of Children's Literature* (2011), and numerous articles. She is currently at work on a book about size and scale in children's literature and Western culture more generally.

JOHN WALL is a professor and the chair of the Department of Philosophy and Religion with a joint appointment in the Department of Childhood Studies at Rutgers University-Camden. He is also chair of the Childhood Studies and Religion Group at the American Academy of Religion. He is a theoretical ethicist who writes on moral life's relation to language, culture, religion, and age. His books include *Ethics in Light of Childhood* (2010), *Moral Creativity* (2005), and the coedited volumes *Children and Armed Conflict* (2011), *Marriage, Health, and the Professions* (2002), and *Paul Ricoeur and Contemporary Moral Thought* (2002). He is currently working on two further monographs: "Being and Making" and "Childhood and Democracy."

Index